D1531468

WIN OR LOSE

Also by Stephen Longstreet:

HISTORY
The Wilder Shore *(San Francisco)*
City on Two Rivers *(New York)*
War Cries on Horseback *(Indian Wars of the West)*
Sportin' House *(Storyville)*
The Real Jazz Old and New
A Treasury of the World's Great Prints

NOVELS
The Pedlocks
The Beach House
The General
Geisha
Man of Montmartre

PLAY
High Button Shoes

WIN
OR LOSE

A Social History of Gambling in America

STEPHEN LONGSTREET

THE BOBBS-MERRILL COMPANY, INC.

INDIANAPOLIS NEW YORK

Copyright © 1977 by Stephen Longstreet
All rights reserved, including the right of reproduction
in whole or in part in any form
Published by The Bobbs-Merrill Company, Inc.
Indianapolis / New York

Designed by Victoria Gomez
Manufactured in the United States of America

FIRST PRINTING

Library of Congress Cataloging in Publication Data

Longstreet, Stephen,
  Win or lose.

  Includes index.
  1. Gambling—United States—History.
2. Gamblers—United States—History. 3. Gamblers
—Psychology. I. Title.
HV6715.L66   301.5′7   77-76884
ISBN 0-672-52253-5

For Three Friends
Gamblers All

John Huston
Billy Pearson
Nicholas Andrea Dandolos
(Nick the Greek)

CONTENTS

INTRODUCTION

There is the often-told story of the Western gambler, marooned in a small town by a flood. When told he was playing in a crooked card game, he replied, "I know, but it's the ONLY game in town . . ."

I sensed that I was going to write this book from the moment the kindly looking housewife-type shoved me aside at the dice table at Harrah's Club in Reno and said, "Give me them dice and let a real crap shooter handle them." No, she *didn't* make six passes in a row and astonish us. She crapped out on the third roll, shrugged it off, and smilingly went off with a paper cup of quarters to play the slot machines. Two casinos down from Harrah's I watched my friend Nick the Greek, the legendary gambler, win $32,000 in an all-night poker session. (He was to lose most or all of it the next two days.)

Between such two extremes I felt there was a theme—the story of the gambling going on among men and women in America since the discovery of the New World. Told free of the usual myths, and shucking off the biased and romantic attitudes that cling to those citizens of the republic who believe that the odds in their favor could come up to produce, if not a fortune, some folding money (in gambling circles also called dough, mazuma, gelt, lettuce, bread, china, green goods, the roll, and greenbacks, as well as skinplasters).

In putting together this book, I have, as a genre historian, stalked facts in the world of the professional gambler, but I have also paid a great deal more attention to the average American whose amateur standing as a gambler is neglected, for usually it follows no set pattern of conduct. As Will Rogers said, "There is a wide gambling streak in nearly every American man and woman, a fat streak, fat as a prize hog's bacon."

This uncharted section of our population is well represented; it includes the gambling urges of the lower- and middle-class city dweller, the country-fair folk, the suburbs commuter. These people represent a large segment of our national life and are as common as church picnics or the filling in of crossword puzzles.

From Columbus's sailors and their playing cards, George Washington's diary of winnings and losses at the table, and the river-boat gamblers' aces to today's Las Vegas, Texas poker, and the numbers lotteries, the men and women of America are a nation of gamblers. There are office football pools and church bingo games; millions of dollars are laid out yearly on the Irish Sweepstakes, legal and illegal track gambling, and Las Vegas dice and roulette tables; and vast sums change hands in the various closed and private card games of the Southwest millionaires, the Greeks, and the Arabs (who are now the highest rollers in many of our nation's gambling centers).

Americans have been gambling since the first frontier hunter aimed his Kentucky rifle at a tied-up turkey in a wager that he could knock off its head at 200 yards. We continue to gamble right up to this morning's placing of two bits with a hustler of the numbers racket in Watts or Harlem. The Gardena, California, poker parlors are legally wide open, mostly to little old ladies with blue-white hair. And in Reno a professor is usually around with a "sure thing" system to beat the wheel's *rouge et noir*.

Americans bet on horse, frog (as Mark Twain discovered), and turtle races, on the roll of a pair of dice, on hopes of a royal flush in poker, on points given on football, and on baseball scores. Professional gamblers' syndicates have several times fixed major college basketball games. The White Sox World Series was rigged in 1919 when a gambling group bought nine baseball players to throw the Series. Today the airlines sell you insurance, betting you will get to your destination alive (a bonanza to your relatives if you lose). As William Faulkner said, "The free and easy American is a born gambler—didn't he as a colonial bet he could beat George III?"

This book studies gambling and gamblers in detail and is fully documented. The facts are: women bet nearly as much as men; stud poker is an art; the house odds can be figured out.

Of the twenty-six most popular games of cards, the leaders are chuck-a-luck, keno, ecarté, monte, and thimblerig; poker and blackjack were once bet on as much in New England as in the far West of men in Stetsons and cowpoke boots. There is a growing organization called "Gamblers Anonymous" that is as much needed as Alcoholics Anonymous. Addiction to gambling at its peak is a disease, a deadly habit like dope or alcohol.

Great or notorious names are connected with gambling in America: George Washington; Richard Canfield (art patron, *bon vivant,* king of the gambling houses, prince of Saratoga); Bet-a-Million Gates (his barbed wire fenced in the West); Hetty Green, the great woman gambler of Wall Street; Lillian Russell, a splendid horse handicapper; Nick the Greek; Lyndon Johnson; Richard Nixon (a poker shark in his Navy days), and many others.

Some gambling games are simple (often *too* simple—like the shell game); others, like faro, are very complex. On the track, winning the daily double (complicated two-race betting) is the dream of the two-dollar bettor; handicapping a pro football game on points is almost a science, and often a racket. Gambling in many parts of the nation is mostly permitted by the local political powers or law enforcers sharing out the gambling rights for a cut of the take. True are the tales of some legendary poker games, some running four to five days.

I have spent a great deal of time in Reno, Las Vegas, Chicago, Saratoga, Hot Springs, New Orleans, New York, and Miami, where what is labeled "big-time U.S. gambling" is at its best. I have also interviewed some of the men who control the telegraph and telephone race result services, who print the tout sheets, and who are experts in the handicapping of everything from a Pebble Beach golf tournament to a mile race of maidens at Belmont race track. I learned a lot of the details about the use of "the battery" (electric shocks), drugs, and "boat races" (fixed runs) on some horses.

Like most social historians, I found evasions and subterfuges when I had to separate the truth from legend and myth. Gambling stories grow in size and content from one retelling to the next. I have tried to get at least two reliable sources for what I used—both verbally and from available records that could be trusted. I have gone through unpublished journals and letters, besides newspaper files and committee reports. I have also sought the opinions of doctors, psychologists, neurologists and psychoanalysts who have treated compulsive gamblers—some with success.

Medical and professional psychiatric ethics being what they are, I have in some cases changed names where there has been discreet cooperation on data I needed.

I have also used interviews with wheel men, floor managers of casinos, and pit bosses, most successfully with a pit boss and gambler now retired after fifty years of manipulating and presiding at dice and card games at many of the most famous gambling spots in the nation. I can only thank him as "Charlie Ross," for the syndicates that control so much of the gambling in the nation might resent the information he had to offer me.

I also want to thank the jockeys (among them Billy Pearson, the art-loving $64,000 winner of television show fame, with whom I worked on his book *Never Look Back*). Among the departed: Cy Rice, biographer of Nick the Greek, and W. C. Fields ("Yes indeed—I've been known to place a few piasters on the nose of some spirited nag"); Milt Gross, whose knowledge of the Roaring Twenties and the era of Jimmy Walker, Dutch Schultz, Frank Costello, Texas Guinan, and Belle Livingston was of great help. Some meetings with Elizabeth Arden, Pittsburgh Phil, Damon Runyon, and Nicky Arnstein helped, as did talking with Larry Hazzard, the best race track handicapper I ever met. Conversations with Wilson Mizner, Will Rogers, James J. Walker, Bernard M. Baruch and Walter Winchell helped immeasurably.

Several members of my writing classes at the University of Southern California, where I teach Modern Writing, helped with their personal knowledge of the numbers pushers and floating crap games in the black and Mexican-American sections of our cities. Thanks are due to Billy Pearson, John Huston, and the late Al Jolson on matters pertaining to horses.

I had the family's permission to use the letters and daybooks of my Uncle Rod, relating to card games of all sorts. Thanks to Helen Wurdemann, director of the Los Angeles Art Association, who did so much to help find and supervise the art work and the hunt for old prints.

No such book as this could be completed without the texts available for checking and studying by those who have written on the subject, and for these I thank the Los Angeles County Library staff and the Library of Congress. In the Bibliography at the end of the book, I have listed sources and authorities that were helpful and pointed me in the right direction for some story or detail. I have also gone through files of many old newspapers and magazines.

In some places I have made the customary substitutions for proper names where there might be danger to some of my sources who are or were once deeply involved in professional gambling. Also, for ethical reasons, the names of some doctors, psychiatrists, and physiologists, as well as case history identifications have been altered.

This book takes no moral stance for or against gambling. Its main purpose, as I saw it, was to relate a peculiar and interesting condition of mankind that gives so much pleasure to many, yet brings to others a regret for folly committed. I tell of both: what William Blake called "The winner's shout, the loser's curse." Whatever else gambling is, it is drama, and like most interesting plays it has its high comedy and its mark of tragedy.

Las Vegas, Nevada / 1973
Miradero Road, California / 1977

Nothing ventured,
nothing gained.

Fourteenth-century Proverb

WIN OR LOSE

1

LAS VEGAS WEEKEND

Lester and Gloria Russell own a small hardware store in the San Fernando Valley, in a community of middle-class life and habits. Lester is thirty-two, a veteran of the Vietnam war. He and Gloria (once called Gloria-Bess) have been married ten years and have two children: Mandy, eight, and Lester Jr., five. Every year for the past six years on their wedding anniversary they spend a weekend in Las Vegas. They are a self-confident, affable couple. Lester spent two years at U.C.L.A.; Gloria is a high school graduate.

I have known them for five years, and they are among the solid, fun-loving, hard-working Americans of their age and class who are excited by a weekend in Las Vegas. They are mild gamblers (except for the one year when Lester's father died and Lester drank a lot and lost his control at a crap table and they had to take out a small loan to cover a $3,000 gambling loss). They go to Las Vegas, they insist, for the food and the shows, but, still, Lester is a man who likes to handle the ivory cubes; and Gloria, who has a loss limit of twenty dollars a night, will usually lose it at twenty-one (blackjack) in the three nights in Las Vegas, after hours of play of winning, then losing, because of the house advantage.

They don't always lose. Three times they have been ahead about $200 on leaving for home. Once Lester hit four rolls of the dice, later to brag to his customers in the hardware store that he came out "800 clams ahead." Both, of course, admit that if they added it all up, they would find that their yearly visits to Las Vegas have cost them "a couple of thousand."

You can fly from Los Angeles to Vegas (the *Las* drops away after your first visit to the place), or you can drive the long

Mojave Desert road past salt flats and moonlike rock formations, a road bone-white and mostly straight and unchanging as an arrow shaft. Either way it's over 290 miles from Los Angeles to Las Vegas.

We flew. I held Gloria's betting money (seventy-five dollars) and I was *never,* she insisted, to dole out to her more than twenty-five dollars a night. "Okay?" Her eyes focused on me like amber held to the light. "I've no controls, once the dealer starts laying down the cards and my day's horoscope has been favorable."

Lester, who was big and blond and had a broken nose from college football, carried his wallet buttoned up inside his jacket. He didn't need "a poke-holder," as he put it. He would win or lose about $200. He'd be pleased to break even, after transportation, food, hotel, taxis, and visits to other casinos to catch their shows. He'd drop some bills downtown at the Golden Nugget or at the slots at the Fremont, which are supposed to pay off a larger percentage and more often than the fancy Strip casinos.

A folder informed us of the current Vegas entertainers. They are well-worn, even shopworn show-business names— nothing new or novel. The visitors seek nothing out of the ordinary on stage. They want the old and tried safe acts that they have seen on television. That and a bit of nudity will suffice for their simple tastes.

The plane talk was general: the bastards in Washington raising their own salaries while taxes go up; what shows they were going to see in Vegas; where were Sinatra, Skelton, Barbra Streisand appearing? There was also an exchange of information as to food, service, and the weather. But in the main the talk was of winnings, of dice passes made, of lucky roulette numbers that came up, of card sense needed at twenty-one, and about a jackpot payoff from a slot machine. There was almost no mention of losses. Most of the passengers like Lester and Gloria were middle-class small businessmen, office managers, salesmen—not professional gamblers. They were seeking that inexplicable dream, "a good time."

There was nothing spectacular about the airfield at Las Vegas. This one was owned by the late Howard Hughes, as were about half a dozen giant casino hotels and about two dozen gold and silver mines, virtually none in operation.

A taxi took us to the casino hotel where we were to spend the weekend. (I shall call it the "Great Babylon.") It is over-ornate, a forward push of modern forms with no taste or reticence; a *Phantom of the Opera* decor, its façade identified by a great sign of neon tubing by the mile and light bulbs by the thousands, already sending out kinetic patterns and the letters GREAT BABYLON.

There was nothing in scale, or real, about the Great Babylon. One of the passengers called it "a diamond-studded poolroom." Everything was in odd taste (*bad* taste no longer exists here—it's all camp or Disney Nostalgia now). While we waited, Gloria rushed off to play the slot machines. It was dusk in the desert outside, gray dust swirling down the main street (and highway); dust was gray on shrubbery and tinted the rows of beach chairs by the large pool. Inside, the air conditioning was on. To the left of the lobby, open to view, was the main casino. It was, as the folder proudly stated, "as large as a football field." The walls were windowless and were ranked by platoons of gleaming slot machines, with people pulling the metal arms after they dropped in their coins. The main gambling in progress was at the roulette, twenty-one, and dice tables. Faro is no longer played at most casinos—it's too complicated—and poker games are played in private suites. There was a race track service for placing bets at various tracks.

Strangers exchanged social amenities; barriers were down. Waitresses in black lace tights and very little else flitted about carrying trays of drinks. Hard-eyed men stood about looking very comfortable in good tailoring: security men—Pinkertons, some said; others said the FBI was checking on the take to limit the *skimming* (removing a good share of the winnings before counting them, to avoid state and federal taxes and to pass currency on to unnamed partners).

The play was heavy and steady; everyone seemed serious.

Who were the players? What would they find in Las Vegas?

Twenty million tourists appear in Las Vegas every year to feed, drink, buy love, and of course to gamble. Eighty percent of them come by plane, train, or bus (a few hitchhike) from Los Angeles. The goal is this glittering Strip where the great hotel gambling casinos light up the desert.

The Strip has its dozen or so great hotel casinos in a style that has been called "dice table Baroque": the Desert Inn, the Tropicana, the Stardust, the Dunes, the Hacienda, and others. There are certain things these places have in common: no clocks in view of gamblers, no windows, and few doors leading away from the tables. Gambling is peremptory and absolute. Players are not—within their hearing—called suckers or marks. The most catered to are the high rollers who are big-play gamblers, or show-business, film, or TV folk. A gambler can be labeled as a "dropper" (a big loser) or a "producer" (in industry or big business) or a "no producer" (just a gambler with no other known trade). A note against a hotel file card can also identify him (or her) as one who spends ("puts out") when winning or looped, or is a board chaser, a boozer, or a whore.

The oldest tired joke in town is that the tourist has three things to do: drink, gamble, screw. Actually, some demand fine food. In a few places the food is good (not as good as it was twenty years ago, or as cheap). There are swimming, golfing, and visits to Boulder Dam (somehow no one seems to care to call it Hoover Dam). There are even dance floors. They are, however, very small; they detract from gambling. And of course there are the stage shows, from Frank Sinatra to Ella Fitzgerald to Don Rickles. As one casino boss expressed it to me, "It's the sugar we trap the flies with. The stage shows, they're headaches—those effing actors and singers—and overpriced."

There is not much else to Las Vegas but hot desert and harsh winds blowing outside. Some visitors combine gambling in Nevada with a divorce or a wedding. But the gambling casinos furnish the true reason for Nevada as a solvent state. One is welcome if armored with cash or credit cards; if one is broke, the law will run you out by sundown. If you protest, they may provide a bus ticket.

Glitter Gulch is really the most fun, the downtown of two blocks of Fremont Street, where there are casinos, keno parlors and surreal neon façades. The establishments, for all their glitter, are like Western dance-hall saloons as seen in Western movies—noisy, with a lot more Western garb, from fake Stetsons to Sears, Roebuck cowboy boots. The women are more painted, and the men often chew on cold cigars in the aphrodisiac scent of money. Here you find sheepmen, ranch hands, clerks and typists, nurses, showgirls looking for work, jazz men seeking a gig, moochers, and panhandlers. Lots of old folks on Social Security, Medicare, pensions, and other senior citizen benefits play the slot machines by the hour, their coins held in plastic drinking cups, right arms active on levers. You meet them everyplace: the Golden Nugget, the Horseshoe, the Lucky Strike, the Jackpot, and the Pioneer, testing their ability to lure Lady Luck. Usually the satisfaction of excitement is their only reward.

It recalls Mark Twain's first look at Nevada ". . . the lawyer, the editor, the banker, the chief desperado, the chief gambler, and the saloonkeeper occupied the same level of society. . . . No greater moment could succeed without the countenance and direction of the saloonkeepers." Turn saloonkeeper into casino boss and perhaps Mafia front and you have a picture of Las Vegas today. It is costly saloonkeeping; it's been figured out that about half a billion dollars is invested in Las Vegas in casinos and room space.

For all its natural nonconformity, there are lots of churches and a few Jewish temples in town. The church, more broad-minded here, is not above taking a hand in the atmosphere. For years the Catholic church's Father Richard Anthony Crowley conducted an early morning mass (at 4:30 in the Stardust's Crown Room) for anyone still gambling at that hour, and for the cocktail waitresses, security guards, pit bosses, croupiers, and resident hoods. The good father excused it all by saying, "After all, there was gambling for the Robe at the Foot of the Cross." Losers with a credit rating can get credit. They sign IOUs, or markers, as they're called, to the house. There are also handy pawnshops to issue loans on watches, rings, cameras, or portable radios. A missing Motion Picture Academy Oscar was once in pawn. State law forbids pawning of items needed for bodily health: dentures, eyeglasses, hearing aids, trusses, and crutches. There was also a rumor of the refusal by one pawnshop to lend money on a glass eye.

Strange things happen to the visitor—to his state of mind—no matter how staid and stern he or she is at home. In Vegas many move into permissive new areas, perhaps long desired. For here is a town built on dice, cards, and numbers that calls itself "Liberty Hall." The balance of most repressed sensual desires becomes upset; money, gambling, available sex, food, and theater are all there at one's elbow. The atmosphere does not affect just the visitor. The pit bosses, the entertainers, band men, waitresses, chefs, busboys, waiters, and parking-lot attendants very often squander their pay in gambling. So do many of the star acts.

Nevada almost creates a psychological need for gambling. There is a gambling casino area in the State Prison at Carson City. Here the inmates can play for brass checks, which can be cashed when an inmate leaves the prison. There are tables for twenty-one and crap shooting as well as a wire service for placing horse race bets on any track in the country. As one guard at the prison put it: "It keeps 'em preoccupied working out systems to beat the cards or the crap table odds."

Eight times a day the Mint Hotel's gambling school (no charge) gives courses in the simpler aspects of roulette, crap shooting, and blackjack. Gloria had attended several times. There are films, and actual experts demonstrate. Gloria, like other students, was given a "Diploma of Gambling Knowledge" and some chips to play with at the casino. No mention, she told me, was made of the odds and the house percentages, the actual odds against becoming a big winner.

The pit bosses are the most valuable employees. The maitre d', with his sanctimonious snobbery, is the person to know for the would-be diner and show viewer. The maitre d' is paid hardly anything; he too gambles on his luck with bribes, and nearly every year the Internal Revenue insists he makes from $60,000 to $150,000 a year in tips and offerings. Lester said it would be foolish for any visitor to enter any of the dining-theater rooms of the Strip without pressing at least ten bucks into the bastard's well-cared-for hand. "Otherwise your seating might as well be in Los Angeles."

The rest of the help, strongly unionized, expect fairly high tips. It is they who caused millions in losses by closing the casinos in their last strike in 1976. Las Vegas casinos lost an estimated $10 million, the Nevada Gaming Commission reported. While the Las Vegas area clubs suffered, clubs in Reno, Carson City, and Lake Tahoe areas showed huge gains in revenues on card and dice games, slot machines, and other gambling devices.

Casinos in Clark County, which encompasses Las Vegas, took

in $206.6 million from gamblers in the first quarter of 1976, for a 10 percent gain in taxable gross revenues. In the Reno–North Tahoe area within Washoe County, the casinos showed a tremendous gain of nearly 30 percent in revenue from gamblers. It would seem that the Las Vegas and the Reno–Tahoe rivalry for who is bigger may see a new champ.

If there is one visitor that Las Vegas welcomes not only with open arms but with fruit baskets in his or her room, fresh drinks, and special attention, it is some genius who has worked out another system to beat the house. It is always claimed to be a foolproof system and works absolutely perfectly on paper. No matter—the house *never* loses at the slots, and the house's favored percentage insures them against great winners. The visitors pay 80 percent of the state's taxes; without gambling, Nevada would probably go back to the Gila monster and the tumbleweeds, existing merely as a way station for freight trains. The lure may be greed or hope, but it is also that last American wide-open frontier.

Before it entered contemporary history, Las Vegas was just desert, hot and cold by turns, inhabited since prehistoric times by Gila monsters, rattlesnakes, and sometimes not very aggressive Indians called Paiutes. However, the site seems to have achieved a name by the nineteenth century, for in 1844 Captain John C. Frémont entered a note in his journal about "a camping ground called Las Vegas." Clearly, mountain men, wagon trekkers, and an occasional outlaw had found a haven there from time to time.

Las Vegas didn't officially become a settlement until 1855, when Brigham Young made a deal with the United States to rent out Mormon soldiers—thirty of them under William Bringhurst—to build a fort to protect the U.S. mail and shelter settlers moving west to the gold fields. The Mormons were also to do missionary work on the Indians—"to convert and baptize." They planted crops and orchards; cabins were raised up and a dam and bridges added.

But as a Mormon mission the project failed. The Indians seemed content with their own version of the Great Spirit. Besides, the Indians raided and looted the settlement's fringes; in the end, the Mormons went back to Salt Lake City.

The Mormons, as practical people, had tried to mine lead

around their mission, but the damn stuff wouldn't melt properly. They didn't know it, but it wasn't lead at all: it was silver ore.

When the Civil War, unemancipated, moved west, the site became Fort Baker, with a company of bored infantry that played cards, shot crap, and practiced killing rattlers. The three companies of cavalry at least had horses for company. Finally, rich mineral discoveries were made, and gold and silver mining took place. In time, nearby Eldorado Canyon produced a goodly amount of gold and silver.

Las Vegas didn't really come around to being a town until May of 1905, when the San Pedro, Los Angeles & Salt Lake Railroad which owned the land, got a few thousand people to attend a meeting under a mesquite tree. Here they announced plans for a rail division point and a train system through Las Vegas and the Southwest. The railroad officials were really there to auction off land for a fat profit—a gamble to the buyers that the empty sun-baked desert would amount to something. During the two-day auction, a healthy $265,000 was paid, or promised, on 1,200 lots.

First came wagons and buggies bearing settlers, *and* land lawyers to torment them; then tents lettered POST OFFICE, HOTEL, BANK; and a score of structures proclaiming: GAMBLING, CARDS, WHEEL OF FORTUNE.

"The rest," the townspeople like to say, "is history." It grew slowly in solitude, dust, and boredom. But it grew, and the railroad came through. Soon gambling and sporting houses were the mainstay of the town. There was a little cattle-dealing, and some lungers came to cure themselves in the dry desert air. By 1911 Las Vegas was incorporated as a city.

In the 1930s the need for power caused the construction of the huge Boulder Dam (later renamed for President Hoover). The work on the dam, and its thousands of workers seeking fun, games, companionship, and drink, boosted Las Vegas to its first prosperity. It was boosted so high that in the 1970s it has a permanent population of about 325,000, and the boosters claimed that $2 billion was invested in hotels, casinos, homes, and industries. In an average year 22,000,000 people come to gamble and enjoy themselves, spending about $250 million.

Once the boom started, nothing could hold it back.

It all began so simply. The golden geese were latecomers to Las Vegas. They did not mature in the state until after 1940, when Clark County (which consists of, besides Las Vegas, a dozen little towns and about five miles of U.S. Highway 91) had a regular population of 16,000 weathered folk. They were mostly road workers, ranch hands, village loafers, and prospectors. Some saloons and a cathouse or two were provided for the casual drifter. The entire state had a population of under 100,000.

There was gambling back then, but it brought state taxes of only about $28,000 a year. By the 1970s, gambling was paying about $16 million a year to the state, $5 million to the county, and $2 million to the cities. Sales taxes added about $20 million more.

Much income is based on a dozen busy casinos, a feisty downtown offering about 20,000 slot machines and providing 1,400 games going at once in about 300 versions. It also makes possible nearly 27,000 legitimate jobs and an unknown number of pickpockets, muggers, and thieves. Add to this a $10 million yearly income from divorcing people after their brief token stay. Also consider the marriage chapels, ministers, and justices of the peace, all working hasty marriages ("witnesses in residence"). The business, in that major gamble of holy or unholy matrimony, ranks as a splendid and not too minor activity in the state.

For the available whore, Nevada may provide an income second only to the gambling take. There is no effective law against prostitution in the state. There is only local option, and in a macho society backed by something called the Mob by some, and the image of the Western male as a stud, legal whorehouses do exist. However, the law states that out of respect for children, the pious *and* the traffic, "it is a misdemeanor to conduct an establishment within 400 yards of a school, church, or public thoroughfare."

What brought Las Vegas and Nevada's legal gambling into the big league and produced present-day Las Vegas, Reno, and Lake Tahoe was a gangster named Benjamin Siegel, called "Bugsy" behind his back. He was a paranoid psychotic, a killer and a sadist. He was hardly sane; no one dared call him Bugsy to his face. Gambling projects were Bugsy's first interest in

Nevada. They began in 1941 when he was sent out by mobsters to help set up the horse parlors of the Trans-American Wire Service, controlled by the heirs of Al Capone in their fight with a rival horse track service, Continental Press Service. The owners of the few simple pine and adobe casinos in Las Vegas were persuaded to take the Capone service, and in 1942 Bugsy came out himself to cut in on the take of the horse rooms and the casinos using the service. He is supposed to have earned $25,000 a month from this horse play, besides buying some interest in the Golden Nugget and the Frontier Club, where the piano rolls played "I Ain't Gonna Give Nobody None of My Jelly Roll." They gave.

Bugsy was also a fancy dresser, a name dropper, and a very handsome man. He was often told that he ought to be in pictures. Bugsy liked class; his shoes were handmade in England, and even his jockey shorts were monogrammed. Gambling in Las Vegas soon was not all pick-toed steer boots and red flannel underwear.

Bugsy was the boss of mob activities in California, but by 1945 he was bored with the palm trees and with the cash going back to the mob. His thoughts focused on Las Vegas. He saw a vision of a great gambling empire, huge hotels, fantastic casinos— "something to really make Las Vegas get off its ass."

He called his dream blueprint the Flamingo Casino and Hotel, and proceeded with dogged ingenuity. He put the Del E. Webb Construction Company of Phoenix, Arizona, to raising up his vision. He insisted on the finest solid concrete, the best plumbing, rare marbles, exotic woods. He read blueprints and put the pressure on designers and contractors. The first estimate had been for "a mill and a half," but in the end, mixing his money, mob money, and various investors', it added up to $6 million. Black markets had to furnish a lot of the materials (with a world war just finished, certain items were in short supply). Sometimes Bugsy bought the same supplies two or three times; black market hoods being what they were, they were stealing it back as fast as he could buy it. The mob put in $3 million after Bugsy's first million ran out and he was out of cash to pay the contractors. There was trouble with the horse-room wire service, and plasterers were being bribed by Bugsy at fifty dollars a day to finish the casino. Only the success of the Flamingo as a gambling palace could save him.

In December of 1946 Bugsy and his girl, Virginia Hill (she was accused during many investigations of being a money courier of the gambling take for the mob), opened the unfinished "Fabulous Flamingo, Starring Jimmy Durante and the Cugat Orchestra." The place was a failure. Bugsy was busy at the time as a womanizer—waitresses and a contessa, besides Virginia Hill (the official Du Barry of the dice tables)—and that too led to private battles, and Bugsy seemed more bugs than ever.

In two weeks the casino lost $100,000. Bugsy closed it "to get it finished and hold a grand opening." The Mob tried to fire Bugsy, but he outtalked them. "Just wait until we really open the Flamingo properly."

In March of 1947 the Flamingo opened again. For weeks the bookkeeping news was dreadfully bad; a disaster was in the making. Then the tide turned, and in one month the place made $3 million. Bugsy had made history and created modern Las Vegas.

Others followed in Bugsy's handmade leather footsteps. The various mobs with millions in illegal, untaxed money now had a place to invest their loot at very fancy returns.

Bugsy still was battling the people who had put their tainted money into the Flamingo and was talking brashly and loudly. His battles with Virginia Hill continued, and she left for Paris. Bugsy continued to live in Virginia's Beverly Hills house, insisting that she'd cool off and come back to him. On a June day of 1947 he was sitting in the living room with a buddy, Allen Smiley. Bugsy was reading the sports section of the Los Angeles *Times*. Without warning someone fired a .30-caliber carbine through a window, sending two steel-jacketed bullets into Bugsy's movie-star features, destroying them in dreadful fashion. Two slugs went into his torso; five others missed him but damaged a nude painting and a gold-leafed piano.

Two odd things were noticed about this assassination: Smiley, sitting on the sofa with Bugsy, was not hit; and, twenty minutes after Bugsy died (his body not yet identified and with nothing on the news wires of the event), certain men in contact with the

Mob took over the running of the Fabulous Flamingo. The Daniel Boone of modern Las Vegas, of Nevada's rise to gambling fame, was not mourned.

The biggest hotel and casino dreamer to follow Bugsy (until the mid-1970s) was a gambler and bootlegger named Tony Cornero (Antonio Cornero Stralla). His dream project was the Stardust. He planned 1,032 rooms on sixty-five acres of desert landscape with a sort of comic-strip decor lit by 12,000 light bulbs and a few miles of neon representing the universe, its planets and stars. Tony had once tried to run a gambling ship off the Los Angeles coast, starting in 1938 with the S.S. *Rex,* and again in 1946 with the S.S. *Lux.* Both times the Coast Guard put his high-seas dice and wheels out of business and out of the water. In 1954 he was in Las Vegas offering shares of stock in the Stardust project without notifying the wary Securities Exchange Commission.

In 1955, when the Hotel Stardust was about 70 percent finished and Tony had raised $6 million to help build it, he dropped dead while playing dice at the Desert Inn. The medical certificate read "heart attack," but no coroner's inquest was held. Orders were not to touch the body, and Tony was buried from his Beverly Hills home.

The Stardust went bankrupt; $3 million was needed to finish the place. However, after a lot of legal behind-the-scenes goings on, the Stardust was soon making money for the final owner or owners.

Las Vegas is a safe city. The *mafioso* will not permit any killings of a gang variety inside the city. But records show that there have been assassinations, hits, and disappearances in out-of-town rub-outs related to crimes committed against the organization in Vegas. Often some casino manager or owner, or front for the real owners, is elected mayor and is officially proclaimed "the Mayor of Paradise Valley," which is the area of about fifty-five square miles of semipopulated zone containing nearly five miles of U.S. Highway 91, the Strip, and a black district near the great gambling meccas. Nick the Greek Dandolas, the famous gambler who died broke in Las Vegas, insisted: "Mayor of Paradise Valley? That's about as important a public office as being an admiral in the Swiss Navy. But it has lots of guns."

While there have been movies made about holding up some
casino for a slice of the visitors' losses in the casino counting
rooms, there has been only one recorded attack on the vast
sums of money taken in daily by the casinos. The unholy event
took place in June of 1951, in the commission book layoff room
where track betting was done. Five armed hoods out of the
Kansas City underworld burst into the place at ten in the
morning, guns ready to out-face the four bookies on duty.
They grabbed up $3,500 in bills and fled, one of the gang
dropping his straw hat in his hurry. Although partly disguised,
two men were recognized and an alarm went out. They were
arrested in San Francisco. Out on bail, the hoods fled to Los
Angeles, the Mob in hot pursuit. The Mob insisted that it was
only interested in seeing that the men had enough money for
their trial lawyers. Lured to a meeting, the bandits each got
four slugs in the back of the head. There have been no attempts
to raid a Las Vegas casino since.

While the Great Babylon in its publicity claims to cater to film
stars, millionaires, rock-and-roll performers, Washington lobbyists, mysterious Swiss bankers, and robed Arab oil kings, what
we saw were mostly middle-class Americans, some pale from
Northern cities, some tanned from sun lamps or Southwestern
sunlight. There were a few exhibitionists and overdone Texans; there were slurred Southern accents and Middle-Western
drawls, but there was also Bronx crispness; visitors came by bus,
train, plane, or auto.

In any other setting these people would fit into Rotary Club
lunches or small town-hall meetings. Mostly middle-aged,
they are often accompanied by sons and daughters. At times
there was an apparent attempt at false youth with toupees, wigs,
and show-business makeup. Some overfeeders were of gargan-
tuan proportions; others controlled their youthful figures.
They were all well dressed; the men wore sports shirts in
carnival colors and patterns, and wide Western belts with fake
Wells-Fargo buckles. The women showed their legs or wore
pants suits. Some held roulette table chips in their hands or
played the slots.

The lower middle class was not here in any great number.
They were at slightly rundown hotels and casinos, or one of

those places that, having passed through several hands, was suspected of having Mafia connections. These usually offered ten to twenty dollars in chips "free," good only on their premises to their guests.

I was greeted by a disbarred lawyer named Fred, a compulsive gambler. "Could you let me have half a C note? I'm expecting a bundle on a horse I hit today at Santa Anita."

I said I didn't think so. Fred, like so many lawyers who get disbarred, had a remarkable criminal brain. He settled estates, took a great deal of the money in huge unethical fees, and lost it at the dice tables. Lawyers, one medical man told me, are in large numbers among the compulsive gamblers who go wrong. My father saw lawyers as the lowest form of life that crawled. But not in Las Vegas. The smart lawyers serviced hotel and casino owners, or mob figures and gangland investors, the owners who first moved into the city and built a lot of it. They have managed to so confuse the ownership and stock holdings and the true backers of big-time gambling as a business that no one really knows for sure *who* owns *what.*

Lester had signed us in, the bellboy had our bags, and Gloria was back with a fistful of half-dollars.

"I hit; I hit a slot machine. It's a lucky start."

"You're a pistol," said Lester.

The silver dollar—not smaller coins—used to be the true sign that you were in Las Vegas. The heavy little towers of silver cartwheels were everywhere and all change was made in silver; the dollar coin was a pleasure to riff through your fingers or to load up in your pants pockets. The silver dollar is now hoarded by the gnomes known as coin collectors. Somehow the gambling tables aren't the same without it. "A plastic chip," Humphrey Bogart used to say, "has no soul." You can buy a silver dollar for three dollars in small coin shops around the city.

I had a small room facing the air-conditioning tower. Lester and Gloria had a larger room across the hall with a huge double bed. When making reservations you can note whether you want two singles, a double, a queen, a king, or a vibrating spring and mattress, and mirrors on the ceiling. Casino managers believe an active libido encourages gambling excess. Everything is done to make life a fantasy, so that resistance to any sense of reality is weakened at the gambling tables. As one gambler told me: "You feel you are in the grip of necessity to bust loose."

I sat in my room and listened to a wall radio. The Great Babylon does not have television sets in its rooms, but you can ask for one from the desk clerk for a normal fee. You're not here, the management hopes, to look at Archie Bunker or Sonny and Cher.

Outside the window was the beginning of night; the distant desert appeared prehistoric, a blurred blue and black, sterile. Below, in the casino, I was sure the crush had become thicker around the gambling tables. The nighttime frenzy takes over joy seekers, the fortune seekers, like werewolves, going hysterical as twilight comes.

I had first come to Las Vegas years ago when it was just starting its strange climb to fame. I had studied something of its history along the way. William Faulkner put the whole situation simply: "From an addled acorn a very damn strange oak grew."

There was a time when a decent room and good food in Las Vegas were a bargain for the quality of the service and what was served, but in the early 1970s a change was evident. Hotel rooms and the prices of meals were in line with the usual rates of the rest of the nation. Now, a dinner at the big Strip hotels would run from ten to thirty dollars a head, and the quality was no longer there.

Lester, Gloria and I ate our meal at the dinner show, while on stage the star expressed his gaucherie and charm. Then the comic came on—"a huge squat toad," Gloria insisted; his work was low and vulgar, but it was enjoyed by the audience, who giggled and gasped at four-letter words and perverse sexual jests. It was an act these visitors would not have accepted in their own hometown, and there was in their mirth, I noticed, a nervous expectancy, as if they were visiting the damned and wondering why they were enjoying it.

The meal, the drinks, and the show over with, we joined the rush to the gambling tables. There would be another show near midnight. Some visitors took in both, but the gambling was the stronger attraction.

Gloria went at once to the blackjack tables, and I gave her the last of the cash I was holding for her. Lester went to work with a pair of dice, and I placed some small bets at roulette, where a boisterous, breezy group was watching the wheel. I won a little, lost a little. A big man with a cigar and a crucified expression continued to write down winning numbers: a system searcher.

The slot machines were all busy, and every once in a while someone would howl at the tinkle of coins announcing a winner. The bar girls were passing out drinks from trays to fervid players. Lester was attracting attention and a cluster of watchers; partisans and bettors were packed around him as he threw dice. The table was well guarded under the eyes of a pit boss; two uniformed security men were within call, and I knew there were one-way mirrors in the ceiling behind which keen-eyed observers watched the play and saw to it that the dice-table handlers and croupiers pushed the bills exchanged for chips into the slot that collected them in a locked container.

I dropped ten dollars at the wheel, playing my favorite numbers: 3, 6, 9, which were no luckier than my unfavorite numbers, 7 and 11.

Gloria was at my elbow showing two fists holding folded money. "I'm doing it. I'm going to make our expenses . . ."

I knew better than to ask Gloria to hold back half her winnings for the next evening and to stop when she had lost the other half. She smiled at a British couple who were dropping aitches like hail.

"I'm trying a new dealer. Come along and watch Mamma win our hotel bills."

"Marvelous, bloody marvelous," said the male Briton. He said he and the missus might risk a shilling or two.

Gloria was a good blackjack player. She took chances, but I had explained the odds and the game to her on other trips to Las Vegas. Why then did she leave after a weekend visit without winnings? One has to see the game from the house side and not from the view of the gambler to understand that.

Charlie Ross, now retired in Florida, who had been one of the best blackjack dealers in the gambling world for over thirty years, explained to me the house advantage in all games of chance, but particularly in twenty-one.

"It's so easy any bright kid can play it. The dealer deals you cards. You can stop him anytime you feel you have come as close as you can to adding up to twenty-one. If you call for another card and you run over twenty-one, the house wins. You also risk the house's getting closer to twenty-one with the cards it deals itself. You can bet a dollar to five dollars a game. The simplest rule for the player is to figure he can win with 12 but lose with a 17 by calling for one more card. Several people can play at once against the dealer. The odds against you are smaller than in most casino games, and if you play with sense, don't plunge, or play hunches, you can sometimes—not often—come out ahead."

Can you beat the twenty-one table with science? One enigmatic personality, a mathematics professor, Edward Thorp, in the early 1970s used a portable computer to figure the odds as certain cards were dealt out of the working deck. This gave him, with his machine, certain percentages for and against the house. It was reported that using his system in one session, he had beaten a casino out of $2,000 in four hours of play. The casino bosses figured that he wasn't their kind of player, and he was barred from play at many blackjack tables.

Charlie Ross said, "Some people *can* count cards without a computer system. Sometimes they beat the law of averages by winning. These card freaks are called 'counters.' As a dealer I figured the only way to beat a counter was to play very *fast* hands, create a lot of talk, a lot of smooz—keep riffling the deck and do anything to break the wise guy's concentration, toss off his timing against the laws of probability. Another way to beat the counter is to use two or four deck of cards, *not* one."

Most counters I talked to were trying to sell their system. They claimed they were barred from play because their sure thing winning method hurt the casinos. Actually, such talk is a come-on to peddle their systems. Few counters have ever actually been barred from the blackjack tables.

At one o'clock I wanted to go to my room. Gloria was losing and changing tables, muttering of deceit and prevarication. She said to me, "Don't watch me play. You jinx me."

I agreed—it's a tradition that watchers jinx their friends.

Lester was ahead at the dice tables, but he was making no steady wins, just winning and losing, taking side bets that he'd make his point. But he was still ahead and having a fine time rattling the dice in his cupped hands and sending them at a gallop to bounce off the backboard.

Come on dice, treat me nice
Roll, roll, you lucky dice.

I would have preferred a chant based on a remark attributed to Mark Twain in Virginia City: "The best throw at dice is to throw them away." I noticed the expressions of those around me; there are few occupations more tense than expecting to make quick money.

Lester must have caught my stare, for he gave up the dice and came over to me. His face was shiny, his voice truculent. "Oh, man; I was hot as a two-dollar pistol. Old buddy, it was going big there, ahead eight hundred bucks. But I cooled."

"You're still ahead."

"Just a couple hundred. I still feel hot tonight. I'm going to play the wheel."

If you've been around gamblers long enough, you've learned that you can't reason with anyone who has been gambling for a few hours; you cannot impress him with what passes for reason and logic; his logic has mostly evaporated. Lester was an ardent roulette player, but the game never favored him as well as dice. He told me he had lost more at roulette over the years than at dice. Tonight, playing red or black, he seemed to have a streak of luck.

Roulette is, of course, played with a wheel that spins a small ivory or plastic ball into numbered slots, 1 to 36, with a 0 and a 00, played on a table laid out with these numbers in squares. It's an old game, some authorities claiming the Greeks and Romans played it by spinning the numbered spokes of their chariot wheels. Pascal, a genius, a religious figure and a mathematical expert, may have fathered the modern roulette wheel in the sixteenth century while trying to perfect a perpetual motion machine. He did invent the first practical adding machine, and his models of that still exist, but not of his roulette wheel.

Roulette reached England in 1820. It would have come over sooner, but Napoleon, nearly always at war with England, didn't encourage in the English a love of "a Frenchie gambling device." There was an English game with a wheel called "even odd," but roulette seems a more interesting gambling game. It came to America via New Orleans, when the French held that city before Jefferson bought it in what came to be known as the Louisiana Purchase.

Great craftsmanship goes into a bowl-shaped wheel, inlaid

and gussied up in rare woods. The croupier spins it by hand, counterclockwise. He tosses in the little ball clockwise. As the wheel slows, it seems to be picking a favorite slot for the ball as it bounces about; then the ball drops down into either a black- or a red-numbered space set up in alternate order. A lot of players often attend a table. Each player buys chips of a color that denotes their value; values from twenty-five cents up to whatever limit the house has on a chip, usually a $100 value or more. A straight bet, *if* your number comes up, pays 35 to 1. You can split a bet by placing your chip on a line between the numbers; that gets you 17 to 1. The house advantage works out to about 5.26 percent for them on most spins and 7.89 on a five-number bet (spreading your chips on lines dividing numbers).

Charlie Ross was amused at the idea of systems to beat the wheel. "Been thousands of systems created to beat the house. Sure, they work nicely—on paper. They add up right to some cockeyed mathematical genius, but none have yet worked in actual play. Take that sucker system—for all the fancy algebra, that insists on betting a *bigger* sum every time you lose. It's a dud. Don't ever try that. These system makers, they work out long rows of figures, they carry notebooks, keep scores, list winning numbers in series. So? Once off the paper the answer is no—back to the drawing board. Some of them bet on red only, some bet on black only—figuring by the laws of chance they have to hit big as they double each loss."

Are wheels honest? As honest, Charlie insists, as the Vegas casino people *and* the state inspectors can make them. "It's very easy to rig a wheel, and lots of wheels in the old and the new West were and are being rigged. Hardly ever in Nevada, and certainly not by the big casinos in Reno and Vegas." Still, now and then the word is out of a rigged wheel being picked up. Of course no reports of this are ever issued.

"Why cheat? The casinos' take in the posh places seems to be a happy one with a fat house percentage. Baccarat they discourage; it gives them a smaller percentage. They would rather the guest played the slot machines."

Las Vegas loves the clang of its one-armed bandits at work. It takes in about $700 million a year at its casinos, less what they pay the winners and the cost of running the places.

The history of the American slot machine begins in 1887 in San Francisco with a Bavarian mechanic who made one that paid out in nickles and was set up in saloons among drinkers of steam beer and eaters of crab stews. The house take was 25 percent. As gambling devices cannot be patented, in Chicago one Herbert Mills with dogged ingenuity began to make and set up slot machines all over the country. From 1906 he was Mr. Slot Machine. In 1920 he added the jackpot—a special win of hard-to-make patterns. The average slot machine is a mechanical marvel of over 600 metal parts, springs, plastics, *and* a trustworthy method of adjusting the house percentage of the coins dropped in for play. The exterior is often as gaudy as a Barbary Coast trollop, and just as greedy.

When the bootleggers in the 1930s were put out of business by repeal, the Mafia went into the slot-machine rackets, and soon most states had laws outlawing the slots. Legally they can be displayed and played only in Nevada, where about 40,000 of them are in active service. It takes no brains on the players' part, no figuring of odds or numbers. It's just drop in a coin and pull a lever. Some machines in deft and devious design have two levers and take two coins at the same time.

You can't figure out any system to beat a slot. It does not respond to any ardent prescience to win. There are, on a three-reel machine, 8,000 combinations. A four-reel machine can come up with 160,000. No "English," pulling hard or slow, hitting it, or kicking it can change the result—your disappointment or rare exhilaration. In Nevada the slot machines are usually reasonably fair and are state-inspected. The best odds are downtown rather than in the big casinos. The worst payoffs are in trash-food eating places, diners, gas stations, and drugstores, or wherever the slot machine isn't the main ripoff.

What odds does the gambler get? In theory, the casino machines are set to pay back ninety cents for every dollar put in. Most are usually set at a 75 percent payoff, and some go down to 50 percent. Each slot machine can be set as to the percent of payoff. Long-time players insist that a tight machine means less payoff; a loose machine means a better percentage. It is said that a machine will often be fixed to pay off 95 percent to excite the playing interest of the crowd. But if so, it's usually planted among 75 percent payoff machines, since players like to play a row of machines. The odds are heavy against your beating the slots if you play long enough. It's all figured out by percentages. A professor from USC, in Vegas for a week, told me: "Go beat Euclid. House odds always win, over any period of time. Once upon a time there were nickel-and-dime machines. Now it's mostly quarter, half-dollar and dollar machines. You can write the history of inflation just by the change in the cost of playing slot machines, juke boxes, the expected tips."

Can someone cheat the house by fixing a slot machine? The casinos insist with tranquillity that it can't be done. But a few years ago someone figured out a way of drilling holes in a slot machine with a battery-operated drill and with long wires adjusting the machine to pay off jackpots. Some have claimed magnets can be used to control a slot's innards for the right combination of reels. For the average player who drops in coins over any long period of time, all he'll end up with will be a well-developed arm and wrist.

What encourages players are items such as: A seventy-year-old man who invested $200 "fishing money" reaped a jackpot of $90,000 on a Harrah's Club slot machine. The winner, who identified himself only as a retired service-station operator from Bridgeport, California, lined up four "men in a barrel" on a dollar machine.

"Too many people know me," he said, declining to give his name. "I think I'll get a motor home and go fishing in Alaska. There's a lot of fish up there."

What are the odds of lining up four images to match on a slot machine? One player told me a million to one—maybe a million and a half to one. But when it happens, play goes up about 30 percent.

The Great Babylon also had a baccarat room, which it would put into play if enough demand was made for it. There are people who seem to have seen so many movies of play at Monte Carlo that they feel baccarat has class. But the players at baccarat I have seen in Vegas do not resemble the film aristocrats (dress extras), the sinister Oriental or Latin faces (character actors), and the international Mata Hari types (usually typists and carhops hoping to be noticed by a director).

Mostly the people were watching the box dealing the cards, or the thin oar with which the croupier or table manager picked up the bets of the losers or swept over the winning chips. It's all an unreal drama to Americans; it lacks the earthy pitch of the crap tables, the circus quality of twenty-one; or, as Lester put it, "Where you seem to be playing against a carnival sharper who you think you can outsmart."

The Great Babylon's baccarat room was open, but at first Lester declined to play. "You know, I feel I'd be sitting between David Niven and James Bond, and someone would hand me a silver-plated pistol if I lost."

But in the end he took a seat.

Charlie Ross remembers when baccarat first came to Las Vegas, in 1958. On the first night of play, according to casino managers, they lost a half a million dollars on the opening of the tables. "This you take," Charlie insisted, "with a great deal of salt." The game is actually close to one or two other games which are somewhat similar: chemin de fer and baccarat banque. It is supposed to have started at the court of Charles VIII in the fifteenth century. Gamblers tried to bring it into the United States at the turn of the century, in Saratoga and Palm Beach, but it didn't catch on.

"To some, it is a class game of social status. Bets run from five dollars to $2,000, which is usually the top permitted. You hear stories of great winnings and great losses at baccarat. I remember the chatter about this character, one of those mystery figures of the Greek Syndicate named Nicholas Zatrophos. He is said to have won half a million in three hands of play. Maybe; maybe not. I've seen the famous Dolly Sisters play. They had a patsy; he was Gordon Selfridge of London, who backed them at baccarat over a period of time, during which the gals maybe lost $8 million of his loot. André Citroen, builder of the French automobile, lost half a million at one sitting at baccarat.

"Actually the Las Vegas baccarat came up from Cuba, not Europe. In Havana it ruled the Mafia's tables before Castro put the dealers and gamblers to cutting sugar cane, or they escaped to Florida and joined the FBI or the CIA.

"The table layout looks complex, and in an honest game it

gives the player a fairly even chance, tilted toward the house in its percentage. A table can hold twelve players and three dealers. You are betting on numbers. Nine is the highest winning number, and the highest hand that comes up wins. The dealer slips out the cards from a box called a 'shoe.' Don't be impressed by the terms 'bank' and 'player.' It's just betting on whatever set of cards turns up. You play as bank or player, but it doesn't mean a thing. Suits mean nothing. The face value of the card counts, and highest cards take the table. Actually it's all mechanically simple—any bet you make is just as good as any other. Don't be carried away by the sucker's hope of using the Martingale system, which is nothing more or less than doubling your bet every time you lose. The doubling up gets too high ever to win it back in a few rounds."

(For the intimate details of baccarat, study *The Weekend Gambler's Handbook,* by Major A. Riddle.)

(Chemin de fer is not popular in the United States, but it is a big game in Europe. It differs from baccarat only in that the bank passes from player to player, and the gamblers are wagering against each other, the house taking its cut from each winning bank.)

Lester came away from the table holding up two ten-dollar chips. "That's how it ends tonight; a double sawbuck."
I asked, "What did you start with today?"
"Hundred and fifty."
"And two more nights to go."
"Like a good-running race horse, I hold back at the start."
"Let's go see what Gloria has."
Gloria was ahead eighty-two dollars. Lester forced her to stop play. "It's two-ten in the morning, honey."
"I coulda made a real bundle," she insisted all the way up to our rooms. But it was clear Gloria could hardly keep her eyes open. At their door I said, "Want to stash your winnings, Gloria?"
She stuck her tongue out at me.

The next two nights (and days) were a mere reenactment of the sensations of our first appearance in Las Vegas. We ate too much of the food, mixed with the visitors and the staffs of the Great Babylon and other hotels, and saw two more stage shows. Lester and Gloria won and lost, and while they were shy about admitting it, I figured they were out $400 in losses at twenty-one, dice, and roulette. But it seems they had been prepared for such an outlay for the fun of the weekend—viewing the scantily attired tall show girls and raucous comics—and for tipping heavily without wincing.

On the last night (we were flying back to Los Angeles in the morning) we went downtown, where there is more noise, more electric signs, and a more outgoing crowd (hard to believe, because the people at the big Strip casinos were not held back by any shyness, or by even a small measure of good manners).

The garb was more movie-Western with a touch of sleaziness. Whiskers, long hair, regional accents were more plentiful. A sense of strain was apparent on some faces. Glitter Gulch in mood and method is closer to the old-time medicine show and snake-oil peddler. There is a more vivid appeal to direct sensation. For months one gambling parlor exhibited $1 million piled up in hundred-dollar bills in its lobby (under glass and guard).

While all forms of gambling games are played downtown (one even finds a faro outfit on display), the major game is keno. It is played with sound and fury, mainly by the middle-aged and old folk of both sexes, the women often with rhinestone-studded shades, blue-rinsed gray hair; the men in straw "Stetsons" or baseball caps.

Serious gamblers and wise visitors avoid keno. Charlie Ross sneered at it. "It proves that you can set up any kind of rube game, from a rubber pea and three walnut shells, to offering shares in the Brooklyn Bridge, and you'll get willing takers knocking you over to get taken.

"Keno is the sucker's game. The house starts with a 25 percent take for itself, and that's only the lowest take. It can take more. You don't really stand much of a chance of ever making the $25,000 top payoff."

The Chinese brought keno to America when they were imported as cheap labor for building the Central Pacific Railroad. It was an old game, some say over 2,000 years old. It was a popular game in the early Western cattle and mining towns. It is theatrical, a group effort, and a good way to meet people. Some play it with imperturbable phlegm, most with energetic, determined watchfulness.

Gloria and I bought keno cards, while Lester wandered off in search of a dice table.

A keno card usually is lettered "Keno $25,000." It's a bit of cardboard with ruled boxes holding eighty numbers. You buy a keno card from sixty cents to one dollar, even more in some games. A device called a "goose" picks twenty numbers at random. If five or more numbers—up to ten—on your card are called, you're a winner. Of what? The house percentage in each game, as I've indicated, is from 25 to 40 percent. On a ten-spot card only six out of a hundred players win anything.

Charlie figured odds on winning as "on a five-spot odds are one in twenty; six-spot, one in eighty-eight; seven-spot, one in 620; nine-spot, one in 161; and on a ten-spot, one in nine million.

"If you have a sixty-cent card and you cover five numbers, you get five dollars. An eight cover pays twelve fifty. On any fifteen basic tickets there are millions of combinations. Sure, it's a comfortable game to sit and enjoy, but the odds are so against the player, it's hardly a game of real chance."

Lester found a faro outfit in play, but only for show. Faro is hardly ever played anymore. The game was popular in the old West. Thirteen cards are used, a deck is dealt from a "shoe." The second card is a loser, the third a winner, and so on through the deck. It is a time-wasting game, and no one wins or loses much, neither the player nor the house.

There are other special games downtown.

The wheel of fortune is the old carnival wheel with numbers painted on it. It's for lookers ("gooney birds"), viewers who come to be in a casino but don't play the usual games. Some do try a few turns of the wheel. It's a sucker's ploy; the house odds are loaded 40 or more percent against the player.

Chuck-a-luck is another one for the lookers. It's a wire cage with three dice in it. You bet on numbers to add up to a score.

The payoff is even money. The house has a 40 percent advantage here, too. It has been figured out that a player in 215 turns of the cage can win only a little over a hundred times. The best part of it all is that the house doesn't use any of its own money; it's all put up by the players.

Even Lester steered clear of the match game. We held Gloria back. ("A pure sucker's game," Charlie insisted. "The great con for the knowing player.") There are fifteen matches in a pile. You can remove one, two, or three matches at a time. The one who has to pick up the last match is the loser. Charlie described the play: "The con artist, if he goes first, takes two matches. The sucker usually is forced to keep picking up an odd number against the original fifteen matches. He loses. A lot of suckers end up taking the game back home and playing their friends as suckers. It looks easy to let the con artist end up with the last match, but it isn't."

Sunday afternoon the visitors begin to leave. Nightfall sees a bigger exodus. Monday morning is the end of the weekend. Eighty percent of them are losers, as a casino pit man told me. "They lost money, but most had a limit they exceeded a little bit. No sweat; they could handle it. Half of them could have run a hundred over what they expected to lose if they weren't in luck. Ten percent, I'd say, got hit but heavy. Two or three percent—it varies every weekend—are into the casino for money up to five to fifty grand *if* their okayed moniker on the IOUs holds up. Usually 'Dragon Breath,' the manager, takes these markers only from people he feels he can trust to pay up. But there are welshers; actors are the worst. Sometimes an IOU goes as high as seventy-five Gs. Sure, sure, there are collectors. No strong-arming. Maybe just a little leaning. But in the main the IOUs get paid off. However, the average visitors lose only what they have on them, or have decided to drop."

Most people preparing to depart looked tired, some were in crumpled clothes, staring weary-eyed, but as they gathered there was little griping. They had had themselves a time, they told each other. A little old lady agreed as she lifted up two ash trays to deposit in her handbag while she waited for a bus to the airport.

As the hotel guests prepared to depart, some superficial philosophies were exchanged with addresses between new-made friends. Gloria was sleepy but happy. She was ahead sixty-two dollars. Not from blackjack winnings ("I bitched it there . . .") but from a lucky tap of a slot machine at the Fremont downtown. Lester was not talking of losses. "I didn't do so badly, I'm *not* complaining. I mean I had the fun and the excitement."

After paying the hotel bill and the charges for services, a lot of hardware would have to be sold to make up for the Vegas trip of the Russells. They felt it was worth it. Lester said, "You know, my father used to hand the train conductor the fine, a ten-dollar bill, and pull the emergency cord. That's how we are."

Most of the Monday morning crowd at the airport seemed to feel it was worth it, too, and if any wounds were to be licked, they didn't show.

Net bags and plastic containers held rock and ore sets, toy pistols, gifts for children and grandchildren. Some tourists cherished the ornate dinner menus of the Sands, the Grand Hotel, the Sahara. The males had bought leather cowboy belts, "Indian" cuff links and tie pins. Some had even gone to Hoover Dam and "walked from Nevada underground right over to Arizona and back."

Greyhounds and Trailways buses passed with visitors taking the desert road home, as did passenger cars and a great many trailers. The air was crisp; the heat of the new day was rising, and a far-off mesa was beginning to show a cloud, blowing sand. A solitary bird, hawk or buzzard, circled motionless in the air currents and then moved off toward a private dump to seek for tidbits among the bashed-in gilt party hats, condoms, empty cigarette packs, discarded containers of Charmin toilet paper.

Aboard the plane Gloria settled down with a paper bag in her lap, expecting a rough trip. She closed her eyes and said as she exhaled, "It was fun."

"It was," said Lester as he handed me part of the Los Angeles *Times* bought at the airport. We took off with a bumpy swoop. Once released of their safety belts, some of the passengers began to talk among themselves. Several seemed to be asleep, and some didn't care to be talked to.

Across the way a man with an American Legion button in his lapel was explaining how well he had played a hand of poker at Caesar's Palace and how near he had once come to a royal flush in Seattle. A woman was repacking Indian dolls and a toy roulette set in a yellow shopping bag lettered GUCCI.

I turned to the newspaper:

FOUR LAS VEGAS CASINOS
OWNER FINED $77,000
by Al Delugach

Las Vegas—The Nevada Gambling Commission levied $77,000 in fines against Allen R. Glick and his four casinos after finding they violated state laws in connection with $1.6 million in losses.

Glick personally was found guilty of illegally accepting a $500,000 loan from prospective buyers of his Airport Casino and fined $25,000.

The balance of the fines were against his companies that operate the Airport Casino and the Stardust, Fremont and Hacienda casinos for failure to report other loans.

Glick confirmed to reporters outside the hearing that he has entered into a "letter of intent" to sell the Hacienda to what he described as a Texas group headed by Joseph Gennitti. He declined to comment on the reported price of $21 million.

Gloria said, "Next year?"
Lester signaled the hostess for drinks. "Next year, honey."

2

IN THE BEGINNING

Perhaps the first gambling in the New World took place aboard Columbus's ships. His crews carried playing cards and dice to while away the long and fearful voyage. As the fear that they were dropping off the edge of the world increased, they threw overboard their sinful playing cards and dice as an act of exorcism of the demon called gambling.

On reaching the shores of what they thought was India, they felt the loss of the cards, for like most sailors they were inveterate gambling men. One story relates that they marked and cut out crude decks of cards from the leaves of the copas tree.

When Cortez and other Spanish and Portuguese gold hunters moved in on the New World, the most valued items the soldiers carried, next to their weapons, were cards and dice. *Amapatolli* (*amati*—paper and *patolli*—game), as cards were known in Mexico, have been traced back to still-surviving cards listed as *Nueva España, 1583*.

Playing cards were certainly the easiest kind of gambling game to carry with one to the New World, even if the church preached against gambling. As for dice, they could be molded of clay, marked with dots and tossed into the campfire to harden; or they could be carved from wood. But the dice handed down from early white men in America were usually carved from sheep joints and cow shins; there is a rare set made of whale ivory said to have been found in Florida at an old Spanish fort site.

Betting on horse races also came early to the New World. The Spaniards brought over those marvelous huge war horses that flattened the Aztecs with fear—for at first they thought that man *and* horse were one animal. Not only did race-running animals cause betting among the roistering colonists, but steeds that had escaped drifted into Indian territory. In time the Indians of the Great Plains became, according to General Sherman, "the best light cavalry in the world." The Indian, be he Sioux, Apache, Cherokee, or Cheyenne, not only rode well but gambled madly for pony herds; the loser could always get up a war party to go raiding for enough of a herd to try to come back a winner in the tribal race meets. Animosities and warfare over horses led to historic Indian wars.

When the Dutch and English came to America in great numbers, cards and dice came along. Priority and position of rank were often decided by the ability to wager large sums in gold. If some of the early New Englanders were a bit stuffy about gambling, the Virginians and Pennsylvanians and other colonists were not. Cards and dice were to be had at all taverns, along with the hot toddies and the rum flip. The planters of the South spent as much time on their racing horses or hunts and breeding farms as they did on their tobacco and indigo and cotton; often a whole season's crop was gambled away.

Eventually, laws were made to control or forbid gambling. Washington Irving mentions that cards were used by the early Dutch settlers, and card playing "during church services" was forbidden in the settlement of New Amsterdam. The grim New England Pilgrims were not free of the "vice." The Plymouth Colony laid fines against card fiends caught at play: forty shillings in 1656, two pounds each in 1661. Servants and minors handling the pasteboards could "be publicly whipt."

Even the Puritans and the Pilgrims had a few rough types that insisted on betting on games of chance in the hope of winning, and tried systems to avoid losing. The Massachusetts legislature insisted that "cards and dice are dishonor to God." And in Connecticut, it was firmly ordered, "No woman shall kiss her child on the Sabbath, or Fasting day. No one shall make minced pies, dance, play cards . . ." Obviously, some were pathologically opposed to pie and four aces on a day set aside to sing hymns.

It was not just the young or the elderly, the high livers and the struggling farmer or hunter who played cards and brought on the stern glare of legal disapproval. The Virginia Assembly in 1624, pointing out that often the clergy were also guilty, decreed: "Mynisters shall not give themselves to excesse in drinking or yett spend their tyme idelie by day or night, playing at dice, cards or any unlawful game."

That didn't stop the shops from carrying cards, some imported from England, some true American-printed products. In the early eighteenth century a good deck cost a shilling, and a card table, costing from twelve shillings up to six to ten pounds, was a proper social status symbol for every well-furnished house. Shops advertised "Bibles, common prayer Books . . . playing cards . . . sand glasses [hourglasses], Leather Breeches. . . ." Others advertised "Ben Heston's Snuff, glassware . . . playing cards, etc." or "The sale of Mogul and Andrew cards."

Cards were given fancy names such as Mogul and Andrew (also known as Merry Andrew). Popular stylish names were Eagle, Harry VIII, Superfine Eagle, Highblander, Refuse, Columbian, Steamboats.

All Americans know about the infamous Stamp Act that in the end "fired the shot heard round the world" at Concord. But few are aware that the act contained the clause of a tax ". . . upon every pack of playing cards and all dice . . . sold or used within said colonies or plantations, the several stamp duties following. . . . For every pack of such cards, the sum of 1 shilling . . . no playing cards or dice shall be sold or used in play . . . unless the paper and thread enclosing them shall have been sealed and stamped as provided in pursuance of this act."

The general whom the Continental Congress selected to fight the British in that War of Independence was a Virginia planter, sportsman and gambler named George Washington. He kept an account of "income and expenditure," a record of horse betting and his gambling at cards—winnings or losses.

"January 18, 1768. At home all day at cards—it snowing. . . . By cash set aside for card money, five pounds. . . . September 5, 1776. At home all day playing cards."

Yet at Morristown in 1777, fighting a war, Washington issued an order: ". . . the commander in chief . . . forbids all officers and soldiers playing at cards, dice or any games except those of EXERCISE for diversion."

Washington's private records show he was sometimes more

of a loser than a winner at cards. Usually playing whist, he lost 19 shillings one night at play, over 6 shillings at another time, and two pounds eleven shillings the next time. Catherine Perry Hargrave, in her fine book *A History of Card Playing*, lists Washington's losses for a period of four years to be seventy-eight pounds five shillings and ninepence, and his winnings seventy-two pounds two shillings and sixpence, a loss of only about seven pounds. Clearly Washington was not a man to ruin himself gambling.

It is possible that Paul Revere designed a pack of playing cards. An early deck shows Paul Revere's eagle design framed by the ace of spades. Over the eagle are the words USE BUT DON'T ABUSE ME, and below, EVIL BE TO HIM THAT EVIL THINKS. But final proof of Revere as designer or engraver is lacking; the printer of the cards may have only copied Revere's eagle.

While any printer might issue or set himself up as a card maker, eventually a handful of firms that were card specialists dominated the trade. In one set of cards printed around 1850, the ace of spades sported large portraits of George and Martha Washington. This was also about the time round-cornered, satin-finished cards began to appear. In 1879 the respected firm of Tiffany & Company in New York published (card makers preferred that word to "printed") a series of playing cards with comic cartoon figures known as the Harlequin Playing Cards.

The names of the early packs were usually English, but by the end of the nineteenth century decks of cards had American names. One finds cards listed as Congress ("gold edged"), Tigers, Sportsman, Army and Navy Mascot, and Tally-Ho. The name "Bicycle Playing Cards" covered a whole range of packs for sports lovers (Nick the Greek favored them). Baseball playing cards featured big-league stars of the game long before bubble gum was invented. In 1903 The United States Playing Card Company issued a deck featuring the head of the American Indian.

When men had worn out or lost their decks in rough places far from civilization, they would often improvise cards from whatever was on hand. Spanish soldiers in Mexico had painted card faces on leather. A letter from one of the forty-niners in Hangtown, California, said: " . . . so it beeing bad weather we hacked out and marked some book end papers into a fairish deck of kards and I loss 3 ounces of gold dust from my poke and have got to swear off gambling here as my partneers must have got to know very well the cards from the back. . . ."

Both men and women gambled. In high society, a soirée or fête of proper protocol would pad out the boredom of colonial life. Betting on dogs or bull-baiting or horses provided entertainment. Benjamin Franklin produced and printed playing cards and sold them in post offices.

Right from the start America was involved with the problems and pleasures of gambling. The Spanish and the French in Louisiana and Florida had no Puritan guilt about betting on cards and dice, lotteries, horse races and cockfights.

A British officer writing back to England noted: "The menn are given to great gambling, and most shan't have a coin left, even parting with their shirts at the dice and sundry carde games."

The white man brought the Indians whisky and diseases from Europe, but gambling was a pastime the natives had always engaged in. They had a form of dice made from plum and peach stones, some with white sides, some with black. From a bowl the dice were thrown half a dozen times; the number of black or white sides decided the winner. Some of the games even included chanting.

George Catlin, the great Indian painter, reported hearing that some Indian tribes made playing cards out of tree bark, painted images on them, and slapped them down on the ground in the manner of poker players. However, he added that they had no idea of how the white man's game was actually played. In the Northwest on the Columbia River, Indian tribes had a fearful kind of a gambling cult called potlatch. This has been defined as "a distribution or exchange of gifts during a festival, often involving the squandering of *all* one's belongings, even wives and daughters." It was reckless gambling in reverse. The first player began by giving away some of his belongings, and the receiver in return began by giving away his. The contest seems to have consisted of each giving away his assets. Weapons, boats, tents, pots, blankets, and even one's family could be given away. It appears to have been a race to see which player could become a pauper first. But unlike modern losses at gambling, everyone often ended up with a new estate. The game had actually been observed in which players had been left with nothing. The loser would be the Indian who walked off with everything in the tribe.

"Cock pittes" existed in all the colonies, where trained and deadly birds tore each other to bits with steel spurs attached to their legs. The betting was heavy. Many a colonial library contained a print of William Hogarth's "Cock Fight" in which even a blind gambler is laying a wager on a cock.

It was an age when animals were seen only as objects of sport. The native bear was sometimes baited by a bull, or savage dogs were set against a bear. The Puritans frowned on this sport of bear-baiting and banned it. As one wry historian wrote: "Not because it gave pain to the bear, but because it gave pleasure to the spectators."

The colonial people bet on wrestling matches, target shooting, and dog and rat fights. Dog fights were a common sport, with specially bred and trained pit dogs; dogs against dogs or dogs in a pit against huge rats. The betting was heavy on some champion rat-killer, or on a dog able to stand against another dog to the death. A general surface of satin and laces, polite bows, and high rhetoric hid a desire for blood sports.

Lighter moments were corn-husking bees, where the young and old gathered to husk the harvest with music, hard or soft cider, and bets on who could husk the most corn. Wagers were on the best husker, based on a given time. Often, too, a husking bee encouraged marriage. According to Mark Twain, a corn husking could produce as many babies nine months later as a religious camp meeting.

A tug of war between fire companies, militia, or citizens with muscle was heavily bet on, often causing civil riots when some folk not part of a team took hold of the rope and all of them lost their amiable dispositions.

Horse racing was a most popular sport. Every farm, plantation, village or town had a horse that could beat any other horse a measured mile on the county pike. An unidentified clipping in a scrapbook notes: "We do hearby state by Jehovah and the Continental Congress that the spotted horse, Pompey, owned by Sq. Welton, can out run any horse in Middlesex County and will meet on the village green this Sattaday [sic] to show it."

The breeding of blood lines, the pride in prime horseflesh, and betting on its speed and endurance was a popular pastime. One bet gold, silver coins, furs, hogsheads of tobacco, or teams of oxen, but there is no record (as with some Indians) of the betting of a wife or a daughter.

Horse racing was a privilege reserved for gentlemen. In Virginia in 1769 only gentlemen, seen as such by law, could race horses. A tailor named James Bullock was fined one hundred pounds of tobacco for invading a "sport of gentlemen" by entering and running a horse. After the Revolution, however, anyone could race horses.

While horse racing must have existed on these shores almost from the start, it was a Colonel Richard Nicolls, the first English governor of New York, who set up the first race track—as far as records go—the Newmarket track on Salisbury Plains (near Garden City today). The date was 1666, and the tout and the bookie seem to have appeared on the scene almost at once. A page from the daybook of a New York merchant and fur dealer notes:

"This day did go to Nu. Mark. for the race matches. Had news of a strong steed, Caesar, from Ned Wells the draper. Did place 3 pd. did see Caesar be out run. Drank pear cider with Ned. Swear to Goody [wife?] will wager no moor. . . ."

As there are bets recorded in other pages of the daybook, it would seem that the fur trader–dealer, like most gamblers who swore off, didn't.

Until the American Revolution, gambling in the colonies was on the English pattern, modified by the changes needed in a new land. Types sent to America were the poor soldier or idle apprentice, once doomed to the gallows, playing at cards with his last coin. Transpose these scenes to the colonies where, in bloody Kentucky, they played at "kyards." Then there were the "lobsterbacks," the Hanoverian soldiers of George III who were later to fight at Waterloo, and at New Orleans against Andrew Jackson. We hear echoes of the rattle of their dice and their curses at the new land as they deal their tattered deck of cards.

With a new nation and its currency "not worth a continental [dollar]," the Congress, in 1776, to rally a kitty for the war, organized a lottery of $5 million in prizes. However, winnings over fifty dollars were to be paid in promissory notes, not to be collected in some cases for years. The whole project was a disaster. It was mismanaged by honest people and exploited by the dishonest. Very few holding winning lottery tickets got anything at all.

No wonder "The Lottery Song" was popular in the eighteenth century:

> *In the fish pond of fortune men angle always;*
> *Some angle for titles, some angle for praise,*
> *Some angle for favor, some angle for wives,*
> *And some angle for nought*
> *All the days of their lives. . . .*

One collector of Americana has shown me an original lottery ticket of the 1776 issue where across it the buyer has written lines by George Herbert:

> *Play not for gain but sport. Who plays for more*
> *Than he can lose with pleasure stakes his heart.*

And this note: "A man gets no thanks for what he loseth at play."

Benjamin Franklin, ever the practical man, had helped organize a Pennsylvania lottery in 1748 to raise three thousand pounds for military supplies to defend Philadelphia against Frenchmen and Indians. He had succeeded where the Continental Congress had not. The Congress also appeared to refuse to face facts when it issued orders to stop "extravagance and dissipation, horse racing, and all kinds of gaming or cock fighting." Yet George Washington, even in the darkest years of the war (1776–79), continued to play cards, sometimes losing nine pounds a night, while ordering "all officers, noncommissioned officers and soldiers . . . positively forbid playing at cards, or other games of chance . . . at this time of public distress men must find enough to do, in service of their God and their country, without abandoning themselves to vice and immorality."

There is noted in one letter from a soldier freezing and starving at Valley Forge that the Americans were rolling dice for acorns as food.

Jefferson took the high road and had petulant resentment for gambling. "Gaming corrupts our dispositions, and teaches us a habit of hostility against all mankind." But in June of 1776, when Thomas Jefferson was working on the draft of the Declaration of Independence, in three weeks of his private record of his losses and winnings at gambling, he marked down: "Lost at Backgammon 7/6. Won at Backgammon 7d 1/3. Won at cross and pyle, 3¾d [the match game?]. Mrs. Jefferson, lost at cards 1/3. Lost at lotto (a form of bingo), 18/d."

It is one of the American myths that Southerners were greater and more passionate gamblers than Northerners. This is hardly true if we search journals, old letters, and the police records. Yet most of the names one comes across in popular histories speak highly of the Southern gambler as a man of emotional expansiveness, a knight in white linen.

Certainly Andrew Jackson, victor of New Orleans and an American president, gambled and bet heavily. He once wagered a favorite horse in a dice game and won the roll. Jackson was a chance-taker in 1805 when he acquired a horse named Truxon, a beautiful bay, fast, with a reputation for being able to run any other horse off its legs. Jackson bought the horse from an owner who thought Truxon was out of condition. Jackson was short of cash; most of the country nabobs were, being rich in land and horses and slaves but not in gold coin. Still, he bought the horse and somehow got the $5,000 to pay for him. Truxon was matched to race Greyhound (who had once beaten him) in the spring at Hartsville, Tennessee. The talk was that the Jackson horse was tired and overtrained. The odds were hard against him with the bookmakers and the bet-takers. Farmers bet their tobacco, plantation owners their cotton. Jackson, having little else to wager, bet his dueling pistols, and also, in arbitrary consistency, bet $500 in "wearing apparel." (It is so recorded—which must have made a pile of greatcoats, waistcoats, nankeen pants, boots, and fancy beaver toppers.)

A drum started the horse race. Off ran the prized creatures—to howls, cries and cheers. The race was close; everyone cheered again and filled up on beer, flip, and whisky. Truxon won in a good fast mile. A report item notes that some ladies bet some of their wearing apparel, and many men went back home on foot, having bet horse and buggy and gig and buckboard on the wrong horse. As far as can be learned, Washington and Jackson were the only American presidents who raced horses. President Andrew Jackson remained a gambling man. He often attended the National Track just outside Washington, D.C. At one meet, one of his horses was shipped up from the Hermitage, his Tennessee plantation, and set to running. Jackson bet and lost $1,000. Vice-President Van Buren also lost a bundle. Jackson bred his own gamecocks, fought them, and bet on them in Maryland, across the river from Washington.

With gambling by congressmen and officials at cards, dice, and horses at the track so prevalent, it was often difficult to gather in a quorum to vote. Mark Twain's *The Gilded Age* gives us the whole color and sound of the period: the gamblers, the pressure players, the fast women, and the gambling spirit that existed in Washington, D.C., with its wooden sidewalks up to the Civil War and after.

Of course there was betting on elections. Van Buren had bet $40,000 and a suit for evening wear on his chance of becoming president. During the years Franklin Pierce was president, cards were played in the White House. But the Washington gentry preferred the "Hall of the Bleeding Heart," a splendid gambling establishment set up in 1832 by an Edward Pendleton as "The Palace of Fortune." It was a place for gambling, meeting women, and eating gourmet food. Great amounts of gambling money passed hands, often by lobbyists pushing forward their clients' interests with rolls of cash for the proper vote. Pendleton, himself a Homeric boozer, was one of the most powerful lobbyists in Washington, able to influence congressmen who played at his tables to listen to reason while coins clicked within reach and the winning cards slid across the green felt. For a quarter of a century Pendleton dominated the Washington gambling and sporting scene. He was a dude in dress, moved in the highest social and political circles, and manipulated votes in Congress with fastidious deliberation. He held IOUs from many with historical family backgrounds. He married a beauty, Jacqueline Mills. Her father, an architect, helped turn the capital into a minor Rome.

Pendleton's name, one newspaper printed, "should have

been on a lot of bills he pushed to passage by crossing off money lost at his tables by prominent lawmakers." And journalist Perley Poore added that "a broker in parliamentary notes is an inevitable retainer of brokers' votes." Pendleton's partner, a Mr. Marshall, proved an old truth: many gamblers, owners of casinos, take their winnings and toss them away as losers at other casino tables.

Pendleton died in 1851. He was honored by the president's attendance at the funeral. The list of prominent high officeholders acting as pallbearers to a gambler and lobbyist was impressive. His beautiful widow Jacqueline had the gambling establishment auctioned off, with the best people attending.

The widow continued to be popular in high Washington circles, and when in her middle forties she lay dying, sitting and weeping by her deathbed was President James Buchanan. He wrote—or had written—a most mournful obituary, which he recited at the burial of the gambler's widow.

Payoffs to politicians, as today, were not too subtle. As one reporter wrote: "What representative could vote against the claims of a man whose money he had been winning in small sums . . . all winter?"

James Fenimore Cooper, who had observed the gamblers' power in national politics, wrote: "Contact with the affairs of state is one of the most corrupting influences to which men are exposed." Emerson went even further: "Men in power . . . may be cheap for any opinion, for any purpose."

Nineteenth-century visitors to America were shocked by the gambling and social manners among the natives. Frances Trollope and others were abashed by the table manners on steamboats, at railroad eating places and in boardinghouses. "They used the blade of the knife to convey all kind of food directly into the mouth." Chewing tobacco, too, was almost universal—even high-toned gamblers "chawed," and the hawking and spitting of amber jets into boxes of sawdust or brass receptacles called spittoons (also cuspidors and gaboons) disgusted many visitors. The heavy drinking of 90-proof corn pressings as bourbon whisky and "branch water" or in the form of high-proof rye led some to think "Americans have boiler room stomachs. In some low gambling places and livery stables there is a pail of whisky and a tin dipper to refresh anyone in need of a tot."

But it was the serious gambling that impressed the visitors as they traveled toward the awesomely extensive horizon of the expanding nation. The betting on a dog fight in the street, a chance meeting of two horsemen on a pike wagering who could reach the next toll gate first, the various gambling halls for the lowest segment of the population from Natchez-Under-the-Hill to the ornate gambling palaces of New York, San Francisco, the sporting houses of New Orleans, were all popular forms of gambling. Wrote one visitor: "Betting and gambling were, with drunkenness and a passion for dueling and running up debts, the chief sins of the Carolina gentlemen."

In the field or camp of early wars, there was gambling for buttons, kernels of corn, or matches as symbols of cash value. Playing cards were best sellers, and during the Civil War, when the rebel presses were not able to print good decks of cards, smuggling of contraband past federal blockade runners consisted in part of playing cards by the gross, often with the exchange of Northern playing cards for Southern cotton.

One provost marshal, during the Civil War, wrote on the arrest of a suspect, a Colonel W. A. S.: "On his way to Warrenton, having in his possession four large trunks containing four thousand packs of playing cards: one box containing tea, sugar, coffee, boots, shoes, dry dress goods, etc. . . . So large an amount of playing cards purchased, and being transported through the lines, would be, in my opinion, a very suspicious circumstance. . . ."

After Gettysburg it was noted that among the dead there was a litter of letters, newspapers, and scattered playing cards, dice, and even jottings of winnings and losses. In winter camp regular faro banks were set up, and chaplains preached in vain against demon rum and gambling and the squandering of money that should have been sent back home to aid some harassed and hungry family. Also, drink and cards cut church attendance. Wrote the Reverend W. M. Handy: "Sometimes the attendance at the gambling tent is quite as large as under the [church] awning. . . ."

(During those dark days of rebellion, the gambling and sporting-house section of Washington, D.C. was so patronized by General Joe Hooker that the district became known as "Hooker's Division," and the whores as "hookers.")

Catering not only to the soldiers but also to the stay-at-home folks who were most inflamed by the war, the printers of playing cards came out with special Civil War sets; stars, flags, eagles and shields replaced the usual hearts, diamonds, spades and clubs. Liberty replaced the queen; a general replaced the king. Jacks were lesser officers.

As for the art on the backs of the cards, it was highly patriotic, consisting of stars, flags and eagles. One pack had Lincoln as the king card and members of his cabinet for the other picture cards.

The Confederates also had war-glorifying cards imported from England and carried as cargo filler by blockade runners slipping into rebel harbors with goods to exchange for cotton. One deck carried Confederate colors, the bars and stars, and other rebel state flags. Actually the bars and stars were not usually carried into battle; most regiments marched to war with their state flag. The bars and stars were mostly missing at Gettysburg. Pickett gambled his charge under the flag of Virginia.

3

GAMBLING
ON THE MISSISSIPPI

Deeply imbedded in the American sporting life and the native folklore is the legend of the gaiety and splendor of the Mississippi river boat and gambler. The gambler was the darling of sporting houses and the ladies, a creature careful of his dazzling wardrobe, a man slim and handsomely sideburned and mustached, usually with a thin cheroot held casually in his mouth. A man able to handle a pistol as well as a deck of cards, a pair of dice, a bet on a horse, or the odds on the result of a steamboat race.

That he actually existed in some form close to the myth, even if not as handsome or as slim, and hardly ever fully honest or as brave, pointed up the fact that there are times when some popular genre tradition is based close to fact.

The Midwestern steamboat came into popularity when the river pirates were dead or retired, when the belching high boat stacks were pumping up black smoke and the decks were crowded with the quality, the lower regions holding other folk, slaves, cargo and crew. These boats were the queens of the Mississippi and its tributaries; swivel gun at the bow, paddle wheels turning, and the flamboyant pilot the hero of the texas deck. Few captains would leave either St. Louis or New Orleans without a professional gambler on board. It was bad luck, most claimed, to steam up without the gamblers. As a sport or a profession, gambling was a profitable business. Americans were betting on horses, on their dogs, on the faro table and roulette wheel, on dozens of frontier card games played with a soggy, ancient deck. So, on the river the three-card monte man, the thimblerigger, and the experts with performing dice or a shaved deck of cards were part of the scene.

Certainly among the river travelers with money and time, life was good: they were being barbered, overfed with fine food, played to by Negro slaves, and taught racy French dance tunes, passengers all the while sipping bourbon or the mint julep made with crushed ice brought down from the Northern lakes the season before and kept underground in sawdust packing until needed.

The river-boat gamblers were quick of hand and eye, and nimble; they had educated fingers and a sense of when to take a chance or shake the odds. The salons were kept busy. Their green felt tables were filled with players; the oil lamps were adjusted just so. The polite hiss of sliding playing cards and the clink of moving gold coins created a very pleasant world. The best boats offered the embodiment of the pleasant, ardent life.

Most gamblers and the people who played with them were often lovers of a splendid, plentiful cuisine. The bigger boats served 250 passengers at one time off Sèvres china, with solid-silver knives and forks. Gentlemen did not eat peas on a knife or sip coffee from the saucer. Besides the main courses, there were *glacés*, nougats, cold aspics, *pièces montées*, ices, and charlotte of peach in cognac sauce. And always a great deal of drink (and rarely the brown Mississippi water). The rivers, bays, and sea furnished scrod and Cotuit oysters; the Vieux Carré (the French Quarter) gave up its recipes for shrimp, gumbos, and mallard duck. Food was served with wine for the ladies and whisky toddies for the gentlemen. The hot toddy was considered a medicine.

Gambling, talk of hound dogs, race horses, the *code duello* was man talk. The women gossiped of opera, cotillions, wild sons, babies, French lace, and love affairs. The pilot on the texas deck stood with a cheroot in his mouth, hands on his gold watch chain, while some proud apprentice, like Sam Clemens of Hannibal, handled the big wheel and worried over shoal water, snags, and the steam screaming in the gauges. Luck of some gamblers ran out. Now and then a steamboat blew its boilers, and a river disaster made big news. The Indians were no longer dangerous, but talk of John A. Murrell and his mysterious gang, the legend of the Cruel Harpes, still made a river trip exciting. At times there were even pickpockets and cabin burglars.

In the early days of steamboating, if a wreck killed some of the passengers, the gamblers were "buried separately." But as gambling became a tradition on the river, the gambler gained a certain respect: he was looked up to as a man who knew how to dress, how to act the man of the world; one aware of events and special sporting information and gossip.

The gamblers' working areas on the boat were the ornate main salon and the bar, with its soft-spoken serving darkies and the aroma of good Kentucky bourbon and native rye—no one drank Scotch in those days. Even the barbershop had a few tables among its scrollwork-framed mirrors and scent of bay rum and hair grease for those gamblers waiting for a shave with the long razor or a trimming of the muttonchop whiskers, long locks, or plantation goatees. One seemed to live to one's full physical capacities on the river boats.

By years the high tide of river gamblers' Camelot days can be charted from the middle of the 1830s to the firing on Fort Sumter in 1861. The river boats survived the Civil War, but never again in their old style and glory or in such numbers. The great days were gone when 800 gamblers were regularly working the river boats with that delicate, easy precision that is the gambler's skill at its best.

The river-boat and New Orleans gamblers were mostly hard-shell professionals, playing in austere simplicity what was called "sure-thing games"—games rigged or braced—so that the gambler (in seemingly impassive detachment) was in control of the play. He could be a card handler who would deal from top *or* bottom of the deck, or he could have key cards hidden in his clothes, and be able to put them into play when needed against a gentleman with a thirst for diversion. The gambler could mark the cards by indenting certain ones with a thumbnail, or by a ring with a small spur on it. "Readers," so called, were cards marked on the back by some tiny change in the design pattern. "Stripping," too, was common. A deck was shaved down a bit on all sides except for a few high cards, so that these stuck out just a fraction of an inch. All this was practiced under an imperturbable facial expression.

All doctored packs of cards were left with the barman, so when a fresh deck was called for, the barman would hand out one already marked or prepared by the gambler, with dire implications for the soon-to-be losers.

From the launching of the first floating palace until Mr. Lincoln called for men to save the Union, the presence of a gambler, picturesque and courtly, was a sight no traveler would forget. In prints and old journals and letters, the gambler always seemed to be pictured in black: the best black broadcloth, a soft black felt hat with a romantic twist to its brim, or in summer a flat-topped, wide-brimmed Panama. The cravat could cover the chest, or it could be only a black string tie. But the shirt was always white, always starched glossy; and here and there a man would dare a ruffle or some lace at the cuffs. Frilly and frizzy detail made a shirt a masterwork. The waistcoat, not then called a vest, was the place for color, for a liberation of decor, for the art of embroidery. Signs and omens of luck, hounds and horses in full action, glowing patterns, even whole landscapes could march across a gambler's waistcoat. The high-heeled boots were kept to a satin polish; they were narrow at the toes and had built-up heels in back. Coat buttons were of gold or silver, and at times waistcoat buttonholes featured diamond fastenings, or at the least pearls. This was all window display, aided by diamond rings; three were usual, five or six a bit flashy but expressive. The cravat would usually boast a "headlight": a big diamond stickpin. How many of these were true gems and how many false, no one ever knew. It was all to suggest a kind of narcissistic attitude of self-confidence. The watch—sometimes two watches, one in each waistcoat pocket—was as big as a turnip, with double gold lids, key wound, and picturing a hunt in full cry, or women and satyrs from Greek or Roman tales. Watches were set with gems and looped to gold chains that encircled the gambler's neck. In his coat or jacket or bootleg, the gambler carried a small pistol called a derringer, or his coat boldly bulged with a Colt or Smith & Wesson handgun. The boot could contain a dagger, dirk or knife. But the gambler hardly ever carried the deadly broad

Bowie knife; that weapon was for mountain men and crude brawlers and tavern slashers. For quick, violent dissent, a gentleman gambler preferred a well-aimed slug.

The game among gamblers was to see who could work up the most class: a rich, individual identity—to scatter tips like a nabob from India and maintain a cold calm at all times, even in adversity—was the gambler's aim.

The honor for the best-dressed gambler was held for a time by a New Orleans man, James Fitzgerald, who worked out of that city in the 1840s. He was the dude of the river boats, attired in audacious sophistication of fabric and cut. Gossip said he had four overcoats or mantles and suits beyond count, and that his bookmaker lived in Paris. All could see that his gold watch chain was as thick as a lead pencil. Jimmy Fitzgerald was a symbol of sensuous plenitude and taste. He was attended on his river trips by three Negro slave valets, who brought on board, with the aura of ritual, his bags and luggage, his suits and boots.

Poker and faro were the Fitzgerald games, and he lost as often as he won, for what he gained on the boats, he dropped in the gambling parlors ashore. There he lost all sense and was reckless and wild. He would come out of some St. Louis or New Orleans gambling hall after a night of play, not only having lost his gems and his wonderful gold chain, but also having wagered away his slave valets. He always followed the persistence of hope that is the gambler's shipwreck.

So back on the river boat, and a few weeks later, Jimmy Fitzgerald would sport new jewels or redeemed ones, a thicker gold chain, and fresh valets, having made a new fortune on the boats. He lived an existence of high and low hopes, transfixed by chance. One of Jimmy Fitzgerald's rivals was a splendidly dressed gambler named Poley, his full name being Napoleon Bonaparte White. Poley had drifted to New Orleans from Washington, D.C., as a boy and had gotten on the river by working for a short time as an engineer on the river boats. But his heart was not with the log-burning furnaces and their hissing steam vents but with the fine life on the upper decks, with the flipping cards and the stacking of gold eagles and double eagles by fingers flashing diamonds. How he envied the gamblers smoking their Romeo y Julietas, their hair smelling of verbena. Soon Poley played the river boats himself, dressed splendidly, and when the Civil War cut down river travel and rich travelers, he became the host of a gambling house on St. Charles Street in New Orleans. Poley had also married; it seemed best to stay put and no longer search for gentlemen looking for "a little interesting game."

If Poley was lucky as a boat gambler, he was unlucky as a father. He had two worthless sons who caused him great grief. They were called "desperate characters" by the local press. Benny and Jimmy White made the gambler's life a burden. The sons were very handy with guns and pistols. Benny, far gone in drink, died in jail while waiting to stand trial for a gun killing. Jimmy drifted out to California and killed two men over the possession of a bottle of bad wine. There is no information as to his fate, but rope was cheap.

Poley's destiny was tragic; the one-time dude of the river boats was not lucky on land. By 1889 he was without money. An antigambling ordinance was in effect. Suicide appeared the only decent way out for the old gambler, but he lacked money for even a handgun or an overdose of drugs. A kindly barman on Royal Street gave Poley some money, and the old man bought himself a lethal dose of sulphate of morphine and a working pistol. He cheerfully made the rounds of old friends, former river folk, ancient pilots, and gamblers at leisure; among the gossip exchanged, he said he was going to take his life that day. The reaction to this unique expression was not spectacular; it was passed off as part of the old gambler's try for public interest. Home went Poley, and with drug and pistol, in characteristic geniality, he ended his life.

Most gamblers remained gamblers, win or lose; they never did much else until forced to by chance or age. Just before the War Between the States, "Colonel" Charles Starr, another finely dressed gambler, embellished his image by talking of his slaves, plantations, and boats, all of which brought him a vast income. He managed, however, to dispose of it by his stakes at the gambling table. He bragged so much of his slaves, cotton bales, and landholdings that among other gamblers, he was labeled "the biggest, fanciest liar on the whole goddamn river . . ."

To authenticate his dream acres, Charlie Starr stationed Negro slaves at steamboat landings where the boat would stop to put passengers ashore or take on fuel from the wood boats.

The Negro would yell out, "Massa Kunnel Starr, sah! Ise from yo' plantation up yonder!" The colonel (most all river colonels were honorary or self-created) would lean over the rail, lighted cheroot in his mouth, and ask what the boy was bothering him for. The slave then would ask what the "kunnel" wanted done with certain acres of cotton, some horse studs, the turpentine, and the slash-pine lumbering. The colonel would shift his cheroot and loudly give orders as to what should be done: what crops sold, what acres put into tobacco—and that more slaves were to be sent up from New Orleans to clear brush. All this was done in a loud voice, while the boat whistle hissed steam, the bell rang, and the boat slowly pulled into the middle of the *café-au-lait*-colored river.

But the colonel was well liked in spite of his imaginary holdings, for he had a ready wit, was a close observer of man's blemishes, and had a lively line of talk. His wardrobe was impressive for many years; that at least was real, and often, so were his jewels. Colonel Starr made a great deal of money, but, like so many gamblers he lost most of it at the faro tables ashore.

When all was lost and his days as a great gambler were over—gone with the last of the great river steamers—he became a shabby moocher, hanging around for an offer of a free drink or sneaking food at the free-lunch counters before being driven off by a callous barman. He was always trying to borrow and to cadge food and whisky. He offered himself as an object lesson in the impermanence of all things.

In one fancy restaurant where as Colonel Starr he had once entertained extravagantly with perfumed women and vintage wines, he entered one cold night and sat down, beckoned a waiter, and ordered a sumptuous meal. The manager came over to his table and, without the old genuflection, stated: "You'll have to pay for that meal in advance, Colonel." Charles Starr rose from his chair and went out without a word. Soon he was back, showing a fistful of bills which he gave to the manager. "Give me the best dinner this money can buy." He had pawned his overcoat.

The waiters came and set out silver platters and their best china with its savory steaming array. Colonel Starr looked about him. Pride, unlike virginity, can be regrown. He stood up and began to turn the dishes over, placing them with their dripping contents upside down on the crisp linen cloth. Nodding with an expressionless poker face as the other diners and waiters stared, he walked out of the restaurant without a glance. Colonel Charles Starr died that night, as if to point up the proper climax to his final dramatic act. A few oldtimers remarked that it was "just like Charlie" to put up a big front, acting to the last as if he still owned all those imaginary plantations. They remembered an old story about the colonel in his rich days when a desperate, hungry gambler had approached the colonel and said, "I need fifty cents for something to eat. I'm starving."

"How long since you last ate?" asked the colonel.

"Two whole days."

"That's hardly starving. But you go without food two more days and I'll give you a hundred dollars for your appetite."

Suckers and card players for mere pleasure got few breaks. These were reputed *square* gamblers, who used only their brain, eye, and skill to keep the luck or chance on their side. One was never too sure the square gamblers were *always* square; they won so regularly. A square gambler by reputation was "Major" George White, who played high-stake cards for over sixty years, from 1825 to 1887. At eighty-two he gave up the profession. He was an industrious gambling man, making it and losing it as was expected in his trade. There were the golden years when his take was over $30,000 a season; and when he wasn't on the river boats, for a time he ran a faro bank in New Orleans, receiving $400 a week as a faro dealer. For all the stress of his work, he lived to be ninety-five; so the danger of getting a pistol slug in the liver from a despoiled loser may have been overrated. There is a unique madness in the basic logic of betting on numbered cards.

More in the romantic tradition of the old-fashioned novel was the Englishman Richard Hargraves, who was the perfect image of the handsome, well-dressed, well-mannered professional gambler. He even boasted the pallor of a man who lived indoors. He came to New Orleans in the early 1840s when only sixteen, which didn't prevent him from becoming a bartender. He watched the big play and was soon taking part in it, separating a sugar planter from $30,000 in poker. This led Hargraves to the river boats, and in just ten years he allegedly piled up $2 million.

As was fitting for such a suave, romantic figure, Hargraves was involved with women, risking his well-dressed skin in an affair with the wife of a banker. The banker found out about the affair and called on the dueling code of Louisiana to satisfy his honor and punish the fornicator in his house. Hargraves accepted the challenge, and in one of those mist-shrouded mornings on the river, seconds standing by, he killed the banker with a perfectly aimed shot. It was a dangerous achievement, for the brother of the newly made widow spread talk around town that he would shoot Hargraves on sight. This sort of talk led to another duel, this one at Natchez-Under-the-Hill, a depraved, wide-open town on the Mississippi. Hargraves managed to kill the brother, and he must have wondered how long this blood-letting would go on if the widow had a large family. It seemed odd that she now should avenge the death of a cuckold she herself had created, for a drama of female sensibility awaited him back in New Orleans. The woman stabbed him and then, in a grisly mood, committed suicide. No Victorian novelist could have put together such an overripe melodrama. Hargraves, however, did not die. The material of bad fiction in his life extended itself. In Mobile, while attending a gambling session, he rescued a girl from a burning building, plucked her to safety like ripe fruit, and married her.

Hargraves's sense of adventure still unsatisfied, he went to Cuba as a soldier of fortune. In the Civil War, Richard Hargraves fought on the Union side and rose to the rank of major. He finally settled in the wild city of Denver, a town still quaking from its gold and silver rush days. He died there in 1880 of tuberculosis. Of all the gamblers of the period, he, more than most, lived out the pattern of popular romantic fiction.

For a gambler who was involved in politics, one can turn to John Powell, born in Missouri, who had a fine education and wore the best clothes. He was so tall and handsome that, with his fine manners and charismatic personality, he was found to be a social success. Powell came early to politics between dealing cards. Stephen A. Douglas and Andrew Jackson were happy to call him friend. He could have gone to Congress from Missouri but decided against it.

In the 1840s and 1850s Powell was given the honor of being called "the best and wildest poker player between St. Louis and New Orleans." His reputation was that of a square player who didn't cheat.

By the time Powell reached his prime as a big winner, he was deep into St. Louis real estate. Besides owning a theater and New Orleans buildings, in Tennessee he had $100,000 invested in horses and slaves. In 1856 Powell entered into legend with a famous poker game on the river boat *Atlantic*. The four-handed game consisted of Powell, two other gamblers, and a very rich Louisiana plantation owner, Jules Devereaux. The play began easy but solid with the usual strategies and moved on at such a pace that after sixty minutes $37,000 in gold coin and paper was stacked along the rim of the table, divided among the four men. Powell won $8,000, making the pot on the first hand dealt. The game went on for three days, with each man leaving the table only to take care of the needs of nature.

There was little food, but wine was ordered from the bar from time to time, and the cost of that ran to just under $800. On the third day, Devereaux was done for. He had lost $100,000, and Powell had won about $60,000 of that, proving for the planter that the illusions of chance were delusions at times.

Soon after that famous game, Powell acquired some very fancy British luggage, along with $8,000, in a game with a young Englishman who was traveling to see the new nation. He seemed a decent enough chap as a loser: bushy-tailed, chin up, and not at all put out by his losses of cash and luggage. After breakfast next day he shook hands with the passengers, a tight English smile in place. Then he casually took out a pistol, placed it against a temple, and shot himself through the head.

It is said that this gory event broke Powell's run of luck and that he sent the money and luggage on to the Englishman's family in England and retired from gambling for twelve months. It hardly seems likely, as the story goes, that he never again won another pot at play. But what is certain is that he did have bad luck at the card table, and in a year's time he was stripped of his houses, land, horses and slaves. He left the river in 1861 and settled in Seattle, where he died ten years later in dire poverty.

Gambling was not all poker. Faro, a complicated card game, was popular; twenty-one (or blackjack), seven-up (also known as "old sledge"), and a form of whist, forerunner of bridge, were played. The simple suckers were most often taken in three-card monte, in which the handler manipulated three cards, showing their faces from time to time and then asking some gilly to pick out the queen of spades for an agreed wager. The hand was quicker than the eye in all cases, and the queen was never where it seemed. Three walnut shells and a pea or small rubber ball was the same kind of game, the pea usually being palmed by the operator. A shill warmed up the crowd by showing how easy it was to find the queen or the pea in the right place. "Now you see it, now you don't. Show me no mercy—I'm here for your pleasure. . . ."

The best-remembered of the shell artists was "Umbrella Jim" Minor, who worked under a spreading bumbershoot, rain or shine, and had a song to start things off with:

> *A bit of fun just now and then*
> *Is relished by the best of men. . . .*
>
> *Pore Jim's chances now are two to one.*
> *But appears your chances sure are slim*
> *To win the prize from Umbrella Jim.*

It always inspired someone to prove Jim wrong. He never was.

George Devol is often given credit for the most famous of all gambling anecdotes, but it is actually the story of a gambler named William Jones, called "Canada Bill" by his fellow gamblers and all who knew him. As the story goes, he was stranded in a dull little Southern town for the night and set out to search for a card game. He found one in progress and sat down to play. Someone who knew him whispered, "It's a crooked game, Bill."

He shrugged and whispered back, "I know it. But it's the *only* game in town."

Canada Bill was not one of the dude fashion plates of the river gamblers with any exquisite sense of grace or manners. He was not of a fastidious, capricious nature, nor was he given to compulsive or gallant actions. Canada Bill played the role of the loose-jointed country clodhopper. He looked as if he'd just finished plowing in the north forty with a team of mules. He lacked impressive size, and Devol writes of Bill as being a "chicken-headed, tow-haired sort of man with mild blue eyes and a mouth nearly from ear to ear, who walked with a shuffling, half-apologetic sort of gait and who, when his countenance was in repose, resembled an idiot. For hours he would sit in his chair, twisting his hair in little ringlets. . . . His clothes were always several sizes too large, and his face was as smooth as a woman's, with not a particle of hair on it. . . . He had a squeaking, boyish voice, awkward, gawky manners, and a way of asking fool questions and putting on a good-natured grin that led everybody to believe that he was the rankest kind of sucker—the greenest sort of country jake. . . ."

A great monte artist, Canada Bill could change a queen into an ace while seeming to just toss down the cards. Bill was a traveling man, and he played the steam cars as well as the river boats. On his trips into the Southland, from Charleston and along the eastern shore, then from Richmond to Atlanta and Memphis, he figured out a scheme. Suppose he cut the Southern railroad systems in for $25,000 a year in return for their permission to work freely as a card sharp and con man without hindrance from them? He figured the railroads would jump at the added income with no cost at all to them.

It seems that the generous offer was refused by the railroads. Canada Bill is said to have amended his offer: "What if I *only* let preachers play?"

Canada Bill kept to the tradition of most kingpin gamblers by dying a pauper. He was buried in Reading, Pennsylvania. Some Chicago gamblers put up the money for his funeral. Two gambler friends were present at the event, watching the sad drama of the coffin being set on the fresh earth.

Said one gambler, "Bet you a thousand dollars against five hundred."

The other gambler watched the casket being lowered into the grave. "On what?"

"That Canada Bill ain't in that there coffin."

"No bet."

"Why not?"

"I've seen Bill squeeze through tighter holes than this here one."

There were professional gamblers everywhere, of course. In the big cities, in the great spas like Saratoga and French Lick, in Denver, and in the Tenderloin on the Barbary Coast. But the pickings were often better in the South, in regions from Washington, D.C., down to Alabama among plantation folk, all the way to the Florida Keys. If the people liked excitement and often got little of it, a man passing through with some decks of cards carried in a red silk handkerchief, or laying out a monte rig on the piazza of the Planters Hotel, could interest the quality and the gentry in chuck-a-luck, red dog poker, seven-up or even a faro layout.

To the sporting man, the gambler, the confidence artist, the American South was a vast territory of charm and fatted calves, a Promised Land of Plenty beyond the Mason-Dixon Line. All along the Mississippi shore, from Cairo, Illinois, down past what is now Faulkner country to the Delta where it melded into the Gulf and the Caribbean, it was easy pickings. Gamblers' letters revealed the good life: how the Southern gentry on the eastern shore retained an interest in fine colonial cooking and French gourmet dishes, influenced by recipes brought back from the European Grand Tour. An early Byrd of Virginia imported much in the way of continental menus, clarets and ports, as his diaries show.

The gamblers found much loot to convert to card debts. The First Families of Virginia lived a rich life off the land through tobacco, rice, and indigo. Through their London agents they traded their crops for furniture, silver teapots and fine spoons and forks, and even now and then brought over a trainer for their horses. All this could be lost in one night at poker and signed away with a polite smile.

Gambling Fever

Even Mark Twain, a grand Mississippi River pilot at the time, admired the fancy-dressed gamblers who worked the cities of

St. Louis and New Orleans. These gamblers spent their vacation time in Chicago, often losing their gains at dice, faro games, roulette, and other devices in the Chicago gambling establishments, playing without expression, dressed impeccably, their waistcoats laced with gold chains.

The best-known gamblers came North during the war years from Natchez, Vicksburg, and the Delta, traveling via the chimneyed steamboats. Other gamblers filled the plush seats of the steam cars entering Chicago. The city had so many of them because, for all their Southern sympathies, going to war for the Confederacy seemed just a bit foolhardy to men who knew how to figure the odds; one could get killed. Chicago, too, was a plum ripe for plucking. It was a town busy with wartime profiteering, carried on in gold coins and easy money from land deeds and bank notes; in short, money looking for the action. New millionaires made their money by sending condemned beef packed in brine and hardtack filled with weevils off to army camps.

The gamblers showed them how to enjoy getting rid of their profits. Writing a history of the 1860s in Chicago, Frederick Francis Cook referred to the Southern gamblers selling the Southern side of the war, "among the unthinking younger generation about town . . . went far in giving the impression that Chicago was a hotbed of disaffection. Indeed, so far did this Southern gambling influence extend, that of all the resorts for men-about-town, the Tremont House was about the only place where one invariably heard outspoken Union sentiment. And while there was among all classes (the German element excepted) a goodly number with more or less avowed Southern sympathies, it was the gambler who above all gave an extraordinarily aggressive tone to the local opposition to the war. . . ."

Both the local gamblers and imported tricksters found splendid prey in Chicago during the war years. Paymasters, officers, and men back from battle with unspent pay played cards. And young men, going back perhaps to die, sought excitement. Women and whisky were not enough. Gambling did not pall or weaken one as did drink and whores. Lady Luck fascinated all. So army contractors, pork packers, the new rich, real estate sharks, the praying-mantis shape of sharp lawyers in their tall hats—all came to fill hundreds of Chicago's gambling houses. For the poor drifter and the tattered soldier, any plank could be a poker table, and any street loafer could handle a pack of soiled cards or rattle a pair of dice. Even those citizens of noted respectability at times got wartime gambling fever.

The really impressive gambling establishments were on Hair-trigger Block, Randolph Street between Clark and State, and Gamblers Row—Clark Street from Randolph to Monroe. The newspapers cried out that the district was "so contaminated by these execrable vagabonds that respected persons avoid them as they would a cesspool."

Yet some respectable persons bragged of being known or taken by the most famous of the gamblers. George Trussell, Cap Hyman, John Brown (not the one of Harpers Ferry), Watt Robbins, and Frank Connelly, who ran a place called the Senate, the most luxuriously furnished of any gambling house beyond Saratoga, were well known in Chicago. St. Louis sent up Gabe Foster and Ben Burnish to deal cards. Survival was a problem at times. James Watson, known as Sir James, was killed by White Pine Russel, who dealt faro; Jim Elliot was killed by Jere Dunn; John Sutton died in a Clark Street saloon. Gamblers led precarious lives, no matter what their standing in the pecking order. Dave Stanley was low class—a burglar, thief, pimp, and small-time gambler. But Theodore Cameron was high class, serving game, *lapin en blanquette, fricassée de poulet,* and wine suppers to his patrons at no charge. Cameron made a million dollars in eight years, and left town nearly broke. Gamblers usually were victims of other gambling establishments. They had no sooner lost all than they were back to plucking pigeons. But when they had it, they loved to spend.

Their shady women sparkled with jewels that were often borrowed back after a run of bad luck.

Did the glamorous gamblers—the kingpins of the profession—cheat? Most of them could—with skill, prudence and decorum. Some of them did.

4

SARATOGA IN THE SEASON

While the city fathers swear that Saratoga is the Iroquois Indian word for Place-of-Swift-Water, there is some doubt that the translation is correct, if it is a translation. What is true is that the first white man to see the place and know of its mineral-water springs was a Father Jogues, who in 1646, laboring to bring Christ to the primitives, had his skull split by a Mohawk tomahawk in a not too clearly enunicated theological debate as to whose god was the more powerful. In 1709 an English fort was built on the spot, after years of wars in the region affecting the French, British, Algonquins, and Mohawks. Settlements were not created by platitudes but by blood and effort.

Saratoga received its first major historical attention when an English army, led by Gentleman Johnny Burgoyne, was defeated in the Battle of Saratoga in 1777 by generals Gates and Arnold. (Gentleman Johnny was a classic scholar, a playwright, and a lover of the hedonistic life. He traveled to this battle from Canada with his wine cellar, his hunting dogs and his mistress. In some ways he set the pattern for the gambling life of Saratoga in a later era.)

The water at High Rock Springs, it was early decided, was supposed to have healing qualities, and a list of its reputed merits is impressive. It was said to cure jaundice, dyspepsia, rheumatism, poor appetite, gout, dropsy, scrofula, and paralysis; later, hope was added for sufferers of heart ailments,

stomach disorders, bad nerves, skin troubles, glandular distur-
bances, and general rundown conditions.

In 1783 Saratoga was visited by General George Washington,
Alexander Hamilton, and Governor Clinton of New York.
They were waiting out the withdrawal of the British troops
from New York City. The three men started for the springs at
High Rock but got lost. Someone finally showed them the right
path. Washington is said to have been interested in buying
some land there. But he was put off by a survey of a General
Williams, who reported that in Saratoga "the accommodations
are very wretched and provisions exceedingly scarce."

Not frightened by such talk was Gideon Putnam, who put up
a sign over a cabin:

PUTNAM'S TAVERN & BOARDING HOUSE

In time, as Putnam expanded, he could house, bed, and feed
seventy guests who came to taste the waters and expect cures.
Miracles appear, however, only for those who believe them
beyond reason. If there were no cures, at least the air was
healthy. Putnam must have been positively telepathic, a man
who knew a good thing. He kept on building.

Old Gideon Putnam in time fell from a scaffold while working on his projects and died. Soon his tavern altered again—
and again—to become the famous huge Grand Union Hotel
where in its prime an oligarchic society took its ease and pleasures.

Saratoga was properly incorporated in 1826 as a township
fourteen miles wide and six miles long. In its early days, its most
celebrated female—a fairly respectable lady—was Madame
Jumel, wife of Stephen Jumel, a rich French merchant and
shipowner, originally from Santo Domingo. Madame is described as big, handsome and blonde. She was born Eliza
Brown, or perhaps Betsy Bowen; her early history is misty. It
was her hope that her husband would succeed in his grand
scheme of bringing Napoleon to Saratoga after the defeat at
Waterloo. And while talks to that effect had already begun, in
the end Napoleon decided to give himself up to the British
instead of his friends, and so ended up at St. Helena, thus
missing treatment for his stomach troubles with the mineral
waters at High Rock.

The Jumels spent a Saratoga season at the Pavilion Hotel. Their New York house was to become a low saloon, but later it was restored, not as a gin mill but to an imitation of colonial grace. In 1820 the Jumels acquired what was to become the Jumel Saratoga Mansion on Circular Street. It was a white Greek-architecture–styled building with the proper white columns. Madame, in ecstatic joy, named it "Les Tuileries" and set herself a goal of becoming the society queen of Saratoga. She tried hard, blending impulse with a drive for attention.

The main event of a Saratoga day, aside from early-day racing, gambling, drinking, and concessions to frivolity and seduction, was the carriage parade down Main Street. Taking part gave one definite social status. Madame Jumel had a golden coach pulled by eight horses and decorated with liveried outriders. But even so, she had a hard time leading the parade. The style and dash of one's horses and carriage were a primitive *Social Register* of the time. A fairly good carriage could cost $12,000 and a fine horse $1,000. Of course livery stables had them for hire: $35,000 worth of horses and carriages, buckboards, gigs and sporting shays, from which the high beaver hats of the sporting gentlemen protruded like gray and white mushrooms and the parasols of the ladies twirled, while liveried coachmen, outriders, and footmen added to the colorful scene on the unpaved streets and roads.

Once, while Madame Jumel was leading, some wits hired an old Negro to dress as a woman of fashion and drive a mule cart just behind Madame Jumel to mock her as she led the parade. The next day she appeared in all her finery, in glacial haughtiness, with two loaded dueling pistols in her lap. The party in drag took warning and was nowhere in sight during the parade. Madame Jumel, after the death of her husband, married Aaron Burr when she was seventy-eight years old. Burr was still as feisty as he had been when he killed Alexander Hamilton in a duel. In time Madame Jumel divorced him.

People of comfortable means set up houses in Saratoga, for the early hotels were not known for their comfort. *Lèse-majesté* was often the rule. There were no baths in the hotels, but for twenty-five cents there were bathhouses available for the finicky. The hotel rooms were lighted by candles and serviced with a pitcher and washbasin; the walls were whitewashed. The privy was out back and a chamber pot was under the bed; these were the accepted comforts. The food for some years was poor, and people didn't linger over meals. One visitor clocked a roomful of diners (one ate at long tables) and found that breakfast was finished by most in ten minutes and dinner in twenty-five minutes flat.

Eighteen forty-two brought the cholera to Saratoga, and the next year the railroad—the Saratoga & Schenectady. The three cars were horse-drawn and did nine miles an hour. But soon two puffing little steam locomotives were brought over from England for the Saratoga & Schenectady Railroad. Before long there were 8,000 guests a season to quicken the hearts of the rapacious local inhabitants: hotel and horse-rental people and gambling and mineral-water folk. It was beautiful country, with green trees moored in fine landscapes. There was a small track for racing, and gambling took place in private houses.

The new nation prospered. Men became rich by way of land ownership, growing crops on plantations, manufacturing, spinning, weaving, and sending out whaling ships. There was a search for someplace to spend leisure time and make sport. Saratoga hit the spot. As one drank better whisky, bought scrolled mahogany bedposts, or chased the fox or raccoon, one began to travel, to seek others.

Saratoga was a place noted for its health waters, gambling, and clean upstate air. True, it had been the headquarters for the first Temperance Society in the nation in 1808, and prayer meetings and Bible readings were held in some of the boardinghouses and hotels. Until near the middle of the nineteenth century, the Union Hall Hotel began the day with morning prayer and Bible reading. But other places had hard cider and cockfights, the quadrille and the polka. There was a growing sporting side, hired rigs for viewing or spooning, and always the mineral waters to be absorbed for health and vigor.

Soon the card players, the sportsmen, the seekers of excitement and sumptuous diversions were coming from New York and Philadelphia to Saratoga; and whole families of Southern plantation owners, cotton growers and tobacco shippers came to escape the summer heat and dust. They, along with their relatives and their black slaves, mammies, and coachmen, valets and cooks, gave tone to the town with their well-mannered, proud attitudes. In white linen and wide-brimmed Panama hats, the men calmly smoked their long cheroots, explaining in their Southern drawl, "Our darkies? Why, they're just like the family." They were to repeat such cant until the Civil War, when the hundreds of Southern families were prevented from coming to Saratoga to drink the "watters," gamble, listen to the music of Offenbach and Stephen Foster, inspect horseflesh, and, for the men, "go down the line" and chat with the madams and take a whore upstairs. As one keeper of a journal put it: "All the world is here, politicians and dandies, cabinet ministers and ministers of the gospel, officeholders and office seekers, humbuggers and humbugged. . . ."

Up to 1825 gambling and card playing had been a private sport; then the billiard halls and other gathering places began to put in faro setups and chuck-a-luck games. Off an alley near the grand old United States Hotel, a small house was dedicated just for gambling by one Ben Scribner in 1842. Saratoga moved tranquilly toward its destiny. It did not hang back.

The man who brought Saratoga to international fame as a gambling town and race track second to none in the nation was a strange rough diamond, beloved by many, hated by some. He was named John C. Morrissey. His parents brought him over from Ireland in 1834, when he was three, to Troy, New York. He grew up to become a gang fighter and went on to use his muscle for Tammany Hall. He got his pet name, "Old Smoke," when he was set on fire (from an overturned stove) while engaged in a fist fight. Migrating west, he fought as a prize fighter in California, was exceedingly good at it, and came back to New York at last to become "the heavyweight champion of the world" at age twenty-two. In 1852 he opened the notorious saloon and dance hall, *Bella Union*. He settled down and married a beautiful girl, Susie Smith, whose father was a Hudson River scow captain.

As a vote-getter, ballot-box stuffer, and voter of repeaters and bums, he gladdened the sly, dishonest hearts of Tammany Hall. John Morrissey took to smoking twenty cigars a day and became the owner of sixteen gambling houses in New York City.

But he nurtured massive aspirations. He was seeking to establish himself in society at no loss in income, which brought him and his wife to Saratoga. He knew gambling houses, he knew how to please, and he liked "class." People said he had lots of principles, "most of them bad." He came to Saratoga to make a big impression and to show how refined and splendid a gambling house could be. He set up the best wheels and skilled croupiers, handsome card dealers, elegant surroundings, good bourbon and cigars. He was in the temper of the age: the life of action preferred to the life of the arts. Soon it was said that Old Smoke, John Morrissey, had opened wide a good place for gentlemen to gamble. Some townfolk tried to drive him out, but John gave so much to churches and charity in Saratoga that it was said he divided "the profits of his sinning with the good people . . . with a generous hand."

By 1870 the gamblers controlled Saratoga. Over a dozen high-class gambling establishments were active at working hours during the season. The play was for hundreds of thousands of dollars. The gamblers knew politics and elected a fellow gambler, Caleb Mitchell, to public office.

By building his Saratoga Club House, Morrissey showed the town just how plush a gambling palace could be. Encouraged to greater efforts, he built the famous Saratoga race track, where races are still run. The Saratoga Club House was considered the finest gambling casino in America. The Club salon, a rendez-vous for the best people, was widely publicized. The faro parlors and drawing rooms had rare carpets and bronze statues by near-great masters. There were beautifully designed toilet rooms for the ladies and well-attended johns for the gentlemen. A visitor could write that it was all created to "hold the blasé and allure the naïve." Patricians, gamblers, rakes, politicians, people with new money in pork or cotton or railroads, in mines and shipping, enjoyed it all.

Old Smoke in his seigneurial power had two rules for all the ostentation he offered: no citizen of Saratoga was allowed to play; no ladies were permitted to enter the gambling rooms. But the grand salon and the drawing rooms in their exquisite taste attracted and entertained them; about 25,000 ladies a year came there, showing their fashions and feathers, their long-trained gowns, their laces and high-buttoned shoes. Poker and most card games were played in private rooms. Planters, bankers, confidence men, senators, and anyone able to afford high stakes could call for a fresh deck and say, "Gentlemen, would you care to sit in?"

Morrissey, helping the metaphysics of chance in gambling, is said to have made a profit of half a million dollars his first two years with his new Club. But, as with all gamblers, he had his own way of being a sucker—Wall Street was his will-o'-the-wisp—and on Black Friday his holdings in the New York Central cost him half a million in losses. His adviser in that venture was the pirate, Commodore Cornelius Vanderbilt, who had loaded John and his friends on stocks he controlled, then cleaned them out by manipulating the market with diabolical precision.

Morrissey and his beautiful wife tried to enter the upper reaches of society. He took to wearing a longer, claw-tailed coat, striped morning trousers, patent leather, white kid, and a splendid beaver topper. Mrs. Morrissey was hung with jewels to the point of impudence and turned her opera glasses (solid gold, studded with pearls and diamonds) on the best people. But, in crude gamblers' terms, it was "no dice." Society shunned the Morrisseys. When Morrissey was not permitted to buy a house in a fine section of Troy, he built a soap factory nearby and drove the stink over into the neighborhood of the best people.

If not society, then politics would work for John. Close to boss William M. Tweed, the gambler became a force in Tammany. He controlled whole wards of votes—legally or otherwise—and saw to Tammany victory by any means possible. The organization paid off Old Smoke by electing him twice to Congress. In Washington his voice was loud in debate, and he was always ready to shuck his coat and fight barefisted any congressman who disagreed with him. Once, rising to a challenge, he shouted, "I can whip any ten men in the house!"

It was a time when the U.S. Senate and the House were most corrupt, and Colis Huntington was writing letters to his payoff men in Washington that the cost of bribing Congress was costing him half a million a year and the damn bastards wouldn't deliver all he needed. Mark Twain, who was a Washington reporter for a time, wrote: "America has one habitual criminal class, the . . . Congress of the United States."

Later, in an angry mood, Morrissey broke with Tammany,

and they ran more docile candidates against him, labeling him a "vicious thug, a rowdy prize fighter, and a notorious gambler." His opponents were even worse, for Old Smoke won. But he died of pneumonia soon after victory, leaving, like most king gamblers, very little of the $2 million he is said to have won; the estate assayed out to a little over $50,000. For Old Smoke the words of Henry James, "Money is the great American sedative," were not true.

Gambling at the Saratoga Club and the race track fell into the hands of Charles Reed, who did not drink and who attended the Episcopal Church, and one Albert Spencer, who claimed to be an art critic and collector: he sold paintings at auctions. Reed was an oldtime Southern gambler; he had murdered a man and been sentenced to hang in New Orleans. But the brother of Major General Butler, who protected the gamblers for payoffs (which he divided with the general), got Spencer pardoned. Spencer was known in Saratoga as a "saving and avaricious man."

In 1886 Anthony Comstock, who saw evil, sin and vice in nearly everything beautiful or pleasurable, had the power of some fawning politicians behind him. He tried to close the Saratoga Club House. Raids took place around town in the gambling clubs, but other politicians reopened them. To his New York Society for the Suppression of Vice, Comstock sadly admitted that twenty gambling houses had been closed by his raids, only to be opened again as soon as he and his agents left the town. There was a repellent snobbery about Comstock's reading of God's mind.

In 1889 Spencer Trask, publisher of the Saratoga *Union*, tried to abolish gambling in the town. He hired private detectives to gather evidence that people actually did bet on cards and numbers on a spinning wheel. Warrants were issued. Albert Spencer and others were arrested, but were set free on bail soon afterward. That night the gambling houses were operating wide open as usual. Grand juries of local people, realizing that it was gambling and horse racing that had made the town prosperous, refused to return indictments. Publisher Trask, fighting this absolute domination of the town, remained with little to show against this generous collection of *fin de siècle* vice except an unpopular newspaper and $50,000 out of pocket for a lost crusade.

Reed had retired early to his horse-breeding farm in Tennessee, where he bred the well-known stallion St. Blaise, for which he paid $100,000. However, the sons and daughters of St. Blaise never amounted to much on the track, so again a gambler lost out when he went outside his field of action. In 1880 Spencer sold his share of the Saratoga race track for $375,000. The track changed hands a few times, and by 1901 was owned by a syndicate of sportsmen and was no longer in the hands of professional gamblers. As for the Saratoga Club House, near the end of the century Richard Canfield, the most famous gambler in America, became full owner. Spencer went to live in France, where he dabbled in art, often a bigger gamble than cards.

The sun continued to shine in Saratoga in season. Summer rains fell, the countryside continued green, the buggies took ardent lovers down country roads under a moon nearly low enough to bite. And the click of the roulette wheels, the riffling of cards went on as before, while drinks were poured into tall glasses. The air was scented with honeysuckle and the smoke of fine cigars. The skepticism of the town was well salted with irony. One had to close one's eyes to things one didn't approve of.

For those who wanted it and could afford it, there was high living, fripperies of dress and conduct, and wild exaltations. One English visitor wrote that life in Saratoga in season was all "duels, elopements; and worse things are of constant occurrence . . . men dressed in Franco-Anglo-American fashion, driving four-in-hand drags filled with ladies of questionable virtue. . . ." In the early days before the turn of the century, attempts were made to police the track. Unescorted ladies were not permitted to enter until 1914.

At the track would be Jim Fisk, who would try with Jay Gould to corner the gold market; August Belmont, banker, and Pierre Lorillard, who would start a century of cigarette smoking ("Lone Jack" was a cigarette brand of the period). And the generals, Grant, Sherman and Sheridan, came to taste and see.

One letter writer recalls: "There was a visible path in the carpet in the Grand Union Hotel barroom, which was pointed out as being worn down by General Grant's trips to the bar. . . ."

The track, which had been called Horse Haven at first, had been built for 7,000 horse lovers, but on a good day later in its history, when Man o' War and Gallant Fox ran, it could pack in 25,000. It was one of the first important American race tracks, the first actually being built in Charleston, South Carolina, in 1760. One of its early track records was made by a mare named Lizzie who went the mile in 1 minute 47½ seconds. In the twentieth century, when the track was run by the Saratoga Association for the Improvement of the Breed of Horses, they admitted to no knowledge of Old Smoke, or the fact that he had once owned it.

The purses at first did not run over $500 per race. Betting was made by bidding pools auctioned off at the clubhouse. Handbooks for betting through bookies did not come in until 1890. Gentlemanly wagers, of course, could be made between two sportsmen. Some famous horses ran at Saratoga in the early days: Alarm, Inverary, Kingfisher, Fadladeen, Atilla, Preakness, Springbok, and the most famous horse of his day, Harry Bassett.

By the mid-nineteenth century the breed of the race horse had changed at Saratoga and elsewhere. Horses were no longer bred for stamina but rather for speed as sprinters. Leaner, thinner horses appeared, less well muscled stock that did not have to run for long periods of time. There soon appeared a grotesque disparity between the race horse and the average riding horse.

Tod Sloan, the famous jockey, even changed the style of riding by shortening the stirrups, so he rode high, perched over the horse's neck, with one stirrup shorter than the other, making the turn for the finish easier by leaning to one side at the three-quarter pole. Tod was born in Kokomo, Indiana, son of a barber. He grew up small and fierce, with propensities for the rich life. He went on to ride for King Edward VII when he was Prince of Wales, and for Lord Beresford. Tod came to Saratoga to help train Ballhoo Bey for William Whitney, bringing with him ten trunks of English tailoring and two British valets. Arriving at the United States Hotel, he announced to the desk clerk, "I hear Mr. Belmont is not using his suite this season. I'll take it." He got it. It was $125 a day. He signed the hotel register with a flourish: "James Todhunter Sloan and Valets."

Sloan is best remembered in the shady side of racing history for pulling the king's horse at the English Derby for a group of gamblers who were betting that the favorite, the king's horse, would lose. For this, not only was Sloan barred from riding in England, but *all* American jockeys were barred from riding in any English race.

When the bookies came to Saratoga, they were a mob scene. They would arrive a hundred strong, each with four men to assist him, to record and take and pay out bets. They would roll into Saratoga on a train called the Cavanaugh Special, named after a boss bookie. They were not gentlemen and were not averse to anything crooked.

The town looked forward to the racing season as a change, for the winters up there could go to forty below, and six inches of snow could sometimes fall in May. Come spring and the landaus and buckboards, the carriages and buggies would be washed and polished, the horses newly curried and shod and led from their winter feed. The track would be full of sound and color, and the bookmakers would begin to pay their protection and take up the matter of odds.

The biggest, wildest bettor, most think, was John W. "Bet-a-Million" Gates, who bet large and bet often, with no forbearance or repentance. Betting the horses one day at Saratoga, he lost $400,000; that evening at faro he won $150,000. Strange betting stories circulated. A gambler named Bill Cowan, backed by rich men, arrived in Saratoga with losses of $250,000 created elsewhere and in one month's betting won $750,000.

The longest-living active horse bettor was John Stanford, who manufactured carpets and who attended the Saratoga races for over seventy years. He would bet on anything—even before senility set in. He once bet $40,000 on a steeplechase, a race no smart bettor would touch with a ten-foot whip. Like Samson's forces in the Philistine corn, crooks flocked to Saratoga to feed off the rich.

Polo came to Saratoga with Harry Payne Whitney, who played the bang-ball mounted game daily after breakfast and was at his favorite spot at the track after lunch. His record betting loss was said to be $125,000 in one race. He had a benevolent contempt for any money under the million mark.

By the turn of the century the Saratoga track was being run by sportsmen related to the Astors, Vanderbilts, Goelets, and others of top social circles. The track on Union Avenue remained style-conscious, and the ladies, respectable or not, were magnificent fashion shows at the track.

Sportsmen dreamed of those chemisette-clad lovelies, often showgirls from New York or sporting-house tarts brought up from Washington or New Orleans. Fashions often turned realities into dreams. As for male attire at sporting events, creases were being ironed into baggy pants, pressed there because Edward VII had had his trousers pressed thus by a thoughtless valet, and the fashion spread. The iron derby or bowler was popular, with a gray topper for coaching, or a flat-topped pork-pie type for the younger men. Collars were stiff, winged, and high, attached to silk shirts by gold collar buttons. The attached-collar shirt was unknown. Suits were usually baggy, double-breasted affairs with high, small lapels. The cravat was large and anchored down by a ruby or diamond tie pin. Shoes were high-buttoned or laced and came up above the ankles. The low slipper shoe of today was unknown for street wear. The underwear was long, balbriggan in summer, red flannel in fall; and garters and suspenders were always proper. If one carried a cane and led a Boston bulldog on a leash at the track, the outfit was completed with field glasses in a case and a flask of rye or bourbon, a leather cigar case, a gold cigar-cutter combined with nail trimmer, and a knife to remove a stone from a horse's hoof. Added was a heavy gold watch with double lids. Social standing and wealth were expressed by chains across a waistcoat from which hung Klondike nuggets, animal teeth, lodge emblems, fobs and medals. Spats were added just before the First World War, and the Airedale replaced the Boston bull as a sportsman's dog.

It was the age of the mustache in the nineties as the century turned. The sideburns had gone with the eighties, the beards with the post–Civil War disasters of President Grant. Men carried cash, the large old-fashioned currency or bills issued by local banks and accepted as legal tender. Eagles (ten dollars) and double eagles (twenty dollars) were gleaming gold coins from various mints, to leave on a harlot's fireplace mantel.

Richard Canfield's Gambling Life

The greatest name in American gambling and the most impressive and respected figure in all of Saratoga's gambling history is Richard Canfield, a man neither eccentric nor capricious, nor self-infatuated. In 1893, at his prime, he bought control of the Saratoga Club House, which had fallen on shabby times. The rich socialites who made the best pigeons to pluck at roulette and faro were looking elsewhere for their gambling. Canfield soon changed all that. He knew wines and put nearly $50,000 worth of the best into the cellar. He brought in two dozen expert waiters who made fifty dollars a day in tips but got only a dollar a day from Canfield. He also knew that a fine cuisine attracted the rich; even those who couldn't eat it could take joy in seeing and smelling the food of chef Jean Columbin. Jean got $5,000 for the two-months season at Saratoga and was on a retainer the rest of the year to pick up recipes and food secrets in Europe and taste the rare Valpolicella and Barolo wines.

Canfield also raised the prices for this excellent food sky high, knowing that the more exorbitant the cost, the more the rich guest would think he was getting something special. The splendid food was only a come-on for the gamblers to feel satisfied in the stomach before their wallets became thinner. Canfield lost at least $70,000 a summer in the dining room by serving fine food, and neatly made it up at the gambling tables. It was just a few steps from the dining room to the gambling setup where Canfield covered his losses—and much more besides. He made it all seem joyously decadent but not corrupt.

The cuisine was a clever move, and Canfield was a clever man. A patron could order anything at the table and the chef would see that he got it. It was impressive to send up to Saratoga, by train, pâtés and truffles and strange tidbits in aspic; grouse and game birds, buffalo steaks, delicacies from New Orleans; then to see the expressions of joy on the guests' faces as the specialties were set before them, beautifully served by well-trained waiters under maîtres d'hôtel as dignified as Hapsburgs.

A special gimmick was a pool in which fine fish swam, and the guest with a saturated pride could point to a fish and have a servant net it for him. Soon a deliciously cooked fish was set before the guest, who would usually remark, "Nothing tastes like a fresh-caught fish broiled at once." Actually the guest was eating a cold-storage fish from the huge icebox on the premises. The finny darling he had picked went back live into the pool through a pipe leading from the kitchen back to the pool.

By the time Canfield came to Saratoga, he was plump and in his prime. After his fourteen-year reign in Saratoga was over, he was frankly a fat man. Yet he remained a handsome, ramrod-straight figure, and it was no secret that during business or social hours he was laced into his corset for the day's or night's work. He wore a demeanor of decorum and good manners most of his life. As he bowed to the percale gowns and aigrette plumes of his guests' wives, he was also aware of the world's human scuffing stoats and ferrets.

It should be pointed out that Canfield was a remarkable man who would have made a success in international business, on Wall Street or in politics. He was self-educated, but possessed a psychological insight to a degree beyond that of most college graduates of his day. He could have become an art critic, a man of letters, or a financier. Canfield's aesthetic opinions on books and paintings was accepted at Christie's in London. He was a charter member of the famous Walpole Society and an intimate friend of James McNeill Whistler. Canfield owned a magnificent collection of the artist's best work. Whistler painted Canfield in one of his noted portraits.

In New York he ate at Delmonico's, feeding himself a bit too much, smoking too many fine cigars. As a drinker of burgundies and champagnes, he was often blandly intoxicated. His brown hair and gray eyes gave his head the look of a Roman emperor, a man who seemed never to stress the qualities he excelled in. Most of his life he was clean-shaven in an era when the mustache and the beard were still a sign of male virility.

He was a neat, even fussy dresser, owning forty suits and fifteen pairs of shoes. He agreed with Aristotle, whom he read often: "My friends, there are no friends." He ran honest clubs, using no ropers or cappers, and never welshed on a payment. "The percentage in favor of a gambling house is sufficient to guarantee the profits of a house. . . ," he said, explaining why he never cheated a guest.

His knowledge of literature was amazing, and as a constant reader he had a full understanding of the historical processes of his time, far beyond that of most of the rich makers-and-shakers of the nation who gambled at his clubs. Canfield's favorite reading was Gibbon's *The Decline and Fall of the Roman Empire*. Its lapidary style was in a way his own. He believed with Talleyrand, "The gift of speech was given to man to enable him to conceal his thoughts. . . ."

The Saratoga Club House ran seven days a week. Its layout was impressive. The first floor was home for ten roulette wheels and four faro layouts. In the private rooms upstairs, there were two double-end wheels and a faro layout. There was no dice playing in his clubs or other card games. In private, almost in sanctity with some of his best and richest guests, he would sometimes play poker and bridge. But these were not for the general public who came through the club doors that were never locked.

Thirty highly skilled croupiers, case-keepers and guards were under Canfield's eye. Play was with chips valued at $1 to $1,000. Winners were paid by check, unless they preferred cash from the big safe, which was supposed to hold a million dollars, half of it in $1,000 bills. This was hardly likely, but the story made a good newspaper yarn and inspired confidence.

In his Saratoga Club Canfield claimed he did not pay bribes to police or city officials, but in fact he made "friendly loans" to them that were never repaid, so it amounted to the same thing. In New York City the graft was collected by police and city officials from all gambling places: 25 percent of the house take, *plus* $1,000. Canfield himself paid off the boodle to the police collector monthly, usually over a table at Delmonico's. He once quoted Jay Gould there: "Anybody can make a fortune. It takes genius to hold on to one." Police Captain Williams retired worth several million.

Canfield's actual losses when he closed his last gambling house were $250,000 in uncollected IOUs, some from the best families and the richest men. Reggie Vanderbilt welshed on a $300,000 IOU and settled for a payment of $130,000. Canfield himself was a great spender. He was a magnificent collector of paintings, statues and etchings. Chinese porcelain was a favorite, and he had two peachbloom vases valued at $8,000 to $12,000 each. Chippendale furniture also delighted him, and his twelve chairs cost him $60,000. But he was never mawkish or snide about his collection.

Besides the art advice he often gave and the splendid food he served, his clubs usually provided the gamblers with free dollar cigars.

Canfield could never descend to a simple way of life. He was a stickler for full evening dress. To keep up his respectable façade, he made monthly visits to a wife and children he kept in Providence. He voted the full Republican ticket. With Herzen, he agreed: "There are few nervous disorders more harmful than idealism."

Richard Canfield was born in New Bedford, Massachusetts, in 1855. His mother claimed descent from the Howlands who came over on the *Mayflower*. She also claimed that she was related to the notorious Hetty Green, the Witch of Wall Street (whose son became a fabulous sport and gambler). Richard Canfield hinted at an ancestor named Canfield who was an officer in the American Revolution.

As a young man, Canfield's father was crippled on a whaling ship. He then tried publishing a newspaper but failed, and ended up running a saloon. There were six children; Richard was the smartest, and a most persuasive child. He had hopes of becoming a famous runner. After his father died, he attended public school. He was a fine talker and was a commencement speaker. Canfield worked for a time in a Boston store's shipping department, but soon saw this was no way to wealth. When he was eighteen, he and a partner set up a small poker game in Providence, with a dime limit. When the police shook their heads at this way of life, he traveled around New England as a professional gambler, claiming that in 1876 he took in $20,000 in a run of luck. He spent it wisely (he thought) by going to Europe and getting a traveler's polish at Monte Carlo and other casinos. He returned with no assets and became a night clerk in a New York hotel—the Union Square Hotel—run by his mother's cousin. Fourteenth Street had class in those days, and Canfield studied the city with analytical scrutiny.

He was charming to the big town's gamblers, the rich, the playboys who exuded affluence, and the socially prominent he met. He liked the elegant fast-paced life. Canfield gambled at the places they played, but didn't lose his head, nor did he have much capital for high stakes. He never became an insatiable glutton as a player.

He moved on to work at a better hotel in Spring Lake, New Jersey, read a lot of good books, became manager of Monmouth House, and a Knight Templar of the Masons. He felt that it was time to spread out, and he and a partner opened a poker game in Pawtucket, Rhode Island. In 1885 he felt that he was well enough established to marry one Genevieve Martin. One of his faro setups was raided, and Richard, on his thirtieth birthday, went to jail for six months. It was hinted that the hard sentence was not for gambling but for an adulterous affair with the wife of a rich man who had political connections.

With another partner (he had charm and could always get a partnership) he set up a gambling house in New York on Broadway that ran from high noon to midnight. It paid off $4,300 a week with smooth efficiency during the first year. He was liked by the rich gamblers and their entourages of sycophants. The public respected him.

Canfield and other partners went into business at the Madison Square Club on West Twenty-sixth Street. From twenty-five- and fifty-dollar limits, the stakes soon went to $100 limit, and then to higher and higher stakes. The boast was that there was always $50,000 in the safe to pay off winners. Canfield soon bought out the partnership and became sole owner. It was now that he moved in on Saratoga and became the owner of the Saratoga Club House.

Canfield liked to be seen at his Club perfectly tailored, polite and friendly, a man one could talk to—tell a funny story to, or one's problems. He never became blasé. Harry Payne Whitney was often his guest, as was the steel-and-wire king, Bet-a-Million Gates, and the tomato-nosed J. Pierpont Morgan. General Daniel E. Sickles, who lost a leg at Gettysburg (the bones are still on exhibit in the War Department's Surgeons Museum in a little rosewood coffin) was a guest. Sickles had killed a cousin of Francis Scott Key; the man had been his wife's lover. He not only had been acquitted, but he took his wife back. Later, as a diplomat, Sickles had been the lover of the Queen of Spain. In old age the general was head of the GAR, the Civil War veteran's organization, and he was accused of dipping into the organization's till, perhaps to finance his Saratoga gambling.

The Club ran well under Canfield's watchful gray eyes. It was safe for the women in boas and puffed sleeves to wear hundreds of thousands of dollars' worth of jewels to the place. And no man's wallet was in danger·from pickpockets or holdup men. Protection at the Club was headed by Pat McDonald, who had been the Saratoga track manager, and six tough New York private detectives under him. The local police who admired Canfield's generosity patrolled the place in regular rounds. After all, Frank James, brother of Jesse James, was a town celebrity.

If the ladies were most welcome to the public rooms to fill the deep ottomans, they were *not* admitted to the gambling sections; neither were citizens of the town.

One of the female guests seen often at the Club's dining room during the nineties was Lillian Russell. The great plump American beauty was an actress, gourmet, and friend of rich men. Lillian came nearly every night to test chef Columbin's artistry, and he never let her down, nor she him in her flowing-sleeved chiffon. Her abilities at the table were even better than her talent on stage and may have matched her skill in bed among her reigning coterie of males. She favored blazing orange-scented crepes suzette and liked a good, well-buttered Country Gentleman corn on the cob.

Lillian's special lover one season in Saratoga was Jesse Lewisohn, a successful banker and Wall Street operator, an opulent, tough man; but his ardent and extensive attentions to Miss Russell soon wrecked his constitution. With some apprehension he sought medical advice. His doctor made it very clear: "You either give up Miss Russell, Jesse, *or* your health."

Lillian's official escort for many years was Diamond Jim Brady, but it would seem that they were never actually lovers. Jim, being a great feeder rather than woman lover, had no delusions about his sexual abilities. He neither drank nor smoked, but could consume six dozen Lynnhaven oysters, a saddle of mutton, a breast of chicken with caper sauce, a few lobsters, a dozen venison chops, a twelve-egg soufflé, and all the trimmings of a twelve-course dinner, washed down with a gallon of orange juice. Then followed the crepes suzette, which had been invented for him by the great chef Henri Charpentier. Later he'd attack a five-pound box of chocolates. People watching him eat at the Club would bet he'd drop dead at the table.

At Saratoga, Jim courted business from the Master Car Builders, who were in town for a convention and fun in 1898. Jim hired three cottages at Saratoga, got two dozen or more Japanese houseboys to attend the guests, and moved in carloads of fancy food, liquor, White Seal champagne, and the best Havana cigars. Polishing up his diamonds, he said, "If you're going to make money, you have to look like money." Of his diamonds he said, "Them as has 'em wears 'em!" One set of jewels had 2,637 diamonds and twenty-one rubies and was insured for $87,315. One of the Japanese servants stole so many cigars that he was forced to open a cigar store to dispose of the surplus. But as Jim in his time had given away $2 million in gifts, it didn't matter.

Music for the dinners and events Canfield gave was always the best. There was Chauncey Olcott, the Irish charmer who wrote "My Wild Irish Rose" and sang it at Canfield parties, perhaps to please another Irish music maker, the portly Victor Herbert, hedonist and fancy feeder, as good with knife and fork as with writing popular music. One season Herbert conducted the Grand Union orchestra in two concerts daily.

Besides food, drink, and music, Herbert was also addicted to picking race horses, most of whom never won or placed. But he kept betting and losing. Among other duties and games at Saratoga, Herbert was also supposed to be writing a show for the popular star, Fritzi Scheff, a bouncy pin-up girl of the period. His story is that while walking around the grounds one night with a house detective, he heard a girl in one of the cottages sigh and call out earnestly in some disintegration of resistance: "Kiss me . . . *kiss me again!*" Herbert turned the amorous words into one of the most popular of his songs in the musical *Mlle. Modiste.*

Another man Canfield saw a great deal of was George Kessler, who sold Moet & Chandon champagne and other wines to the rich and to the best hotels and eating places. Kessler had a new-fangled red auto car, a well-trimmed black beard, and always plenty of pretty, loose-thighed girls to offer a buyer who was deciding what brand of bubbly to put into his wine cellar, Kessler's or his rival's, Mumms. George invented the idea of sending free ice buckets of champagne—his brand, of course—to the table of those whose wealth or social standing hinted that they would be buyers.

Bet-a-Million Gates was a rough gem who favored jewels the way a Sioux war chief liked feathers. Gates's shirt front was ablaze with three big diamonds, and various buckles and belts had their share of the gems. Gates was a stock-market plunger who had made a fortune as a barbed wire maker when the law required Western range to be fenced in. He told Canfield that at first, the ranchers shot and hanged some of his salesmen; but in the end, they fenced. Gates was a miserly tipper of waiters, even at the Club, but he would always bet huge sums. "Unless I risk getting hurt or can hurt the other guy, it ain't no fun."

Canfield raised the limits of the stakes many times for Gates. In the end Canfield always came out ahead, but there were nights when Gates walked off with $150,000. He usually lost it back, and maybe $150,000 more, betting $10,000 a card at faro. As Nell Kimball, the sporting-house madam, points out in her memoirs, most men prefer gambling to sex—even in her grand bordellos.

Canfield disliked stingy rich men or men of means who played timidly. Decorum, yes; prudence, no. He had such misfits turned away. He always kept men who couldn't afford to play for big stakes from the Club. Canfield remembered the two tinhorn gamblers who bought only twenty dollars' worth of chips, lost them, and went around saying that the roulette wheel was fixed and wanted their money back. The big losers seemed less impressed by their losses. Senator Pat McCarren, lobby-fed by trusts and monopolies, lost $100,000 in one night; Fred Hostetter lost $213,000, but it took him three nights. The racing man, Mike Dwyer, dropped $90,000. Another U.S. senator, Edward Wolcott, paid off with an IOU that was never honored. "Men who cheated their country saw little wrong in bilking a gambler," said Diamond Jim Brady.

Constant players at the Club were William Vanderbilt; Joe Seagram, who made it big with whisky; and Percival S. Hill of the American Tobacco Company. Once Vanderbilt, waiting for a couple of beauties scented with frangipani to get ready for the evening, wandered into the Club for a few minutes "to make a bit of money for dinner." He dropped $130,000 at the roulette table, then made a belated night of it with the two charmers.

Canfield was always improving the Club, and bought up surrounding land until he had ten acres. He hired Clarence Luce, the architect, to make a park of the place at a cost of a million dollars. Canfield wanted an Italian garden with fountains, a lot of statues of real marble, tempting nymphs and lusty satyrs. His pride was two Tritons spitting water from opposite ends of a big pool beside massed flower beds. The cost for taking care of this garden was $25,000 a year. He also added a grand wing for a new dining room, with fancy stained-glass windows, many mirrors, oak parquet floors, archways, vaulted ceiling, and rows of glowing gas fixtures. In the café annex there was a serving table sixty feet long. No connoisseur of the sporting life or *bon vivant* could be less than impressed.

One of Canfield's most zealous efforts at furbishing the Club was the arrival one day of a flatcar with "the world's largest rug," seventy-two by forty-four feet, specially made up for the gambling room at a cost of $10,000. Everything in the Saratoga Club House was of the best: rare wood gambling wheels, tables, burl panelings, and more twining, flaring chandeliers than most hotels had.

To open this wonderful new setting, Canfield gave a $30,000 shindig in 1903, hiring an orchestra "all the way from Paris," he announced. No one dared to tell him for some weeks that the orchestra had played for years in a New York dive without attracting attention.

He was beginning to have trouble again with the bluenoses. The Club was shut down for the entire racing season. The next year, however, it remained open. But the Canfield clubs in New York City were raided. It was all very complicated. Canfield spent two years in court defending himself. With his New Bedford jail term on record, he could have received a long prison term. He was fined $1,000 and his lawyers cost him about $1,000 more.

For Richard Canfield the clock was striking midnight. More laws and outcries and pressures were put on him, and by 1904 he had had enough. He refused to pay bribes to the police and officials, as the other clubs in Saratoga did. "I'll only open up if I can run the gambling when, if, and *as* I please." He closed the dining room, which was a blow to many gourmets. In 1906 Canfield's Club House opened and closed, then had private gambling upstairs until 1908. Canfield then closed for good. He sold the Club to the city of Saratoga for $150,000. Today it is the Saratoga Historical Society.

Canfield had made a fortune on Wall Street by speculating and was said to be worth $14 million. His take at the Saratoga Club House in fourteen years was figured at $2,500,000. Most of this fortune was lost in the panic of 1907.

Whistler had painted his portrait (today it is in the Cincinnati Museum). He is said to have invented the famous solitaire game known as Canfield.

Richard Canfield retired to a brownstone house in the East Fifties. In 1915, at the age of fifty-nine, he had a rather common accident. He tripped and fell down a flight of subway stairs, taking a bad blow on the chin. He refused medical attention and took a taxi home. He spent the evening reading in his library. His housekeeper could not wake him the next morning. Doctors found that the blow on the chin had also fractured the gambler's skull. Brain specialists tried to bring him out of the coma. It was decided to operate, but he died that afternoon before this could be done.

Gambler friends and a mob of hundreds were at the Congregational Broadway Tabernacle for the burial rites. His ashes were taken to New Bedford for interment in the Canfield family plot.

He left an estate of $841,485. It was very little for a man who had made millions as an honest gambler ($12,500,000 at one time).

He had sold his collection of Whistler paintings to M. Knoedler & Son for $300,000. The three best were sold to the steel czar, Henry C. Frick, and are on view today in the Frick Collection, where no one will admit that they once belonged to Richard Canfield.

The Summer Hotels of Saratoga

The magnificent hotels in America began to die out or become debased with the end of World War I. The *old* Waldorf, the early days of the Plaza, the Palace in San Francisco, Colorado's Antlers, the Broadmoor—all meant true luxury. Wrote a retired hotel manager I contacted: "Legends of the grand service, the perfect tall-ceilinged rooms, the herds of servants are long gone, replaced by slovenly unions, very sure of their

The Ruined Gambler. An early-American print of the tossing away of cards and dice, a vice disposed of much too late. *Author's collection*

A championship dog fight. An old woodcut. Very heavy wagering was done. *Author's collection*

Bettors at a cockfight. Colonial Americans followed the English pattern of betting on animal fights. The center figure is blind, but betting.
Author's collection

A gambler dressed as a "rube" lures a sucker into picking the "right" card.
Author's collection

Raiding a nineteenth-century gambling house. The surprised players wear the top hats. *Author's collection*

If you were for Abe Lincoln and the Union, you gambled with this military set of cards. *The John Omwake Playing Card Collection. Printed with permission of the United States Playing Card Company*

The Lady Lee—a Mississippi river boat—noted for its gambling and its cargo. Note the gentry's carriages on the upper deck.

Ross collection

Bet-a-Million Gates. All the gambling legends about him seem to be true. *Ross collection*

Gambling in a New York City shop, 1865. *Ross collection*

THE FATE OF HUNDREDS OF YOUNG MEN.

1. LEAVING HOME FOR NEW YORK. 2. IN A FASHIONABLE SALOON AMONGST THE WAITER GIRLS
—THE ROAD TO RUIN. 3. DRINKING WITH "THE FANCY"—IN THE HANDS OF GAMBLERS. 4. MUR-
DERED AND ROBBED BY HIS "FANCY" COMPANIONS.—5. HIS BODY FOUND BY THE HARBOR POLICE.

Title page of a story of the dangers of the city. Notice the text below:
"In the Hands of Gamblers," which leads to murder.

Author's collection

LEFT: James Todhunter Sloan, the dude jockey. *Ross collection*

RIGHT: On the left, Wild Bill Hickok, who was shot dead in a poker game while holding a black ace. On the right, a young Buffalo Bill. Center man is not known. *Ross collection*

Bare-knuckled John L. Sullivan and Jake Kilrain fighting it out in 1889. A *Police Gazette* print. *Author's collection*

Gambling scene in San Francisco. The player on the right probably has an empty pocket.
Ross collection

Gambling joint in the Far West around the turn of the century. Only the professional gambler wore the top hat. *Courtesy of the Signal Corps*

rights. Perhaps it's because the millionaire gamblers, the great professional poker players who lived a grand life, have changed into something else. The big gamblers of Las Vegas and Miami lack the proper élan; missing is the feel of gold coins piled up. My father remembered that in those days in the best hotels it was evening clothes, and many a gambler traveled with his own valet. So did the big stake players, he said; men like Colonel Greene, Lucky Baldwin, George Hearst, the Whitneys, the Belmonts, the Virginia City silver crowd like Tabor and others, the West Coast oil men. Champagne was served, not cocktails; and no Mafia or hoodlums in the great days when poker wasn't something to make headlines for Texans. Gambling's Golden Age is gone, with the twenty-dollar gold coins piled *this* high."

Only memory can recall the grand hotels of Saratoga Springs, under trees stirred by lake zephyrs; behind their respectable façades the whispers and laughter in the night. They were an interesting group of structures, examples of majestically ornamented General Grant and Victorian ideas. They were also sometimes dangerous firetraps, as were all noble wooden buildings of the period, protected only by primitive fire-fighting devices. They were marvelous to live in. Large, high-ceilinged rooms, splendid in their steeples, boasted gingerbread trimmings, woodworkers' maddening detail of scrolls, curves, and cast-iron barnacles. Their great airy porches held thousands of rocking chairs. The hotels, the glory of Saratoga, live in memoirs and on hundreds of postal cards. Trees and gardens gave a green setting to railings and courtyards.

The vast dining halls showed that it was an age of spaciousness, when good living insisted on high rafters, wide golden-oak staircases, white linen, figured velvet, taffeta, or brocades.

On the Fourth of July in 1864, with toy cannon banging and fireworks doing damage to limbs and eyes, the Stanwix Hall Hotel burned down, along with over a dozen nearby buildings in the vicinity of Broadway and Congress streets. The remorseless flames joined the rhetoric of the holiday. Someone had tossed a good-sized firecracker into the Water Cure Shop of Dr. Norman Bedortha, and from there Stanwix Hall caught fire at a moment when the Saratoga firemen, volunteers in fine uniform, were enjoying a firemen's picnic on Lake Champlain, with kegs of beer, three-legged foot races, and band music. These glorious hotels were expendable; the flaming pyres were usually rebuilt in an even grander style.

At the Stanwix fire the male guests and a gathering crowd watched the hotel burn as stricken nesting birds fell to earth. Some twenty women took over a hand-pumper and got a hose, spraying a feeble stream of water on the fire. The men cheered and rushed to help. It was a good try against enormous odds. The telegraph message to the volunteer firemen did not bring them back in time to do anything but kick their toes among the embers of fourteen buildings.

The next year, in June, Marvin House, a gambling joint, caught fire and sent flames along to destroy the United States Hotel and its cottages at a cost of $350,000. Fires continued, and after the Congress Hotel and the Columbia Hotel (the firemen were again away at picnics during big fires), it seemed time for a full-time fire-fighting department for professionals. This was done in 1883, and picnics suffered.

However, rebuilding was a boon, for it added more luxury to the hotels: more gilt, turkey-red carpets, grill work, cast-iron railings, plate glass, and much fancier lobbies of marble, rare woods, antlers of spreading gas fixtures, and chandeliers of Venetian crystal.

One of the most talked of hotels was the Grand Union, on the site of the old Putnam Tavern. It was an isolated phenomenon of past grandeur, a vast pile of regal sentimentality and comfortable luxury. It had cost $3 million and had wide mahogany beds, mirrors that were tall French imports for viewing and primping, hand-painted drapes, multicolored marble shipped from Italy, and Waterford crystal chandeliers that hung high and swayed a bit to musical tinkling with the breeze, making polite sounds to accompany the chatter of the guests underneath. Granite from Vermont gave the building strength. The black walnut staircases were native, cut from trees nearby. Artists lay on their backs on scaffolds, painting pure frescos in the method of Michelangelo (if not his genius) onto the hotel ceilings. Art styles went from vaporous Greek to unresolved *art nouveau* when it came along.

The feeding of guests was in a vast dining hall which had no visible supports from floor to ceiling and ran a whole city block.

Fifteen hundred people could be fed in comfort and with polite service, the steaks and buckwheat cakes coming hot to the table, the wine buckets chilled and in place at festive dinners. One could get shad roe and planked salmon, deer haunch and acorn-fed pork. Available were wild strawberries with clotted country cream; also cooling drinks of lemon juice and syrup for the ailing to mix with mineral waters.

The Grand Union grounds comprised seven acres of buildings and landscaping. Someone with a pencil and an active mind once figured out that if set length to length, there was a full mile of porches. The ballroom and the grand bandstand had to be seen to be believed, and when the waltz came in, the strains of Vienna's Strauss mingled with Offenbach and the Virginia reel and the later ragtime. Life was at its very best, with a languor, a grace touched with indulgence.

The ballroom contained one of the largest paintings in the world done at a cost of $100,000 and two years' labor; a popular painting that gave a sense of culture in its mixture of mythology and addled history to the 1,200 guests who occupied 550 rooms. Some visitors were in legal wedded status on the high-piled big beds, some in not-too-furtive sin. All this vast herding and feeding of well-heeled patrons called for 35 chefs and 250 waiters, usually, as one letter writer put it, "darkies dancing in with loaded trays, wearing white gloves, carrying high their trays, the thick laughter of their deep throaty greetings, all still in my memory of the Grand Union, a picture of my childhood I shall always remember." In a letter from Alice C. to this writer years later, she wrote: "The full menus were beyond the ability of any one ordinary person to sample in any detail. Fifty main items were listed in scrollwork type. Just to read them gave Papa the feeling he was spending his money for worthwhile substantial reasons."

One day's appetites at the hotel consumed 1,500 pounds of prime beef, 500 chickens, 1,200 quarts of milk, 20 barrels of potatoes, 200 quarts of strawberries, huckleberries, or blueberries, and vegetables and fruits in season. It was a corn-on-the-cob culture. The fish came from lake and river; the lobsters and shellfish from the ocean came on ice.

With their tradition of nasturtiums, elms and sycamores, the social-status hotels of the knowledgeable people were the

Clarendon and Congress Hall. The Grand Union, however, had the habit of throwing big bashes and huge galas for folk heroes. General Grant got big fêtes—two within four years. Parties woke the finches, the wild canaries and pigeons in the hotel trees. Congress Hall had over 400 feet of piazzas for walkers and rockers. Alice C. remembers: "We used to run and skip among the men swinging their canes on the porches as they inhaled pungent cigars and the ladies in their well-hipped outfits and hats trimmed with ribbons and false fruit and parts of birds. In the sunlight the carriages would roll by at a slow trot, filled with people coming back from the race track, the horses arching their necks, foam on their silver bits, and dropping golden horse-apples. Several times one season Papa, after a good day at the race track, would be helped down from a buckboard or carriage by the hotel servants, having taken too many refreshers from his golden flask. Mama would hold smelling salts to her nose, a nose sunburned because she had, as usual, forgotten to hold up her parasol for protection, or had lost it. Papa would drop gold coins onto the fireplace mantel in our suite and laugh a lot and slap Mama on the rump. We'd all go down to the dining room for big lobsters which the maître d' cracked for us with a silver tool, and the wine steward said Papa had ordered the right wine, Pommery Brut of course. The steamed clams came in big boilers set on the table, and Papa and Mama and their guests got to sipping clam broth and lager beer from big iced pitchers. Me and my brothers were always getting butter in our ears from the corn on the cob. There were big, ice-cold watermelon slices, and Aunt Gussie would start crying about her married life going wrong with Uncle Herbert. Uncle Herbert seldom came to Saratoga. He preferred Bangor."

Another writer, Henry James, in 1870, back for a visit to the United States, set down his impression of a Saratoga hotel: "In the evening when the 'boarders' have all come forth and seated themselves in groups, or have begun to stroll in (not always, I regret to say, to the sad detriment of the dramatic interest, bisexual couples), the big heterogeneous scene affords a great deal of entertainment . . . . brick walls illuminated by a line of flaring gas lights, form a natural background to the crude, impermanent, discordant tone of the assembly."

James was a dreadful snob, happiest at the English tea tables of raddled duchesses. "A few dozen rocking chairs, an equal number of small tables, tripods of the eternal ice pitcher, serve chiefly to emphasize the vacuous grandeur of the spot. . . ." James had been a slacker in the Civil War and had run off to Europe to avoid fighting for the Union. His few visits back home made him fear for his country's progress into a cruder, grimmer industrial age, the final triumph of a dubious class of greedy businessmen.

The United States Hotel again burned down—as if to be in fashion—and was rebuilt. It had seven acres of ground, was done over in solid brick and stone after its fires, and fronted proudly on nearly 700 feet of Division Street. It boasted 65 grand suites with a parlor and up to seven bedrooms, for those who could afford it. Other guests had to make do with over 700 large, well-appointed bedrooms. There were 1,000 wicker rocking chairs for sedate exercisers; and, as one guest observed, these chairs were not, as elsewhere, tossed or kicked about. "If a bellboy moves a chair on the piazza of the United States Hotel, he *lifts* it. . . ."

The cottages of the nineties had a sign placed on their doors: *The rent of this apartment is $20 per day; board for each person in occupancy of this apartment is $2.50 per day.* Gone are those days. Three fine meals a day: $2.50!

Anthony C. Graves was dancing teacher and master of ceremonies when the open reception for the United States Hotel took place in August of 1874. "And what a galaxy of beauty and charm and gallantry were here assembled! . . . the gorgeous costumes of the ladies . . . the soft strains of the 'Blue Danube Waltz' breathing romance and glamorous gaiety upon the brilliant assembly. . . . Women and girls in Saratoga," he recalled years later, "did not have short hair, and when gentlemen smoked, feminine delicacy withdrew to wait, but not to snatch a coveted smoke behind the palms."

However, the professor, who disdained bawdy tableaus, was romancing a bit, for our letter writer, Alice C., reports: "Aunt Gussie, when she wasn't crying over her marriage, was smoking Russian cigarettes, and one night she tried one of Papa's cigars, and said it was strong but had no flavor. Aunt Gussie used to come back to the hotel very late at night, clicking her fingers, kicking at her train. I remember waking up, needing a drink of water, and there was Mama in her long pink robe talking to Aunt Gussie, who was laughing as she sat on the sofa, rolling her head around, and Mama was pointing a finger at her and saying, 'You'll come to no good with those gamblers and those lobster palace people. You'll rue it, Gussie, you'll rue it.' "

Aunt Gussie appears to have been a patron, with her shady gamblers and race track escorts, of the restaurants for the high livers in Saratoga. The early eating places sometimes continued in popularity for decades, some like Meyers, where living bass were kept in ponds on the grounds and the guest could choose the fish he wanted cooked. Moons is said to have invented the cocktail snack known as the potato chip. The legend is that an uncongenial guest kept complaining that the French-fried potatoes were too thick. The chef supposedly sliced them cardboard thin and tossed them into deep fat; the result was the potato chip, which became a favorite in Saratoga circles. Another story at Moons is that someone accidentally dropped a slice of potato into some cruller fat and discovered that the result was edible.

George Crum, son of a mulatto jockey, is credited with the chip invention. In time he set up for himself an exclusive eating place in Saratoga. He liked, in some maniacal delight, to keep his Vanderbilts, Gateses and Bradys, judges and gentry waiting an hour or so for a table. William Vanderbilt brought his own canvasback ducks along to Crum, after a United States Hotel chef had spoiled a pair for him. Crum had never cooked canvasbacks before, so he just boldly put them on the coals for only nineteen minutes. Hot, underdone and bloody, they went to the table. Crum reported: "Mr. Vanderbilt said he never had eaten anything like it in his life." Crum's place had the quality trade and the political fat cats, not just congressmen and judges, but Presidents Chester A. Arthur and Grover Cleveland.

The list of the season's guests at the hotels could include General Ambrose Burnside, famous for his muttonchop whiskers if not for his battles; Jay Gould, the most crooked millionaire of his time; Commodore Vanderbilt, not far behind in callousness and chicanery; Chauncey Depew, a true *homme moyen sensual*, the most witty and obscene after-dinner speaker; and

Pierre Lorillard. The *Police Gazette* suggested that the Lorillard coat of arms was "a cuspidor couchant, with two cigars and a plug of tobacco rampant."

It must be admitted that most men chewed tobacco, a wad kept in one distended cheek, often discreetly. English visitors were shocked at the habit, at the spitting, and at the target practice that took place all the time in lobbies and on porches at the waiting cuspidors. The rich had gold and silver spittoons; the usual, however, were of brass, highly polished at the start of each day and placed on rubber mats for inferior marksmen. It was "a dirty habit, a gross indulgence," everyone agreed, and yet "chawing" did not become a social blot on one's character until after World War I, when only baseball players were forgiven the habit.

In 1876 Judge Henry Hilton acquired the Grand Union. The judge is described as "a stormy figure," which is a polite way of saying what one journalist said in private: "Henry was a mean and poisonous bigoted son of a bitch, and had about as much right to be a judge as a Sioux war chief loose in a girls' school." Some of his reputation for outrageous bigotry was brought on by his ruling that barred Jews as guests at the Grand Union. The Belmonts, Strausses, Warburgs, Dillons, Goldwaters and other American families, most of whom are now accepted as pure WASP but had Jewish parents, all were barred by Judge Hilton as a hotel owner. A good gentile like Moses Thompson once had a desk clerk pull the pen from his Protestant hand when he began to write "Moses" on the hotel register. The judge was in business in New York as Hilton, Hughes & Co., and the boycott that resulted from his bigotry forced the firm out of business. In time Judge Hilton also gave up the hotel and retired to his Woodlawn Park estate.

On a mere judge's pay, Hilton seemed to have done remarkably well in the money department over the years. Besides putting over half a million dollars into the Grand Union, he lived in Woodlawn Park, which consisted of 1,500 acres and 25 miles of private road. The huge, sprawling mansion held a fireplace that cost $18,000, and the mahogany paneling around some of the rooms was nearly three inches thick. His office or den had a plush ceiling with the initials H.H.H. set in its center. As one local wit said, "So when the judge is dead drunk and on his back he could look up and see that his initials were still H.H.H."

At Woodlawn the servants' quarters alone consisted of 28 rooms, and the stables held more than 80 horses. By special permit, non-Jewish visitors could gain admission to the Hilton grounds to ride along in buckboards, carriages or landaus and admire the Green Moutain in the background.

Saratoga today is a placid, debilitated ghost of its former self. Gone are the days when Sam Riddle sent his great race horse, Man o' War, as a two-year-old against the Saratoga barrier in 1919 to take the Sanford Memorial Stakes and five other races that season. Only record books echo the victories of Gallant Fox and Whichone; the stands that once held 30,000 now see fewer crowds and poorer horses.

The great old hotels that ran the spectrum of style and sin are nearly empty or have been torn down. Those that remain are often creaky ruins, the dingy halls with cracked walls, musty rooms in most cases still far from the bathrooms, the water running rusty in ancient brass faucets. The oldest waiters are passing from the scene, still muttering of legendary tips from Diamond Jim, and a few from Bet-a-Million ("a rotten tipper").

The roulette wheels and the faro layouts were made into coffee tables; the cards are worn out. The hundreds of old wicker rockers have been auctioned off, as have the chandeliers and the whale-oil fixtures. The last water pitcher and basin have become antiques. The cigar stores' wooden Indians are in museums.

The women who now come for the waters lack the style and dash of those James Gordon Bennett wrote about: "Beautiful Saratoga . . . realm of a hundred queens!" Now they go for the various medicinal spring waters: Geyser, a table water; Hawthorn, a laxative; Coese, a milder stomach-churner. Lost is the mood of *fetes champêtre,* where the twenty-dollar gold coins were flipped away and $1,000 chips were tossed like peanuts. And gay ladies with aphrodisiac laughter unbuttoned and unlaced and uncorseted themselves for ardent males. Now there is the sipping of the tainted waters that contain—by Saratoga's report—sodium chlorides, potassium, lithium, ammonium, bicarbonates of sodium, calcium, magnesium and iron. Not a drop of Mumms, White Seal, or Moets.

The last survivors lean on their canes and with sad garrulity repeat old lies of past razzle-dazzle. The Chamber of Commerce (not a sideburn or a beard among them) announces: "The tourists and visitors come to Saratoga to enjoy the scenery and drink the waters." (And the orange-juice stands, Disney movies, parking lots and parking meters.) People now walk the once-ornate hotel lobbies in bathrobes and Hawaiian shirts and bare feet. The smell of the best carriage horses is gone for good, as is the aroma of Havana cigars. Walking the streets of the town to the haranguing pop music of transistor radios, you feel a sense of the tail end of something lost: a livelier time, a sporting group of people willing to play for the odds, an audience for the sensual delights available for the bold and the beautiful. Under the August sun in the city park Richard Canfield made, one seems to hear the distant axes chopping down the cherry trees.

5

GAMBLING IN THE WEST

In one old mining town I once discovered a gambling house turned into a church, with a wind-battered sign still on its deserted façade:

IT DOESN'T MEAN MUCH TO GAMBLE WELL IF YOU LOSE

Legends clutter the history of gambling: Gamblers are sometimes inclined to be pathological liars. They are also romantics in many cases, living in a world of fantasy containing lucky cards, fabulous runs of winning plays at the dice tables, and miracles of the right numbers at roulette.

Checking out the background of any gambling myth is often difficult. Was there, around 1847, the Secret Band of Brothers, a group amazingly close to what we think of today as the Mafia? This secret band was supposedly "pledged to gambling, thievery and villainy of all kinds."

So claimed a book by Jonathan F. Green (Philadelphia, 1847). The author insisted that this band was active in the 1830s, with rituals, codes, and a dedication to gambling and crime. Titles ran from Grand Masters and Vice-Grand Masters to the head himself, the Worthy Grand, or Ruling Grand. Like the later Cosa Nostra, the band's masters passed down orders, and whatever gains resulted were shared by all. Members "wandered from place to place, preying upon the community in the character of barkeepers, pickpockets, thieves, gamblers, horse players, and sometimes murderers."

Upon what evidence, besides Green's book, can one base the existence of the Secret Band of Brothers? That gangs of gamblers, tricksters, bunco artists, con men, thieves and pickpockets traveled about the country was certainly true (and still is). Rigging card games, playing the rubes for suckers at gypsy race courses and country fairs, with three-card monte or the shell game, was commonplace. But a fully organized band with Grand Masters, bylaws, and secret ink, with information drops and orders in hollow trees and in caverns, seems like sensational fiction.

Horace Greeley of the *New York Tribune* wrote that the gambling fraternity had "conducted their nefarious business and [its] effrontery [was] perfectly surprising . . . five millions of dollars are annually won from fools and shallow knaves by blacklegs in this city alone; and not less than a thousand young men are annually ruined by them."

He could have suggested once again: "Go west, young man." But the West was hardly the place for a young man with the gambling itch. For in the cow towns, the mining camps, and coastal harbors, men died violently over card tables and in gambling houses, some of them mere tents. Gambling was a raging fever in San Francisco. Hulls of clipper ships were dragged ashore after the crews had all run off to the gold fields. Green himself was arrested and put in the Tombs Prison in New York when one of his book agents accused him of shady dealings. In the Tombs, counterfeit money was found on him, but the Secret Service said that they had given the author the queer currency (as one of their agents) to help them catch passers of bad money.

Jonathan F. Green seems to have been a very strange fellow, a character out of Dickens, and no more real than his "Secret Band." Yet he was used as one of the boosters of reform in Greeley's New York Association for the Suppression of Gambling. Green was the organization's head undercover man and its secret police chief. There was even an "enemy list." Businesses, banks, stockbrokers, and all sorts of merchants were informed by the association if they had employees on the "active gamblers' lists."

The press reported the public outcry against using "spies and informers watching the . . . secret personal habits of private citizens." It did little to stop gambling, but a new law against gambling was proposed. The Anti-Gambling Bill, with the gamblers' lobby against it, "led to official corruption . . . that disgraced the annals of our . . . legislation." In 1851 the law passed. A year later reform had faded, even if, for a little time, some gambling houses closed and gamblers worked other green-felt fields with dice and cards. Soon gambling reappeared in New York, newer gambling houses were active, and the cards flashed across the tables, the dice rattled, and the wheels turned. As Charles Lamb had observed: "Man is a gaming animal." (It is interesting to note that until well past the middle of the nineteenth century, many used the word "gaming" rather than "gambling.")

Those of Mr. Greeley's men who did go west were welcomed by the professional gamblers; to refuse to play was nearly a breach of etiquette.

The names of the old mining camps occur in old journals, in letters sent back east, in files of yellowing newspapers, and often in court records. There are stories of gamblers' luck or loss in places like Frying Pan Camp, Hubbard's Gambling Tent at Sacramento, Pizon Switch, and Hangtown (later legally fumigated to become Placerville). There was Jackass Crossing, the El Dorado in Frisco, Virginia City's Crystal Saloon, Leadville, Goldfield, Ore City, Slim Diggin's, Coyoteville. Not all gambled or panned for gold. In Hangtown a Studebaker brother made picks and shovels and put enough gold in his money belt to return to Pennsylvania and back the building of the Studebaker Brothers wagons. An Armour butchered meat and dreamed of becoming a king meat packer, and a grocer named Huntington charged higher prices for his beans and bacon, figuring that someday soon the steam cars would cross the continent on iron rails and he might be a part of that gamble. These three men were gamblers, out for much larger stakes than the ordinary miner. As one gold-panner wrote back to his brother in Ohio: "It is digging, eating, shitting, fornicating squaws, drinking red-eye whisky and gambling. . . ."

In shaky tents, under dozens of oil lamps, men gambled; $5,000 to $20,000 bets on a hand of cards were common. Everything was costly. Whisky was usually a silver dollar a shot.

Housing was crawly, buggy, and, most of all, dirty. Six men slept in a bed. Men rarely bathed, and undressing was risky, as bags of gold were carried next to the skin. But as one writer put it, it was "an act of bad breeding to go to bed with one's hat on. Better to get to the gambling houses, well lit, lively, with drink, cards, girls on hand."

Many of the best gambling stories of the Old West came out of Abilene, Kansas, during the days of the great cattle drives. It was a railroad town and a cattle-shipping point. Though not impressive or large, it nevertheless catered to the whims, desires, and hopes of a transient population of nearly 300 cowhands, trail bosses and drifters. It offered the thirsty, gullible, raunchy and greedy its twenty gambling halls and its dozen or so dance halls, which in most cases were actually whorehouses. One of the best-known places was Ben Thompson's "Bull's Head." The killings in Abilene were never as deadly as pictured in the movies, nor were weapons always kept on the ready. Ben would take pity on a cowhand who went broke at his tables and would buy his Remington or Colt for fifteen to twenty-five dollars. If the gambler was lucky, he could buy back his hogleg. If not, Ben sold off his collection of weapons from time to time.

But the glory of a town could become definitely passé as rails moved on to open up more landscape. Texas cattle brought $300 million a year into Abilene during its prime. But when the Union Pacific high iron got to Cheyenne in 1867, the gambling play went there with those who called it Hell-on-Wheels. A letter dated 1868 reported: "There is sure nothing what you can't find here, and nothing you can stay 'way from in whisky, women and gambling after all the months working with the gandy dancers [track ballast tampers] so you end up with empty pockets and a head like a pumpkin."

The champion of gambling, by all available comment, was Dodge City. It was named after the Civil War general who was construction boss of the Union Pacific. Besides crowds of cowhands up from the Chisholm Trail, there were buffalo-robed men who killed off the last million of the great herds of bison, railroad workers paid off or fired, and soldiers from the forts and the territorial outposts who protected civilization and property from the Indians. Dodge City was what one visitor called "the wickedest, the most bibulous Babylon of the frontier."

The legend is that when a conductor on the Union Pacific asked a drunken ticketless passenger for his fare and destination, the boozed citizen said, "I want to go to hell." "Well, then," answered the conductor, "you want to get off at Dodge City."

The various fun-seekers, gamblers, con men, and bunco artists all mixed in a wild whisky-haunted crowd. And frontier whisky was often the professional gambler's best helper. It was a noxious brew called red-eye, skull-cracker, p'izon, forty-rod, or panther piss. It was really raw, often illegally distilled alcohol, colored with tobacco juice, made to bite by pepper and sometimes other revolting ingredients. It could be bought for ten cents a shot, and cost a silver dollar a shot glassful at outposts of civilization. Most gamblers drank, and the owners of the gambling places saw to it that the stuff kept flowing to befuddle the player. Often it was merely bottled hard cider with fizz water. One recipe called for baking soda. There were preachers who spread the word at the bars and saloons: "Blessed are the undefiled—Psalm 19." The pious God-pounders spoke out against the wild gambling as they tried to bring the wicked to God. But few gamblers repented until broke, or on the verge of the DTs. To go on playing and drinking with the odds against him got the player the award for being "a dead-game sport," "a square-shooter," or "no tinhorn." The innocent, or those who didn't conform to the West's ideals, were tinhorns, tenderfeet, muckers or mollycoddles.

There were preachers who could take over a gambling house or saloon full of raucous men and recite the Bible in card-playing terms:

> *You just listen a bit, pards,*
> *And I'll show you the Bible in cards.*
> *The ace, now that reminds us of God,*
> *The deuce of the Father and Son;*
> *The trey of the Father, the Son and the Ghost,*
> *For remember all of the Three are but One!*

If the lines were well delivered, a hat would be passed. One of the few pious lines the gambling houses produced was an obituary concerning a man caught cheating at poker: *"Played Four Aces, Now Playing the Harp."*

The professional gambler of the Western frontier was an individual who lived a hard life and was always in danger of being killed. In between seasons of taking suckers, he usually dropped his winnings on the gambling tables of Chicago or New Orleans. The professional either dressed well or played as a simple country rube in baggy clothes, side whiskers, and steel-rimmed glasses, carrying a carpetbag and wiping his face and neck with a red bandanna handkerchief. He also always carried cards. He could be a specialist in three-card monte or the shells, or with a pair of acrobatic dice. Rather than admired, the gambler was feared. He was skilled with a pistol, and often with a knife or dagger, too. Some favored the pocket derringer, a small item that could be concealed in the palm of the hand but fired a large-bore slug.

Wild Bill Hickok, a legendary Western hero, was in reality a drifting lawman and a seeker of wealth in gold strikes. Possessed of steely eyes and a magnificent head of yellow hair, he had a reputation with guns that was such that few ever dared face him when sober. From all evidence, Hickok was not really a great card player. He often drank while playing, and would join in wherever there was a game.

Once Wild Bill was in a game with a crooked gambler named McDonald in Sioux City. It was clear that McDonald was cheating the heavily drinking Wild Bill. There was a big pot of money on the table by midnight, and Wild Bill had bid up his hand with all he had.

McDonald laid down his hand. "Three jacks."

Wild Bill showed his. "A full house, three aces and a pair of sixes."

McDonald looked over Bill's cards. "I only see *two* aces and *one* six."

"Well," said Wild Bill, pulling out his six-shooter, "now right here is my other six, and"—adding a bowie knife with his free hand—"this here is my one-spot."

McDonald didn't change his expression. "Well, that sure is a good hand, Bill. You take the pot."

Gamblers liked to play with their backs against a wall. A cowhand with the idea that he had been cheated could, in his rage, sneak up behind a man and get him in the back. The most famous mistake a gambler ever made in *not* having his back to a wall happened in 1876 in Nuttal and Manns's place in Deadwood Gulch in the Black Hills of Dakota Territory. The incautious man was Wild Bill Hickok. Playing at Nuttal and Manns's in a friendly game of poker, Wild Bill had taken the only chair open in the place, with no wall behind him. The show-off pests of the frontier were those who wanted to create an instant reputation as gunfighters by pistoling down some famous gunslinger. One of these was "Crooked Nose" Jack McCall, who had been drinking rotgut whisky and watching Wild Bill play. There is no record of Wild Bill ever having done McCall any harm or damage. But Crooked Nose moved behind Wild Bill and casually put a bullet into the back of the card player's head. Wild Bill fell dead on the floor, his fingers still holding his card hand: two pairs—aces and eights—and a queen. In gambling circles it became known as "the Dead Man's Hand."

The death of a frontier celebrity like Wild Bill in a poker game attracted attention. But many a gambler went to burial on Boot Hill, name unknown. The song "The Streets of Laredo," also known as "The Cowboy's Lament" in various versions, is a dirge of the dying cowboy who riled the wrong gambler.

Bat Masterson had a reputation as a gunfighter, professional gambler, and later sportswriter for a New York newspaper. In his early life he worked as a buffalo-pelt hunter, town marshal, and army scout, and showed admirable skill at card playing. He played at Watrous and Bannigan's place in Creede in 1890. One night a drunk at the bar turned suddenly and slapped Bat Masterson across the face. Everyone ducked, expecting Bat to blast the damn fool with a bit of fast-gun action. Bat, however, his face livid from the slap, just stared at the drunk and said, "You go sober up. Then come back when you want to trade lead with me."

There is no evidence of a return.

People bet on nearly everything. In the 1890s a Judge Campbell ran his court from his saloon in Benicia, California. After hearing the evidence in a case, he would throw a pair of dice. Double fours could bring eight days or eight months in the cooler, or hoosegow, as a jail was often called. If it was a busy day in court and the judge knew his prisoner and his background, he'd toss the dice without hearing evidence.

While the westward surge was made mainly by pelt hustlers, gold prospectors, home seekers, ranchers, and makers of raw villages and towns laced together—first by trails, then by rail lines—the gambler, the whisky-seller, and the brothel-keeper cannot be overlooked in a true explication of the interwoven relationships of the frontier.

Not only were the railroads preceded and followed by emigrants and footloose folk seeking new land, but, as one reporter put it in 1873, there was on one rail line under construction "three hundred sharpers, cappers and other standbys, all of whom were engaged in conducting . . . games or frauds."

Many a tent or shanty had its card-handlers ready to skin anyone foolish enough to go up against them, and every railroad junction and depot was the haunt of some three-card-monte handler. The larger nineteenth-century gambling establishments that became famous and notorious flourished in St. Louis and ended at the Pacific Ocean in San Francisco, with Denver and Kansas City in between in their own multiform life patterns. The rattle of dice, the click of the roulette wheel, the shuffling of cards seemed almost as much symbols of the new raw West as the covered wagon.

San Francisco was the nearest center for the first gold hunters. It became a wild and desperate city. As the sailing ships were deserted by their sailors leaving for the diggings, landfills extended out into the bay, in time to bury the ships. Some were broken up or hauled ashore to serve as gambling houses, hotels, and houses of entertainment of all sorts.

The El Dorado was the first gambling house (tent at first) in San Francisco, set up at what is now Washington and Kearny streets. It raised up more splendid and solid quarters, and its popularity grew as gold dust was weighed and the crowds of players had to push their way in to get a place at the gambling tables. In the early 1850s there were over a thousand active gambling houses. The *Annals of San Francisco* reported that two sides of Portsmouth Square were "occupied by buildings specially devoted to gambling." This overlooked the even more numerous saloons, which also offered faro, monte, dice, and other games. Old letters recall the names of the first gambling places like the Arcade, Mazourki, Ward House, Bryant House, the Varouvienne (French names were suggestively, sinfully popular). The most popular gambling places paid rents up to $50,000 or $70,000 a year for taking over a floor for gambling.

Bill Briggs ran a fancy establishment on Montgomery Street. He considered it bad luck in a game for anyone to take seriously any coin smaller than a silver dollar (also known as a cartwheel). After a night's gambling, Briggs would collect all the smaller coins, which did not meet his idea of money, and throw them into the street. He was one of the best-remembered gambling-house owners, managing to stay active in spite of the town's usual fires and the police efforts at reform. He was active and survived until 1880.

San Francisco was known for its devastating fires. One reason was that everything was made of wood. Every gambling house or place of entertainment liked to light itself with clusters of lamps, usually swinging freely and burning whale oil. Careless or reckless men had a habit of cavorting when drunk or in a rage and knocking down the lamps.

When the gold rush first provided the wealth to gamble, few places were more than raw lumber with some shoddy attempt at fancy furnishings. In time, gold frames and chandeliers were a part of the decor, and some effort was made to provide good food. But the scene was usually a shambles. The players were nearly all rough males: they not only smoked their cigars and drank their bad whisky neat, but they chewed tobacco, so the interior of a gambling house was usually gamey, smelly, smoky, and muddy underfoot. The players could be gentlemen in imported Bond Street tailoring copied by local tailors, or tattered, whiskered miners smelling like polecats. As one text of the period by John P. Young noted of the places: "The showiest were tawdry affairs despite the almost uniform testimony . . . hardly . . . an attractive addition to the waterfront of a seaport."

Few of the establishments were honest. The magnetized roulette wheel was often in use, and croupiers, called "skinning crews of braced games," always had jobs. But even if suspect, the gambling tables did a land-office business. A popular place like the Bella Union might see $200,000 a night put into play.

But the fabulous sums bet, according to later memoirs, were often exaggerated. A bet of two or three thousand dollars was high. One could play for four bits (fifty cents) to a sawbuck (ten dollars). As one educated gambler wrote home: "Gamblers here move from sacrifice to communion to atonement."

A drunk with a big poke of gold, or some person in the grip of a mad lucky moment, could run hog-wild. One lucky digger bet his all, an eighty-eight-pound sack of gold (worth $16,000 at that time) and beat the house. In a place called Whipple's, gambler Jim Rynders won nearly $90,000 in a night's play but went broke a few days later in the same place.

Oddly enough, poker hardly mattered during the early gold rush. Faro and roulette were louder, quicker, and better (for the house). Poker hardly seemed a game for anyone but sporting gentlemen playing among themselves in a kind of dead-pan etiquette. It was not until 1870 that it really caught on as the town grew a bit more respectable and heavy charges for gambling licenses became a burden. In 1854 the law made running a gambling layout illegal (not that any great effort was spent to enforce it). Police raids became a problem in time, and the number of open gambling houses patronized by the public declined. The rich and well-off continued to have fine places to wager their money, but the gambling mania of the gold-rush days simmered down and the raw nature of the frontier took on polish.

Poker became the Western game. It could be played in hotel suites or discreeet clubs or in the backs of saloons. It remained the popular San Francisco game, although it was pushed aside a bit in time by a growing interest in dice. Poker rooms sprang up, with heavy decor in red velvet, thick gilt frames, and silver spittoons, offering cigars, drink and food. Businessmen breaking for a long lunch could play away a few hours or spend an evening in play with their equals. Up to the turn of the century, cigar stands along Market Street had back rooms for poker parties. The best known of the Market Street places was Mose Gunst's; he took half a dollar out of each pot over a dollar and a half, and hired house players who turned over their winnings to him. In these places, the press reported, "Direct charge of cheating cannot be made . . . the visitor finds it an exceedingly hard game to beat."

Lucky Baldwin built his Baldwin Hotel in San Francisco in the 1870s. In the Cinch Room, big-time poker took over. (Cinch was a card game based on a version of "all fours.") Often a $100,000 pot came up. It was not a game for incipient mistakes or for weaklings. William C. Ralston, president of the Bank of California, and William Sharon, a Comstock Lode millionaire, in a famous game in the Cinch Room (after others had dropped out), soon had raised each other to a $30,000 pot. Sharon, after studying his chances, shook his head. "I quit."

Ralston laid down his hand—a pair of aces. Sharon did not show his hand, but much later he admitted that he had been bluffed out while holding jacks.

Kansas City ("K.C., the railroad town") had about forty gambling houses in the 1870s. On Missouri Street, Bob Potee ran a fine place. Potee was the stereotype of the professional gambler of fiction. Coming from Virginia, he had retained the soft vowels and manners of the Old South. His gambling tables were made of rare woods inlaid with mother-of-pearl and ivory, the drapes of damask and lace, the mirrors from Paris, the carpets soft and deep-piled.

Major Albert Showers ran a gambling emporium on Main Street and was perversely proud of the fact that in Washington, D.C., he had once dealt to such sterling American citizens as Henry Clay and Daniel Webster. The major prospered. But Bob Potee—who appears to have been a self-destructive type— threw himself into the Missouri River after great losses. A letter commenting about that sad event stated: "No gentleman and true Southerner would do what Bob did. The pistol held to the ear—trigger pulled—is the proper way a genteel person leaves this vale of tears."

By 1881 Missouri had a strong antigambling law, and gambling sports moved into what were listed as "social clubs," a coverup for high-stakes gambling at poker. Not all these establishments were honestly run, even for the gentry. One visiting guest at a club, feeling that he had been taken for several thousand dollars, was appalled at the barefaced cheating. He rose from the game and made a speech: "Gentlemen, I was assured that I should find this a gentleman's game . . . be kind enough to tell [me] where I can sit in a horse thief's game; I believe I'll go around there."

Gambling houses that didn't turn into clubs moved across the state line into Kansas City, Kansas. Clayton Maltby was host to the biggest and best known of the K.C., Missouri, places. His faro tables brought in half a million dollars a year.

The gamblers were able to remain open by a coy but satisfactory payoff. The police would raid them from time to time, and, as a Kansas City paper reported it, while "thirty or more men [were] gambling, their names were taken down and the proprietor was required to deposit $10 apiece for his visitors and $100 for himself . . . gambling was immediately resumed." The next day Maltby and other gambling-house owners would appear "in police court and were formally fined the amounts they had deposited. This is the manner in which gambling houses are . . . licensed in Kansas City, Kansas."

Denver, more than most towns, combined gambling with saloons, dance halls, and vulgar theater, a kind of early vaudeville. It was a city of self-confidence, derisive, and given to ornate extravagance. It was a kind of vacation spot for various swindlers in cards and mining stocks, for madams taking a breather from their trade; and in season it sent out flocks of card sharps—experts with marked decks and other brazen gyp games—to many communities of the West. It retained a brash sophistication in the Rockies.

The gambling houses in Denver had interesting names for their establishments: the Bucket of Blood, the Slaughter House, the Morgue, the Chicken Coop. The gambler Soapy Smith once dominated Denver's gambling scene. He lost his crunch there when his brother killed a gambler named Shotgun Smith and Soapy and his friends were run out of town.

Nearly everyone gambled in southern Texas with a three-cent coin called a quartilla or the universal silver dollar. Some would gamble with stakes of three or four hundred dollars. A journalist passing through in 1859 noted: "In this little village a hundred thousand dollars often changed hands in a single night [in] monte and poker."

Perhaps the most violent gambling scenes (closest to the fictional versions of native American gambling) occurred in Texas. After the Civil War, Texans wanting big play preferred San Antonio, Austin, and Fort Worth. Ben Thompson ran a saloon and flourished as a professional gambler. Unlike most gamblers, he was a notorious killer. He needed gun action, as he was a clumsy card cheat. When faced with a man who claimed he had been bilked, Ben went for his pistol. He is said to have gunned more than twelve men as a consequence of cheating. Some considered Ben Thompson the most dangerous gunslinger in the West. In 1884 Ben and another man, King Fisher, a gun handler, were attending a show in a San Antonio theater when killers shot both of them to death from the box seats. Two men were tried for the murders, but a casual jury, aware that they were offending no sensibilities, brought in a verdict of "justifiable homicide."

For some the trade was not a dangerous destiny. Nat Kramer from Fort Worth plied his skills all over the Southwest, including the steamboats on the Shreveport–New Orleans run. He didn't drink or carry a gun, but worked with calm and cunning. Nat was active for half a century. One report of his dying scene has someone asking him: "What are you going to tell Saint Peter?"

"Just going to tell him that I have helped some, and I have skinned some." The dying man paused. "Those I skinned could afford it, and them I helped needed it . . . maybe."

Gambling in the West as a way of life persisted until World War I. In some places the hunt for gold and silver had turned to the great Spindletop gushers of Beaumont, and the Texas Panhandle rotary drills opened up the boom towns of Oklahoma. Beef, wheat, and citrus also created new fortunes.

Some names of places suggest self-reliance but no settled way of life: Deadwood, Cheyenne ("Hell-on-Wheels"), Leadville, Cripple Creek (always pronounced "Crick"), and Tombstone (where Wyatt Earp and his brothers, Virgil and Morgan, took on the Clantons and McLowerys). There was never any bucolic simplicity about them.

The most unbelievable gambling story of the West took place in 1889, when pistol-protected gambling was beginning to simmer down and laws were enacted against gambling. The event took place in the Bowen Saloon in Santa Fe, New Mexico. John Dougherty was a confident gambler, with as independent a spirit as Doc Holliday when they were friends in Tombstone. However, Dougherty was not a gunfighter; he never shot anyone. He took pride in always carrying a wad of $100,000 in bills, and he never played a game with a limit on it, insisting that every player had to be able to put at least $10,000 on the table. The only human touch about Dougherty was his vanity about his small feet.

In the Bowen Saloon in Santa Fe that famous poker game is supposed to have been played with Ike Jackson, a millionaire cattleman from Texas. It was ballyhooed as the "Poker Championship of the West." One hundred special guests were invited to witness the match, including the governor of New Mexico, D. Bradford Prince. (It's amazing the number of men in the West, even today, who use only a letter in place of a first name.) The play began. After a few easy hands, Dougherty and Jackson had $100,000 in cash in the pot. No chips were used. Jackson, running out of cash, drew up a deed to 10,000 steers and his ranch. Dougherty calmly raised the pot $100,000. Jackson demanded to see the money for that raise. Dougherty called for writing materials and wrote out a document which he tossed to Governor Prince. Then he calmly drew his pistol.

"Governor, you sign this or I'll kill you. Now, I like you and would fight for you, but I love my reputation as a poker player better. So sign."

The governor didn't even bother to read the paper. He just took up the pen and signed. Dougherty nodded, took the paper, and tossed it onto the table.

"I raise you the Territory of New Mexico. There's the deed to it."

Ike Jackson cursed and laid down his cards. "All right, goddamn you, the pot is yours. But it's a hell of a good thing for you the governor of Texas isn't here to back *me!*"

My favorite story of the use of a gun in a poker game is the one about half a dozen men in a hot game in Omaha, in which a one-eyed man was playing. One of the players mistrusted the dealing by this man; maybe an ace had been palmed. He pulled out a pistol and demanded a new deck, adding, "I'm not making any insinuations or bringing any charges. I want to say just *this*. If I catch any son of a bitch cheating, I'm going to shoot his other eye out!"

The Saga of Soapy Smith
In the times of the early West and in the snows of Alaska during a gold rush, card-playing reached a fury far from the placid

pastime invented by the Chinese A.D. 1120. Marco Polo didn't have to bring cards back with him. They arrived in Europe in 1299 and were used by some for predicting chance, fate and fortune when turned into Tarot cards. These decks had four suits, the symbols of which were based on social status of those dark ages. There were knights (the highest form of *macho*, grace and bravery) that became the modern king, queen, and jack; lovers, who wore gaudy costumes (hearts in our deck); diamonds for merchants; and peasants, whose symbol was three blades of grass (to be called clubs). In Spain knights were called *espads*, and so one suit came to be called spades in English.

When the cards were used for gambling it meant the risking of staked money, or any object of value, on a chance event.

American card-playing has its own truculent history. The Far West of legend—the historic images created by popular novels, and by now nearly seventy years of films—pictures a lusty frontier that hardly resembles the true images and patterns of actual events or the hardships with which the people lived, struggled and died. Yet there is some truth in those scenes of gambling, when poker games could be deadly. The roulette wheel took gold dust from the miners, and cowhands splurged their pay on bad whisky and bad women. Prospectors and cowpokes were born victims of the professional gamblers.

It was not as gaudy, colorful or melodramatic as depicted in book or film. But it is a fact that Americans in distant places, often under mean or desperate conditions, found gambling a diversion and a hope of gain, though the gain was rarely achieved. The letters, journals, and newspapers of the day give form to much myth-enshrouded fact. "We have more saloons to the population than any other place in the country . . . faro, keno, chuck-a-luck and roulette may be found in every second saloon." (Gold Hill *News*, 1876.)

The Western gamblers set the style for the professional card experts. They copied the river-boat mode, sporting high beaver hats, silk-embroidered waistcoats, and "enough gold watch chain to anchor a small boat." They wore pick-pointed boots and hammer-tail coats. Smoking a cheroot or stogie, the gambler entered genre history in the tales of Bret Harte.

In actual life many gamblers were more like Jefferson Randolph Smith, usually referred to as "Soapy" Smith because he once sold soap as a pitchman from a folding stand on street corners. He was born in a small town in Georgia in 1860. As soon as Jeff Smith was old enough, he lit out for the Long Horn State, where he drove cattle.

Jeff Smith found the cattle drives dusty, mean and dangerous, but found the Kansas end of the trails fascinating and animated. For a Georgia cracker, it presented a way of life to delight a youth who was always keen for the main chance and not too much toil. Certainly the towns that catered to the miner, the ranch hand and the railroader were prepared to entertain and exploit. Newspaper clippings of the day report that "Leadville could brag of 35 brothels, 120 saloons, 118 gambling houses. . . ."

Young Jeff Smith, wide-eyed and observant, mixed with the diamond-studded gamblers and the silk-rustling whores. He observed the town marshal and the sheriff with their tin stars and their belted bullet-studded weapons. The Colt .45, "The Peace Maker," was the most popular. He was impressed by the tents, shacks, dance halls, and saloons that featured cards, dice and the wheel. He already had the concupiscent eye, but no experience.

He began his career by losing several months of hard-earned pay to an artist working the shell game. "Now under which of these three walnut shells is the little pea?" Jeff Smith guessed wrong, for the manipulator of the shell game usually had the pea palmed in his hand. But Jeff, instead of reaching for a gun, joined the gang of swindlers, working with them. He worked with a traveling circus and proved to be a marvelously adept pupil. He could work the shell and pea setup with the skill of a magician; his fame as a practitioner of three-card monte spread. In that game a mark, or sucker, tries to guess which of the three cards the dealer slips onto a flat surface is the queen or ace. The dealer looks clumsy. It's easy to get the mark to put up big money after letting him pick the winning card a few times. The dealer's skill consists of flipping a card off the bottom, but the action is so fast that it looks like the top one.

Reaching Leadville, Jeff Smith became a shill for the soap-game swindle. The spieler offered wrapped bars of soap for sale at a high price, claiming that there were five-, ten-, twenty-, and even hundred-dollar bills under the wrappers of many packets.

Jeff's job as a shill was to push forward and offer to buy a bar. He would unwrap it and, with surprise and glee, wave a twenty-dollar bill before the crowd of onlookers.

The bunco artist would chant:

> Take your pick among the lot,
> Why not invest a fiver for a hundred spot?
> The bacon's frying, come on the lope,
> Come pick your bar of lucky soap.

After the crowd had bought up all the available soap bars, Jeff and the bunco artist would get away in a hurry.

Jeff, already known as "Soapy," became a leading manipulator of anything from loaded dice to street come-ons and three-card monte.

Soapy worked the streets until the early 1890s. There are stories that he killed a few men when someone doubted the honesty of a game or a sale and the victim started for his gun holster.

Soapy opened a saloon with the customary "genuine" oil painting of a nude over the bar. There exists a photograph that has been tentatively identified as one of Soapy dealing cards in a poker game. He is pictured in a top hat and frock coat, smoking a cigar, his poker face intent on the game.

When a rich strike of silver was discovered in Mineral City by a miner, N. L. Creede, the prospectors, miners and others looked for ways to enjoy and spend their money. Soapy was there with his gang to open the Orleans Club. There was even a song about the town's founder.

> Miners, merchants, pimps and tarts,
> Sure-thing men and bunco sharks,
> Men of money, men of greed—
> Every one fetched up at Creede.

Soapy showed the players no mercy. He hooked them with every kind of game, and they seemed to enjoy the excitement of being fleeced by an expert. He was the boss gambler, the king of games of the roaring boom town.

Boom towns, however, faded as mines petered out. Soapy moved on to places where new strikes would feed his gambling urge.

In 1898 there was talk of gold in the Klondike, up in the frozen North—Uncle Sam's icebox, as some called Alaska. There was a rush of clerks, earnest dreamers, cowboys, outlaws, and ordinary citizens hoping for a change of luck. Whores and madams followed them to the gold fields. The miners were called sourdoughs because they learned to carry a bottle of fermenting yeast mixture next to their skin with which to make their biscuits and pancakes just a little lighter than lead.

Soapy began his adventures in Alaska in Skagway, a jumping-off place to visions of gold nuggets at the grass roots, and lump gold big as hens' eggs. Some found wealth, some nothing but frostbite. Many died during the cruel winters. Some went mad; a few ended their own lives. Those who came back with gold, heading for home, passed through Skagway, where Soapy's establishment, called "Jeff's Place," awaited them with whisky, women, and gambling in all its forms. The plan was simple: get the pokes (deerhide bags that held gold dust) from the victims in any way possible. Doctored whisky, whores, cards, dice, and the roulette wheel were all employed. All the while, the "professor" at the piano pounded the keys.

For the few miners who escaped from the clutches of the gamblers, Soapy Smith had a big sign painted and set up over a shack: TELEGRAPH OFFICE.

Miners eager to let people in the outside world know they had made it were charged a good fee to send out messages. No one seemed to notice that there were no telegraph wires going out from the shack. "It's the gesture," Soapy is said to have remarked. "They feel damn good, don't they?"

If some stubborn individual who had gotten gold from the barren waste and the wilderness creek by panning or cradling still didn't let himself be clipped, Soapy's gang would invade his cabin and take his money belt at gunpoint.

There is a time, historians and psychologists have pointed out, when great gamblers rebel against reason. These types lose all sense of proportion. Their ego drive and contempt for the rest of mankind reach a point from which there is no return.

In July of 1898, Soapy Smith reached that point. He felt that he was the power of Skagway, Alaska. The citizens of social and financial position in the town (bankers, lawyers and merchants) and others who had made a good thing of the gold rush decided that Soapy and his gang were fouling the atmosphere with their crude game. They formed a Committee of 101. Soapy was told: "Get out of town, or else." In reply, Soapy set up a Committee of 303. He boldly retorted that the odds were in his favor three to one, and he'd bet on it.

The Fourth of July was fun time in Skagway, as it was all over the United States and its territories. Cannon fire, Chinese fireworks, outdoor cooking, drinking, dancing, and all-night gambling for those so inclined livened up the city.

The big parade got off at noon, with Soapy Smith, in topper and in proper dress, astride a white horse heading the procession in celebration of Independence Day. He had his followers in the crowd, and also those citizens who liked any form of excitement, cheering him on. Soapy felt his power and invited everybody to Jeff's Place. He mocked the Committee of 101.

It was open warfare, and the town knew it. Sniping and direct face-offs took place as fighting began. War started in earnest three days later. Soapy's perfidy caught up with him at last, at the age of thirty-eight. He was killed by City Engineer Frank Reed when he tried to break up a public meeting.

Soapy Smith entered American legend as one of its outlaw heroes, the romantic gambler who staked all on the dealing of a card, the turn of a wheel. Actually he was a ferocious bully without moral values of any sort, and his main aim in life, inflated by a monstrous ego, was to trim the victim in any way possible. For those who care to visit the Pullen Museum in Skagway, some of the tools of Soapy's trade—cards, roulette wheels and chips—are on view. There also is a tour to visit his grave.

Two men gave the Alaska gold rush a romantic glow it had never had, its gamblers' foibles a polish.

Though Jack London and Rex Beach got little gold in the Klondike, they did get material that made them best-selling authors of tales of the frozen North under the midnight sun. Robert Service, a maker of popular verse, added Dangerous Dan McGrew and the Lady Known as Lou.

A figure just as interesting as Soapy Smith who escaped these writers was Tex Rickard, who, unlike Soapy, was known as "an honest gambler." Some have challenged his "Mr. Clean" label, but evidence seems to suggest that he was trusted, and when the city of Nome grew large enough to feel that it was a true city, Tex was elected its mayor. He later reached fame as a boxing promoter, achieving the first "million-dollar gate" when Jack Dempsey, "The Manassa Mauler," fought the South American "Bull of the Pampas." Both names were invented by Rickard and helped gamblers get betting business.

In Dawson, Tex owned the "Monte Carlo" gambling palace and saloon. Like so many gamblers, Rickard—even if as shrewd as a weasel—liked to test the games. He was once involved in a faro game that ran for twelve hours. It was no-limit faro, and he ended up with no more money to put up. Facing four lucky winners, he offered his place, the Monte Carlo, for just one more play against their $50,000. The offer was taken. After a little play he took a card from the faro box and flipped it down. He had lost.

"The place is yours," he said.

He then left town. It was the opinion of many, however, that the real reason he left town after his loss was a redheaded woman named Blanche LaMarre. Blanche was a remarkable gambler who ran games in Dawson and Circle City and wherever she could set up. She had a reputation for using her beauty to the best advantage with those rich enough for gambling. She was a cheerful sort, by all reports, who knew cards, miners, and the ways of the world. She won and lost thousands of dollars.

She had avoided a strong attachment to any man until she met Tex Rickard and tried to get him to enter into matrimony. She made her play, but Tex was polite and frankly not interested. His affection was for a dance-hall girl.

Blanche LaMarre and Tex Rickard remained friends and fellow gamblers, but when he lost his gambling place and saw that the offer of aid by the redheaded female included marriage, he left town.

A Man Named George

Gamblers were hardly reliable writers of their own memoirs, yet George Devol, a three-card monte man, put together a fascinating book in 1887, *Forty Years as Gambler on the Missis-*

sippi, in which he confessed with pride that as a cabin boy he "could steal at cards and cheat [at age eleven], and stack a deck at fourteen." As for his skill with his fists, he claimed to have fought "more rough-and-tumble fights than any man in America, and was the most daring gambler in the world."

George Devol was fifteen when he became a gambler with his pilot cousin on a Rio Grande boat. By sixteen, he had $3,000 tucked away. He made an unconditional surrender to destiny and spent a lifetime gambling.

Devol and three other gamblers once formed a syndicate that took nearly a million dollars off the Mississippi and Ohio boats, based on the victims' hopes that invented dreams are more real than any reality.

In fifty years Devol became a legend. The truth was that he was remarkable for ringing in new-stacked cold decks while dealing. His skill was great. He could ring in four or five new decks of cards in any game without the other players' knowledge. Once, as a joke, he dealt every man at the table four aces, then sat back, lit his cigar, and watched the fun as each holder of the best hand began to toss everything he had in gold, currency and jewels on the table as his stake in the growing pot. When the farce ended, the uproar almost led to bloodshed.

In his fecund and resourceful lifetime, Devol claimed to have won two million dollars, and lost it all playing against the big-city faro games. If his luck at faro was bad, his skill as a rough-and-tumble battler and gun carrier carried him through—he managed to survive to old age. Many gambling dens and barrooms, native bordellos, and street corners tested his ability as a battler. While he carried a pistol which he named Betty Jane, he claimed never to have used it. The only time he needed the backing of lead and powder was when he was in Chicago in an encounter with a faro dealer named Lawler. ("I left Betty Jane in my room.")

Lawler was a kind of madman who, when his faro-dealing went wrong, would butt his head against the wall and try to tear off his ears with an obstinacy hard to believe. Devol and Lawler seem to have been interested in the same girl. One day she told the gambler that Lawler had grievously insulted her. Devol caught up with Lawler on muddy Clark Street and battered him down into the gutter. Lawler left, cursing, changed his clothes, armed himself with a big pistol, and went gunning for Devol. He found him at Clark and Madison; the gambler's weapon, Betty Jane, was in his lodgings. Lawler fired. Devol took a slug in his best card-dealing hand and ducked behind a light pole. Lawler fired three more times, but his chance for a kill was gone. He was arrested and sent to prison for assault with a deadly weapon, but in a new trial he won an acquittal, perhaps on the theory that a man who misses three times is no menace. It is said that his hair turned snow-white in prison, but there is no record that he used his head to butt at the jail's stone walls.

The wound to Devol's hand was not serious, and he was soon cold-decking and laying the bottom stack in card games as well as ever. He never hit a man with his hands if he could help it. Devol weighed over 200 pounds in his prime. In most fights he would simply lower his head and butt a troublemaker senseless with his skull. According to folklore, it was the thickest skull around. Devol agreed late in life that it had to be thick, "or it would have been cracked many years ago, for I have been struck some terrible blows on my head. . . . I have had to do some hard butting in my early days on account of the reputation I had made for my head. I am now nearly sixty years of age and have quit fighting, but I can batter down any ordinary door or stave in a liquor barrel with that old head of mine."

In 1867 the Robinson Brothers Circus played New Orleans, featuring "Billy Carroll, the Man with the Thick Skull!" Carroll, against all rules of materia medica, broke barrels into splinters and went through solid doors head first. He also beat every local head-butter who challenged him in the sawdust arena of the circus.

Friends of Devol pooh-poohed Carroll as Champion Butt Master, compared to the gambler's skill with *his* skull. The Robinson brothers and a sporting man of New Orleans, one Dutch Jake, set up a friendly butting contest between their champions. The contest didn't last long. Devol flexed his neck muscles, lowered his head, and rushed forward; and when the ivory gourds met, the ringing was like a clash of two stone walls. Carroll was down and out. Slowly he recovered consciousness, holding his aching head. When he got to his feet, he walked over to Devol and placed a hand on the winning head.

"Gents," he said, deeply impressed, "I have found my pappy at last."

Devol was comically involved in military glory when the Civil

War came. Gamblers traveled to New Orleans and organized a military regiment that was known as "Wilson's Rangers." Soon everybody was calling the singularly defiant company the "Blackleg Cavalry" because of its rogues, scalawags and confidence men. The press played up the hard-drinking, fast-talking gambler-soldiers and said of them: "We judge them to be a valuable support to our army of Gulf Coast Defense."

George Devol, who was a member of the outfit, wasn't that impressed. "We armed and equipped ourselves, and the ladies said we were the finest-looking set of men in the army. We would mount our fine horses, gallop out back of the city . . . and the first orders we would receive from our commanding officer would be 'Dismount! Hitch horses! March! Hunt shade! Begin playing!' In less than ten minutes there would not be a man in the sun. They were all in the shade, seated on the ground in little groups of four, five and six; and in each group could be seen a little book of tactics (or at least it looked like a book at a distance). We would remain in the shade until the cool of the evening, when orders would be given: 'Cease playing! Put up books! Prepare to mount! Mount! March!' When we would get back to the city, the people would come out, cheer, wave handkerchiefs and present us with bouquets; for we had been out drilling in the hot sun, preparing to protect their homes from the Northern invaders. . . . The citizens called us their defenders; and we did defend them, so long as there was no hostile foe. . . ."

The trouble with wars is that one can get mangled or killed. Devol had a pathological aversion to dying in battle. If it was rambunctious fun, fine; dangerous, no.

When Admiral Farragut came steaming boldly against the Delta with his warships and ironclads in April of 1862, the Blackleg Cavalry was ordered to join rebel forces downstream to protect the forts. The gamblers left the city, loaded with flowers from their lady friends, feeling a bit boozy. They had traveled six miles from the city when Union warships began to shell them. The gambler-soldiers then agreed to retreat to the city. There they dismounted, got out of their splendidly tailored uniforms, buried their weapons, and took up their cards, happy to be civilians again. As Devol put it: "We had had enough of military glory, and were tired of war. . . ."

Fifteen thousand bales of cotton were burning when the

Admiral's ships passed the forts and took the city. Riots broke out as looters began to load up on sugar, molasses and barrels of smoked and pickled meats. There was a lot of smoke and some burning of supplies, but a great deal was carried off. Many people expected the Union forces to sack and terrorize the city; so, as Devol wrote, the shopkeepers decided to make it bargain day. "They threw open their stores and told everybody to take all they wanted. . . . I hired a dray (for which I had to pay $10) and loaded it with hogsheads of sugar, twenty-five hams, a sack of coffee, a box of tea, a firkin of butter, a barrel of potatoes, some hominy, beans, canned fruit, etc. I would have put on more, but the dray wouldn't hold it. . . After laying in my stock, I went down to the river to see the fleet come in, and there were all of our company, but they did not make the slightest resistance. The captain said, 'It's no use trying to bluff them fellows, for they have got a full hand! . . .' "

The Yankees also had money for gambling, and soon the former Blackleg horse soldiers were dealing poker hands to the men in blue. Major General Benjamin Butler, one of the most dishonest men that ever held rank or public office—in an era of grand stealing—took over as military commander of New Orleans. He was an American despot and ruled for seven months before being recalled by the War Department. He earned the name "Beast" Butler; rapacious and unscrupulous, he managed to get rich by cutting himself in on the gambling fraternity, among other rackets.

Butler's method of muscling in on the gamblers was through a military order closing *all* gambling houses, then appointing his brother to issue valid permits, for a fee, to open the town wide to gambling. The Butler brothers amassed huge sums from license fees for gambling permits. They used no sophisticated techniques. Just stand in line, boys, and hand over the cash.

Butler also managed to confiscate all the race horses at Oakland race track. They were worth $50,000. The General's brother then shipped them to the Confederate forces.

The gamblers took great pleasure in fleecing the Union officers and crooked paymasters, along with anyone from the Northern armies or navy who sat down to play cards, watch the wheel spin, or rattle the dice.

George Devol was running the Oakland race track, and some

amazing races were run. Devol was arrested for skinning some
Union officers at three-card monte, fined $1,000, and given a
year in jail. He had served only six months when he was released by General Shepley. The gambler gave a big celebration
when he got out of jail and, to salve himself for his vicissitudes
there, won nearly $20,000 at poker and the three-card throw
from a Union paymaster. By 1864 the gamblers were taking
away so much money from the soldiers, paymasters, and
dishonest officers that General Hulburt closed all the gambling
houses. While it lasted, it had been a great war for the gamblers.

Devol's one-time valet had been a Negro shoeshine boy,
found by him before the war in a top-deck barbershop. His
name was Pinckney Benton Stewart Pinchback, which had been
shortened to "Pinch." He had come from Marietta, Ohio, to
attach himself to the steamboat *Wacousta*. He possessed an
innate shrewdness, a graceful stride, and a scrutinizing wisdom.
Pinch was a bright pupil, and Devol opened up the secrets of
gambling to him. Soon, while Devol and his syndicate were
trimming the quality in the fine salons on the upper deck, Pinch
was below with the Negro roustabouts, waiters and musicians,
taking away their cash by means of a little chuck-a-luck. Pinch
had a more important and impressive career than his master.
After the war he went to New Orleans, looking for oppor-
tunities. Negroes were encouraged to take over the newly won
South. Pinch took charge of the Fourth Ward Republican Club
and began to synthesize black power into an organic unity. He
was on the State Central Committee and was a power among
the Negroes and carpetbaggers who ran the state. Pinch
climbed higher, becoming a state senator in 1868 and
lieutenant-governor in 1871. When the governor died, Pinch
was acting governor for a month. In 1873 the one-time
shoeshine boy and chuck-a-luck gambler was elected to the
United States Senate. But he never served in that exclusive club.
After three years of wrangle and loud talk, the Senate refused
to seat him. Greater rascals and rogues with less brain power
voted him down.
While Pinch was governor of Louisiana, he had come to the
aid of his old patron Devol, who had gambled one of the high
police officials out of nearly $1,000 at monte. The chief of

police, with no sublimated nostalgia for past times, announced that he was running Devol out of town.

Devol hadn't seen Pinch for over fifteen years, but now it was time to renew their friendship. Rushing to the governor's mansion in the middle of the night, Devol got Pinch out of bed and poured out his troubles over a late supper.

One of them, in a gesture of affection, suggested a game, and they were playing seven-up when dawn came to the Delta— playing and talking about old times on the river when they had fleeced the suckers, white and black.

In parting, Pinch walked his mentor to the door and gave him comfort: "Now, George, you get to bed and don't you have any uneasiness. I'll take care of the chief of police."

And he did.

6

DEADLIER THAN THE MALE

There were many women who dealt cards, spun wheels and had a keen knowledge of poker, as good as any diamond-studded dude gambler with his shoestring tie. Calamity Jane, an independent sort not given to tulle ruffles and feather boas, was built like a man and often dressed like one. (There is no truth in the story that she was Wild Bill Hickok's girl.) Calamity played a skilled hand of poker and cursed like a mule skinner while doing it. Belle Starr, "the bandit queen," had a hankering for cards. And Blanche LaMarre trimmed the suckers in Alaska during the Klondike Gold Rush. Mattie Silk, a famous Denver madam, played with the best poker players in the West. Nell Kimball, in her memoirs, *The Life and Times of an American Madam*, tells that when she ran sporting houses in New Orleans and San Francisco, she played in epic card games in her houses for huge sums.

The glamour of women on the frontier was enhanced by there being so few of them, respectable or otherwise. In one mountain mining camp in 1860 there were 4,000 men to 12 women, and a few of those were Indian squaws who could be bought from their mates for whisky. Some of the early females who made the trek west were prostitutes. In film and fiction, they later became the "dance-hall girls." Few had the "heart of gold" given them by novelists. A woman was a novelty among the land sharks, shady lawyers, cold-eyed bankers, cattle barons and lucky miners at the gambling tables. From the start the gambling-house owners saw the advantage of a skilled woman dealing black jack, operating the faro box and the roulette wheel.

Often the ladies combined their gambling-table jobs with prostitution. Doc Holliday, another myth-made hero, had a mistress, Big Nose Kate Fisher. She was never self-indulgent, nor was she irresponsible at gambling. She didn't fear a high bidder, or men who were careless with their pistols.

Nell Kimball and one of her girls, Frenchy, from Nell's New Orleans house, used to take their vacations in Denver to play poker and enjoy the slow season in the Delta sporting houses.

Kitty the Schemer worked the mining camps and the timber towns and followed the line of the marching railroad iron.

Colorado Charlie Utter ran a posh gambling house in El Paso. His mistress, Minnie, was only four feet tall and was called "the best house dealer in the West." When things got too hot for them in Texas, they moved on through Central America, with Minnie still dealing. When Charlie died, Minnie came up to Los Angeles. I spoke to some old folk who still remember her. "Minnie was no taller than a Winchester repeater, but neat and ladylike. A churchgoer at times. Sure, she liked a good belt of rye, but she was always the little lady. I remember when she died. People were surprised when somebody said she had been a hell raiser in El Paso once."

In 1834 the town of Sante Fe had a new item of gossip: Dona Gertrude de Barcelo, the daughter of dirt-poor Mexican field workers. She had fled the fleas, the lean dogs, and the corn *tamal de cazuela*, and *frijoles negros* of her folks' shack. She began, at sixteen, as a whore in Taos. Besides a desirable body, Gertrude had brains. In Santa Fe she became well known at the monte tables as a daring gambler. Having acquired the skill and the nerve of a great card player, she gave up selling herself and turned into a professional gambler. Then she began to buy up or establish gambling houses, always seeking a better clientele. San Francisco Street was the main drag in Santa Fe. It was here that she owned six of the best places, where men could gamble expensively under crystal chandeliers while music filled the place. Now Gertrude lured men with good food and drink. Thick carpets underfoot made her places cheerful and comfortable. The invitation to gamble was subtle, insinuating. By 1843 Gertrude was rich enough and famous enough to be one of the sights for travelers, and was the focus of all gamblers wanting to try their luck. She wore the grand costumes of her time and sported rings on nearly all of her fingers. Of several gold chains around her neck, the longest had a solid-gold crucifix. She was know as "La Tules." She showed her loyalty to the *americanos* in 1846 when the Mexican War began, warning them of a Mexican plot to seize New Mexico on Christmas Eve. The revolt did not take place.

When Colonel David P. Mitchell lacked money to pay his soldiers' needs and to move his troops on to Chihuahua, he went to La Tules for help. She agreed to let him have the money if he would get her invited to a very fancy ball that the Sante Fe snobs were giving: the respectable señoras and señoritas of the great Spanish names wanted no part of her.

The Colonel promised that she would dance the social fandango. At a monte game with some of the richest players in town, she won the funds the Colonel needed. She attended the dance, and the Colonel whirled her around the floor in her most daring gown. Everything ended well. The United States seized some of the Southwest from Mexico with the help of a little gambling money. Colonel Mitchell fought valiantly at the Battle of Rio Sacramento. The American government repaid the money advanced by Gertrude de Barcelo, with an added "thank you" from the United States. She said, "God doesn't want church candles. He wants good deeds."

In the 1870s, when silver was discovered in the Panamint Mountains, every gambler, shady lady, confidence man, whisky-seller, and land lawyer who could manage it headed for the strike. It would mean high-stake gambling, money spent in sporting houses, and lots of whisky moving across the bars. The lawyers would have a field day creating misleading documents and papers on mine claims, which they would file and then defend (or attack) in courtrooms.

Among those who left Carson City for the silver lining was a woman well past her prime, a professional gambler of many years' standing among the sharpies. Eleanor Dumont was better known as "Madam Mustache," for she did boast a dark down on her upper lip, which, however, did little to destroy her appeal, poise and complacency. She has been called "perhaps the greatest of all professional women gamblers." Black-haired, a bit plump even in her youth, and dark-skinned, she was said to speak half a dozen languages and was trained to sing and play the most difficult music. She could roll cigarettes with amazing dexterity. In Nevada City she opened a gambling house featuring twenty-one, or blackjack, with herself as the dealer. She forbade swearing: she insisted that men wear jackets, and no one wore a hat at her table, where food and champagne were served. Eleanor Dumont had such skill at dealing that reputed card players of ability made trips to town just to watch her deal blackjack.

The crowds grew so great that she needed more help to run the games, which included faro, poker, chuck-a-luck and keno. She chose David Tobin. While he didn't have her skill or brains as a card technician, he was over six feet tall, "handsome as a twenty-dollar goldpiece, with more curls in his black hair than on a monkey, and one of those wide mustaches that outgrew Madam's own" (J. Davis's journal). Tobin dressed as a dandy in well-cut black broadcloth. Madam was vulnerable, and she lost to this heartbreaker that part of her love not dedicated to cards.

It was said that she did not become his mistress and that they finally broke up when he demanded her body and a half interest in her establishment. Whatever inconsistency was between them, Madam was French enough to see that Tobin was dangerous and a bother, and a lady-killer who thought himself irresistible. She paid him off and he vanished east.

She continued to work the gold fields, never endangering her virtue. Perhaps this was part of her appeal: a mustached virgin who was unobtainable. "Beware," she warned, "of anything that begins in the heart." As she grew older and times grew harder, she had a run of bad luck at cards. Then she began to take lovers, and her reputation and her life were no longer what they had been. People lost interest in her. A legend had run its course.

She took to whoring. She may have been aware that when lucky gamblers turn into unlucky ones, self-esteem is lost. She aged, she drank more, she turned foul-mouthed; and the men who were attracted to her were no longer well-dressed gentlemen with diamond stickpins, as in the early days. When she settled down to accept life as it was, her house was a saloon and gambling place and a brothel. She had various lovers, but never any long-lasting attachments. There were reports that she still had skill at cards and that she enjoyed riding in a fine carriage, smoking a cigar while surrounded by some of her best-dressed girls. But she had changed with the times. The wildcatting boom towns were in full swing.

Louis Rosche, an old-time steamboat man, remembered her in a dive she ran in Fort Benton, Montana. "She was fat. . . . Rouge and powder hid the sagging lines of her face, the pouches under her eyes, the marks of dissipation. . . ."

The time came when she could no longer face the jarring misery of reality. The Sacramento *Union* of September 9, 1879, carried an item from the mining community of Bodie:

> A woman named Eleanor Dumont was found dead today, a suicide, about a mile out of town. She was well known throughout the mining camps.

There are those who claim that Alice Ivers, known as "Poker Alice," was a more skilled card player than Madam Mustache, and that she had the best poker sense of anyone, man or woman, in the West. She was born in 1850 in Sudbury, England. The family came to America, and Alice was educated in a fine Southern school that specialized in making ladies of breeding aware of their uniqueness and charm. The Iverses may have been remittance folk, paid by some member of the family to stay out of England. The facts are murky. But when gold seemed easy to come by in Colorado, the Iverses were there with their well-raised daughter in a world as bawdy as a Breughel painting. Alice fell in love with and married an engineer named Frank Duffield. After a few years of what seemed a happy marriage, Duffield was killed in an accident. What happened then is a mystery. The respectable, well-brought-up dainty lady turned to professional gambling and became notorious in the late 1870s for her skill at poker and faro. She became a card manipulator, a cigar-smoking queen of the toughest poker tables.

Her accent was upper-class English. She did retain some Victorian sensibilities: she never played cards on Sunday. Instead, she took to the family Bible and spent the day in pious contemplation of life and its spiritual aspect.

Skilled and lucky, she often broke the bank at rival houses. Appreciating nice clothes, she visited New York to see the latest fashions. She enjoyed the city's lobster palaces, went to the theater, and returned home with trunks full of splendid costumes.

Alice was in demand by many well-known gambling houses, for she dealt cards with skill and grace. (She could drink as well as any man, but always played cards stone sober.) At Ford's Exchange she worked for "the dirty little coward who shot Mr. Howard" (Jesse James). She was present when Bob Ford got his comeuppance in his ornate establishment, gunned down by a Jesse James fan who wanted to even the score.

Poker Alice married three times; each marriage was a failure. She ended up in Deadwood, still dealing expertly but supporting a worthless mate. Her third husband was a lush and a barroom loafer who soon drank himself to death. When a reform group—the term was "the bluenoses"—tried to clean up Deadwood, Poker Alice moved on and opened a gambling and sporting house near Fort Meade, where enlisted men and officers could come to enjoy cards and girls.

She continued to drink, and was probably a bit drunk when she shot and killed a soldier in her establishment. She read her Bible in jail. Her defense was confusing: she claimed that it was an accident *and* that she had acted in self-defense. Charged with murder, she was freed by the jury.

Alice did not change her ways. She survived well into old age. Nearing eighty in the 1920s, she took naturally to the era of bootleg whisky, hijackers, and rum-running. Arrested for maintaining a brothel and gambling joint and for selling whisky, she was found guilty. But some of the old men with memories, those who had known her in her rosiest days, appealed to the governor, and her sentence was commuted. Thereafter Alice Ivers faded from the scene. Today there are still arguments among those who comment on gambling history: Was Poker Alice the greatest woman gambler in the West, or Madam Mustache? There will never be a settled answer.

A true Frankie and Johnny story was that of the Chicago gambler George Trussell and "Irish Mollie" (Mollie Cosgriff). George had been a bank clerk, good with figures. Soon he was a gambling man who by 1862 owned two big houses. He was not yet thirty. Mollie had begun a career of improving herself, first as a chambermaid at the American House. But she liked the high life of Hair Trigger Block where the professional gamblers and their women gathered. She became a girl in demand by many men in the sporting set. George Trussell was the type she admired most, and she became his mistress. That they "made a handsome couple," the gambling crowd agreed. They both had tempers, and George, when drunk, would often run down the street firing a pistol. He was a high-strung fellow. He was also a faithless lover, and Mollie heard of it.

On the night the Driving Park track for harness racing opened, Mollie and George were to attend. But George stopped off in a saloon, and when Mollie found him he slapped her face and tried to throw her out. She pulled out a pistol and fired. George fled down an alley; she followed and got in a second shot just as he reached Prince's livery stable. The bullet proved fatal. "George, my own dear George," she cried, weeping over the body. The jury agreed on manslaughter and a year at Joliet, but the governor, who was a gambling man, pardoned Irish Mollie.

Cap Hyman, once George Trussell's rival as king of gamblers, was afflicted with woman trouble, like most of his kind. His mistress was "Gentle Annie" Stafford, a holy terror, a wildcat of a female. Cap had treated her to the ownership of a whorehouse, and a fine place it was. Many patrons remembered it at 155 North Wells Street. Gentle Annie was neither gentle nor slim. She was pointed out to visitors to the streets of sin as the fattest cathouse madam in town.

Gentle Annie learned a lesson from poor Mollie's fatal shooting of a lover. Mollie had called herself Mrs. Trussell, though no marriage lines were in evidence; Gentle Annie decided she had to have those damn lines. Cap, a confirmed bachelor, kept repeating he wasn't the marrying kind.

One September day in 1866, Gentle Annie came roaring into Cap's gambling house on Randolph Street, carrying a mule skinner's rawhide whip. Banging her way up the stairs into his office where Cap was trying to catch some sleep on a satin sofa, Annie brought him back to life with a few swipes of the whip. As he yelled in pain, she drove him down the stairs and into the street, expertly whipping him as if he were a top. A mule whip is a deadly weapon. It took a few more solid hints and punishment, and in a few weeks Cap Hyman saw the advantages of a good, healthy wife. The wedding was magnificent. The best of the underworld—madams and gamblers, ponces, confidence men, and safecrackers—were present. Some came from as far away as New Orleans.

At the wedding, sumptuous and wild, Cap announced that he and his bride were going to run a tavern and high-toned gambling house, a place of opulent hedonism, in Sunnyside.

The opening of the roadhouse was like a Fourth of July celebration, though it was a crisp, snowy night. The best people of both worlds attended. Police captain Jack Nelson and other city and county officials were present. The press sent its best social reporters. Acting as hostesses were Gentle Annie's own girls. One redhead claimed a fine family background and a knowledge of literature.

Cap knew how to run a press conference, long before today's publicity firms gave them polish. He called the boys into his office and set out the booze.

"I'd like you gentlemen of the press to understand that this affair will be straight to the wink of an eyelash. All the ladies are here on their honor, and Mrs. Hyman will see to it that nothing unseemly takes place."

Frederick Francis Cook, who was there as a reporter for the *Times,* noted: "All the rest of the little formalities that distinguish like functions in the *haut monde* were strictly observed. Yes, the make-believe was quite tremendous."

After the reporters had been sent back to Chicago, the guests were free to express their own peculiar ideas of fun. The party ended in a free-for-all fight at dawn, after cases of champagne had been downed. Cap Hyman shot out the lights, Gentle Annie chastised the madams for distributing business cards, and half a dozen girls went upstairs for trade.

The extravagant hopes of the ebullient newlyweds were doomed to failure. The Sunnyside roadhouse, for all its possibilities, lasted less than six months, and Cap and Annie came back to the city, to the gamblers' deck of cards and the strumpets' rallying call: "Girls, gentlemen callers!"

A year later Cap Hyman, probably suffering from the Old Rake, or Big Casino (syphilis), went into a mental breakdown and died insane on the West Side. Gentle Annie Hyman was loyal to the last, holding his hand in his final hours.

Happier sporting citizens and clowns were two gamblers on Hair Trigger Block named Al and George Hankins, who ran a house with extreme simplicity. They were, however, ridden with superstition, omens, and magic gestures. Opening their shop for play, they burned an old shoe every day for good luck and put a pinch of salt and pepper on every player's seat to bring him bad fortune. If anyone really started having a run of luck at the brothers' tables, Al and George would come up with a shaker in each hand and begin to sprinkle salt and pepper onto his head and shoulders. As their house averaged winnings of about $1,500 a day, there might have been something in their hoodoo-making antics. If some winner objected to the pouring of salt and pepper onto his person, the bouncers stood ready to give him the heave-ho into the street.

Chicago was teeming with gamblers, speculators, seekers of pleasure, women in stylish dress squired by men in splendid tailoring, or rough types, hard-cheeked with an enormous quid of chawin' tobacco . . . a city with people dancing the polka, resting from the music as they swallowed *Charlotte Russe de la Reine* and *Pyramids d'Espagnol*, patties of quail and prairie chicken, or even a boar's head.

While a later era was to find that crime paid best when based on the illegal brewing of alcohol, drug-peddling and organized looting, Chicago, in the two decades after the Civil War, found that gambling and prostitution brought the biggest returns, perhaps because so many respectable people owned the properties where it thrived and because both police and city officials were eager to claim a share. So the professional gambler and the madams were the city's most serious problems. Decency experienced a great dislocation as the city prospered and expanded.

Madam Vestal
While the Eastern sportsman and pleasure-seeker usually tried to maintain a kind of decorum about his activities, the Westerners who had made their pile in the mines or with smelters, cattle and railroads, and later in oil and real estate, had fun doing damage to property and to one another in their belliger-

ent joy. A woman who had been washing miners' drawers and serving beans on a tin plate could, by a fortuitous play of chance, find herself possessed of diamonds, carriages and a marble bathtub. A fellow who had led a precarious life, then been lucky and scratched up some metal—gold, silver or copper—with the right backing and connections would soon be able to build himself an opera house or a nabob's mansion, eat food cooked by a French chef, and indulge his fantasies on a bizarre level with an unabashed Rabelaisian audacity.

If Saratoga Springs, Atlantic City and Newport were the proper Eastern spots to spend one's money and erect mansions, Denver in 1876 came forward as the Babylon of the West. The Pike's Peak gold rush had made millionaires of the fortunate few, and the diggings at Central City were boasted of as "the richest square mile on earth."

The Kansas Pacific Railroad had come through just before, and land values rose to monumental heights in Denver. This brought the big-time gambler, the most richly endowed sporting-house madam, the land boomer, the too-eager lawyer, the merchant with an eye for excessive profits, the hotel builder—all who knew just what sort of luxury the denizens afloat in a sea of new wealth wanted.

Holladay Street in Denver was called "the wickedest street in the West," the women "exotic odalisques," the most beautiful and greedy. Gamblers like Ed Chase were willing to take off all limits at games of chance. Certainly Denver gave possibilities to the sporting life.

The most interesting of the gamblers was a woman who called herself Madam Vestal. She had a huge tent set up on Blake Street—building materials were still rare—where she proved to all who could afford to play that she was indeed "the most skillful blackjack dealer in the nation." Her accent was Southern—half honey, half mellow peach brandy—and when she drawled "Cards, gentlemen?" she drew to reckless play men with a poke of gold or a big check, all asking her to hit them again. Watching her flip the cards, it was said by oldtimers, was "better than Lillian Russell with all her clothes off."

She was a professional with depths of experience. She had her own staff of shills to lure money to her roulette wheel, faro table, stud poker game or keno. Madam Vestal got more than her share of the high play and big spenders in Denver's boom times. For the players there was a bar, and while the whisky had no ancestry, it did have a kick and a tendency to befuddle. It was a man's world, and Madam Vestal kept it that way. The so-called dance-hall girls, with their black silk stockings, short skirts, and gewgaws, each hanging on the arm of a spender, were absent from Madam's tent. Madam wanted *all* attention focused on herself and on the games of chance. Let the madams of carnal games in their sporting houses—Katie Fulton, Minnie Clifford, Lizzie Preston—take care of the male who wanted his pleasures horizontal.

Some claimed that there was something familiar about Madam Vestal. The calculated, spacious pattern of her style seemed somehow a part of past history. They were right. She had had several careers and some notorious living before coming to Denver. She had once been well known as Belle Siddons, the Confederate spy, working out of St. Louis during the Civil War. There she was sparked, courted and entertained by the young officers on the staffs of generals like Halleck, Newton, Curtis and others. She had been graduated from the Female University of Lexington, having come from solid old family stock in Jefferson City, Missouri, where she was piously taught that beauty is a silent deceit, a short-lived spring. She believed none of it.

During the Civil War, with Missouri divided, Belle continued to entertain Union officers and was escorted by them to the De Bar Opera House in St. Louis. General Halleck issued warnings against public rebel rousers and Confederate bullies who carried pistols. Belle, more discreet, worked in more comfortable private places and got many military secrets from sexually bemused officers excited by her brown eyes and concupiscent smile. If she offered and gave her body for a cause, many felt that this was the complete commitment to glory, if not to honor. For Belle the fundamental indecencies of unmarried fornication were sacrifices to Jefferson Davis and Robert E. Lee. (How good her military information was, or how valuable, or what it did to help the rebels is a matter of guesswork or the bragging assumptions of her admirers.) In December of 1862, orders went out for Belle Siddon's arrest. She escaped on a horse but was caught at Ste. Genevieve. Documents found on her person were proof of her spying activities. In St. Louis she confessed all to General John M. Schofield, telling in a girlish gush of her friendship with rebel generals Nathan Forrest and Sterling Price. The Union general was immune to her volatile charm. He had her locked up in the Grant Street Prison. Here she managed to meet a weaker vessel of impulsiveness, the provost marshal, who released her after four months' imprisonment on her promise to be a good girl and get out of St. Louis and the state.

With the war over, Belle married Dr. Newt Hallett, an army surgeon, and went to Texas, where her husband died. Soon she emerged as a blackjack dealer in Wichita, Kansas. She ran her own games in Fort Hayes and Cheyenne, but with the gold strike of '76 she set up her tent in Denver as "Madam Vestal" and was dealing to all, including those who had come from the new gold-field discoveries in the Black Hills of South Dakota. As word of the strikes spread, everybody who could pack up and get out went to the new fields. Things slowed down in Denver. The cards remained undealt, the wheels did not spin, the girls slept undisturbed.

Madam Vestal bought a wagon and packed her gear; rounded up her shills and dealers, case men and spindle men; loaded her boudoir furnishings in another freight wagon; and started for Deadwood, center of the new gold boom.

In Deadwood, Belle decided that a change of name would do no harm, and she became Lurline Monte Verde. By any name she was welcome. A celebration greeted her appearance: old and new customers cheered; the rich and the would-be rich were proud to have Belle among them. As a *New York Tribune* reporter wrote of her arrival in Deadwood, she "stood on a board and was borne through the town on the shoulders of four strapping miners. . . ." She soon was to "deal twenty-one and dance a jig with a far-off look in her left eye. . . ." Other reporters spoke of her "flawlessly groomed beauty, artfully jeweled and gowned," and as a woman who didn't touch a drop of hard liquor.

Belle picked a spot on Main Street for her gambling setup. It was a tough neighborhood known as "the Badland," where everyone who had the money could play and sport and spend. Here were federal marshals with head money; businessmen freighting in supplies of booze, beans, duds, canned oysters and gold watches; sharpers buying or selling mine leases; merchants and salesmen; army officers; and the usual frontier collection of mystery men and drifters. There were also armed sadists. Plenty of gunslingers were present, some of whom were suspected outlaws and road agents. All sorts played cards with Belle. There were reports that Wild Bill Hickok himself asked Madam Verde to flip the cards for him. So to banjo music, the reek of rotgut and exhausted oil lamps, play went on.

Belle appeared to be a cool, controlled wise woman who had avoided love. But then Archie McLaughlin came to try his luck at her tables. Archie was big and rough and had been one of Quantrill's cruel and mean raiders—a bushwhacking lout. He was now a road agent, holding up stages and gold wagons. Perilously balanced in frontier society, he spent recklessly what he stole, and Madam Verde was too much in love, for all the wrong reasons, to care. She even aided his career. The guards of the chests of refined gold shipped out of the mines were treated to drink at her place, and from them Archie learned the routes and time schedules and the quantities of gold being shipped. Madam herself got the information at times and passed it on to her lover. Belle seemed to suffer a derangement of reason and caution.

There was another man who came to her tables who seemed fascinated by her—one Boone May. All he seemed interested in was information about the outlaws. May got from Belle the fact that Archie and his gang were to hold up a gold shipment in Whoop Up Canyon, between Deadwood and Rapid City. Because of May's information the holdup failed and a couple of the gang were killed. Some were wounded, and those who were able escaped. Archie suffered a minor wound himself. One of the injured outlaws, a man named Brown, had a festering wound from a bullet. Archie knew that Belle's dead husband had been an army surgeon and that she had worked with him. So he sent for Belle to come and get the slug out of Brown. Belle, perhaps feeling guilty, came to the hideout, probed for the bullet with a bit of wire, and extracted it. As a reward, some of the gang suggested that she be done away with as a witness who knew too much. Archie drew his pistol, vowing that she would return to Deadwood in safety.

The event took an ironic turn, for the rescued Brown, who was soon arrested, implicated Archie in a few crimes. Archie fled, but not far enough, for he was caught in Cheyenne with two of his gang. He and Belle had planned to run off to San Francisco, but luck took one bad turn after another. While the law officers were taking Archie back to Deadwood by coach, five masked men, members of the "Little Cottonwood Creek Vigilantes"—a to-hell-with-courts group—held up the coach a mile north of Fort Laramie and demanded the prisoners. The lawmen didn't protest; they considered court trials senseless and absurd.

The three outlaws were hauled to a grove of trees, where nooses were looped around their necks. The youngest, a teen-ager, screamed for mercy. Archie remained calm. "Go ahead, you bastards, hang me; get it over with. One thing, you'll never find none of that $8,000 loot I got stashed away in the hills."

"String 'em up!"

There was no great outcry at the lynchings. Probably the lawmen and vigilantes had it all planned the way it happened, but all agreed that it did save the taxpayers' money. This kind of anarchy was routine in the mining camps. None of Archie McLaughlin's loot, if it existed, was ever found.

Belle took the news of Archie's death hard. In her grief she swallowed poison. (Of the many suicides in the West by women, most seem to have taken poison rather than death by handgun or rope.) She recovered, however, from the poison, but she had lost her poise. She took to drink and the opium pipe, seeming to move in a fog of doubt and regret. She could still deal blackjack, but in time drink took its toll and she drifted off to San Francisco and into a hopeless existence.

In October of 1881 we have our last notice of Belle. She was arrested and jailed in San Francisco. The news item states that she was destitute and worn down by drink. Dying, she was moved to a hospital where a chaplain came not merely to comfort her but to hear her confession, to raise up all the specters of her past. Her life story as she told it to him soon appeared in public print as a lesson in the wages of sin.

Belle Siddons Vestal Monte Verde was no frontier slut, no maudlin dance-hall whore. She was an educated lady who had a knowledge of books and opera and who had been escorted by staff officers and generals to important social events. By self-discipline and skill she had become an amazing card dealer; she also had the clear business head to run a successful establishment in crude surroundings among lawless men and newly made millionaires in the raw atmosphere of the West.

There are many discrepancies in her life that remain unfathomed. Without putting too much emphasis on the moral that all sins are punished, one might say that her downfall can be blamed on her love for Archie McLaughlin. Had she betrayed him? She was never the same after his death. Her decline was in the romantic tradition of *tableau-vivant* operetta: poison, opium, drink and final destitution that led to a last-minute deathbed confession.

7

THE FIGHTING DOG

Usually the fighting dog was a mixture called a bull mastiff. Bull mastiffs existed long before the orderly crossbreeding of mastiff and bulldog. The earliest recorded hybrids, called keeper's night dogs, were those of nineteenth-century British gamekeepers. Guards needed dogs with a controlled bark, dogs that would attack and hold on to poachers. The bulldog was aggressive; the mastiff had size, strength and the required temperament. In standardization of size and type, the strain was about 60 percent mastiff and 40 percent bulldog. The bull mastiff is heavy, muscular, powerful; the head large, the muzzle broad; and it is usually dark. Ears and tail are natural, the coats short and hard, ranging in color from red and brindle to fawn. Training makes them fighters.

The dog was probably the first wild animal tamed by man. The dog was early admired for its worth as a fighter as well as for its companionship. A few hundred years of breeding for fighting strains was common, and American dogfights engendered as much interest during the nineteenth century among gamblers as did boxing matches. Both had the primitive appeal of visceral drama.

Most of the fighting dogs were imported from England or were bred from stock brought over. English sportsmen over generations produced fighting dogs bred for strength of jaws and body to do pit battle. The bulldog, as he came to be known, was pretty much the standard breed, running from small, agile Boston bulls to huge mastiffs, dogs with such flat faces and deformed noses and bowed legs that they had difficulty breathing, and even walking. By the turn of the century, dogfighting had gone out of fashion as boxing contests—even if illegal in many states—had begun to attract attention. Man in violent contest had become more interesting than beasts at each other's throats.

As famous as John L. Sullivan in his day was the brindle and white fighting dog Pilot, a champion owned by "Cockney Charlie" Lloyd. A challenge with a rich purse was sent out in 1881 to the owner of any dog that could beat Pilot. Richard K. Fox of the *National Police Gazette* accepted the offer to act as stakeholder, with the paper's sports editor, William Harding, acting as referee. The sporting public had an avid appetite for fierce action with no delicate nuances.

The challenger was a dog named Crib, an imported animal owned by Louis Kreiger of Louisville, Kentucky. In most states prize fights were against the law, but the dogfight between Pilot and Crib was openly announced, with no false pretenses of "bettering the breed."

Louisville, near the site of the fight, began to fill up with sporting men from New Orleans, Chicago, New York, St. Louis—wherever there was interest in wagering money on the merits of either Pilot or Crib. The Ohio and Mississippi Railroad sold special excursion tickets for the coming battle. Rambunctious bettors talked of the prowess of their favorite. The sportsmen were greeted at the Louisville Hotel by the president of the Louisville board of aldermen, a gathering of notables, and the genial chief of police, one Adam Bly. Louisville was a notoriously open town, with a façade of pleasant dignity.

Copies of the agreement were passed around: "The said Charles Lloyd, of New York, hereby agrees to fight his brindle and white dog Pilot, ears cut and tail on, against Louis Kreiger's, of Louisville, white dog Crib, ears cut and tail on, at 28 pounds weight, for one thousand dollars ($1,000) a side: the said fight to take place on the 19th day of October, 1881, at or within a point of seven miles of Pittsburg, Ky. The stakeholder or the referee to name the place of fighting. The dogs to be weighed at 7 o'clock A.M. on the day of fighting, and to fight between 7 A.M. and 8 P.M., Richard K. Fox to be final stakeholder and to select the referee. The deposits to be made with Richard K. Fox, of *The Police Gazette*.

"The said Charles Lloyd and the said Louis Kreiger do

hereby agree that should the authorities in any way interfere or try to stop or prevent the said battle, the referee shall have full power to name the next time and place of fighting. It is also agreed that the referee shall insist on the dogs being again weighed, and the said weighing shall be within thirty minutes before the time named by the referee for the fight to be decided. Should there be any after-interference the dogs shall again be weighed day after day, and neither will be allowed to exceed 28 pounds in weight.

"It is further agreed that the handlers shall each taste the other's dog and sponge them with wet sponge. The sponge used shall then be squeezed into each other's dog's mouth in order to prove there is no poison or pernicious drugs placed on them. After the dogs have been tasted neither of the sponges must be changed.

"In pursuance of this agreement the said Charles Lloyd and the said Louis Kreiger do hereby agree to comply with the rules embodied in this agreement or forfeit the money now deposited with the stakeholder. It is also agreed that the battle shall be fought according to *The Police Gazette*'s revised rules of dogfighting."

At dawn on the morning of the fight, the dirt roads were filled with carriages, gigs, buggies and farm vehicles carrying fans to the scene of the battle on a nearby farm. Pilot, as champion, traveled in an elegant closed carriage. Crib was conveyed in an open buggy. Garr's farm, six miles from Louisville on the country pike, was ready. An old barn was the site for the dogfight. A pit 13 by 16 feet had been dug. Mr. Harding, a fastidious fellow, seeing a messy floor, insisted that the barn be properly cleaned for the battle. Cockney Charlie demanded a one-dollar admission, but many got in through holes and loose planks in the old barn.

At approximately seven o'clock the dogs, snorting through their flat noses, were weighed in. Pilot weighed in at 27¾ pounds, Crib at 27½. The dogs were washed in the Garr kitchen, with Mrs. Garr and her four children watching the rites. Pilot, having won the toss to be bathed first, took his bath in warm water, then was rinsed in tepid milk. The owner of Crib tasted the wet dog with his lips to see if any red pepper had been slipped into the milk, an old trick to disconcert or even blind the other dog. Towels and blankets were also examined, and Pilot was dried, covered and muzzled. Crib was put through the same routine. Both animals were brought to the pit where wagering and singing were going on between gulps of Kentucky bourbon. A cloud of cigar smoke hung in the air. Mr. Harding, as referee, had the chief of the local fire department announce that both dog handlers would be searched. There was no naïve acceptance of honesty on either side. Nothing was found that could injure either dog.

Stripped of blankets and muzzles, the dogs, with words of encouragement, were placed in the pit, and the fight began. Mr. Harding, as sports editor of the *Gazette,* reported the battle in detail:

"Both uttered low growls, and then, with one savage bound, Crib sprang in Pilot's corner and attacked his antagonist. He caught Pilot by the nose, but the brindle dog shook him off and grasped him by the right leg. Pilot loosened his hold upon Crib's leg to get a better one upon his throat. Crib succeeded in freeing himself, and once more caught Pilot by the nose, only to loosen it almost instantly and seize Pilot by the back of the neck and ear, throwing him down. While down, Pilot got Crib by the breast and had a terrible hold, but being unable to retain his hold to any advantage, let go and grasped Crib by the left ear. Then in turn Pilot loosened the ear-hold and got Crib's left front leg between his molars. As he pressed his jaws together, the bones in Crib's legs fairly cracked. This terrible punishment seemed only to enrage the Louisville dog the more, for with one great effort he threw Pilot five times in succession with the ear-hold. Crib again seized Pilot by the nose, which seemed to be his favorite hold, and once more downed the New York dog. As quick as a flash he let go Pilot's nose and went to chewing Pilot's front leg. With the fighting that Crib was now doing, the Louisville people thought him a sure winner of the fight.

"But it now came Pilot's turn to do some fighting, and the manner in which he viciously chewed Crib's front leg was terrible to behold. Crib, with a growl, broke loose, only to be caught again in the same way. With another effort Crib once more gained his freedom, and for fully five minutes the dogs fought with ear-holds, until finally Pilot downed Crib, and while holding him by the ear, bumped his head on the floor of the pit. Crib secured a hold on Pilot's throat and, although only fighting on three legs, succeeded in throwing his antagonist. This seemed to incense Pilot, for he threw Crib with a throat-hold and again with a hind-leg-hold. Crib returned with a leg-hold on Pilot, and then a bet of $100 was made that Crib would win the fight. The bet was promptly taken by Cockney Charlie, the owner of Pilot.

"The fight had now lasted forty-two minutes. Crib succeeded in getting from under his adversary, but the poor critter's gameness was gone. He turned to the side of the pit and was in the act of leaping out when he was grabbed by the brindle dog and dragged back into the field of battle. Crib was a whipped dog at this moment, but Pilot, not content with the victory already achieved, determined to kill his antagonist while the opportunity of so doing was at his command. Crib once more turned to the side of the pit, and this time succeeded in getting outside, followed by Pilot, who seized the Louisville pet by the underjaw and, clinging to him, refused to loosen his hold, necessitating the picking up of the dogs together and placing them again in the pit. Pilot threw Crib in the corner with an ear-hold and held him there. Kreiger fanned Crib vigorously with his hat, but did the dog no good, for he was fast failing. From this time on Pilot did nothing but endeavor to shake the little life out of Crib that still remained.

"The fight lasted exactly one hour and twenty-five minutes."

The crowd was well satisfied and felt compensated for their journeys. Pilot's owner and handlers drove to the Louisville depot with their champion and departed for New York City. But "Colonel" Kreiger, owner of the losing dog, came charging cheerfully into the station, and, smiling at Cockney Charlie Lloyd, insisted on standing host to a round of drinks like a good sport.

"I said I'd stand treat if I lost. I'm here now, gentlemen, to keep my word."

Everyone agreed that the Colonel was a thoroughgoing sport; it was just that Pilot was the better dog. Pilot may have retired as the undefeated champion dogfighter of the world.

Cockfighting, with its vigor of sustained speed and action, lasted longer than dogfighting. It originated in the Spanish islands and Mexico. Some European prize bantam cocks were bred to don steel spurs and to battle in sustained fury.

The sport of cockfighting still goes on. Many cock mains are still featured, in secrecy, all over the United States. Recently, the Los Angeles police arrested a cockfighting-gambling ring and took into custody two dozen birds staked at $5,000 to $10,000 a match.

Dogfighting and cockfighting have led to legal action in Washington. The House has voted that the use of interstate transportation and the mails for the promotion of dogfighting and cockfighting is a federal crime. Congressman Eligio de la Garza (D.-Tex.) argued against the ban "because of the ethnic and cultural background of some of us." He represented Mexican-Americans interested in cockfighting. Congressman William M. Ketchum (R.-Calif.) was also against the bill. He said it would not stop dogfighting or cockfighting any more than the 18th Amendment stopped drinking. Final action has yet to be taken on the bill.

8

THE POLICE GAZETTE

In America, betting on sports events was first promoted by a feisty little Irishman named Richard K. Fox who in 1876 took over a faltering weekly newspaper, *The National Police Gazette*, as owner and editor. The paper owed him money and was hearing its death rattle. Fox was to make it the champion reporter of sports, gambling and scandal, in text and daring woodcut pictures. It enlivened journalism by highlighting the sensational aspects of humanity. He shunned the aesthetic. He was also the promoter of the modern prize-fight ring, the giver of grand-sounding awards to champions, near champions, and mere freaks.

Richard K. Fox was born in Belfast, Ireland, in 1846, of Scotch-Irish parentage, and, as his own paper wrote of him (he started as a newspaperman with the *Banner of Ulster*): "The solid grit of one and the mental acuteness of the other are both equally represented in him." The *Banner* was the official organ of the Presbyterian Church in Ireland. In 1874, after ten years with the *Belfast News Letter,* Fox emigrated to New York City.

There were hard times, but before long he was working on the *Commercial Bulletin*. Here he became involved with *The Police Gazette*. He became owner, publisher and editor of the oldest weekly in America (founded in 1845). He was slim, boyish-looking, and just forty years old when the weekly became his. It was a sick publication, devoted to unctuous reforms and advertising of, among other things, "Italian Hair Dye" and "Vegetable Extract for Fits."

There were debts, and Fox borrowed $500 from William (the Great) Mulldoon. Mulldoon was the pride of Harry Hill's Sporting Resort. A splendid-muscled fanatic, an example of a clean-living athlete, member of the New York Police Department, and about to become wrestling champion of the world, the Great Mulldoon was the first of the people in the sports world to attract Fox's interest.

Fox obtained new type and printed the paper on the pink stock soon to become notorious as background for indiscreet woodcut pictures of sports figures, bandits (Jesse James read the *Gazette*), actresses in provocative attitudes, and big-time sportsmen. It became a grab bag of sports-reporting and crimes of passion and soon was an international favorite, with subscribers from twenty-six countries. Richard K. Fox was to make $3 million from his paper.

Outlawed in most states, prize fighting was in disgrace. Serious newspapers paid little attention to the sport beyond a sneering comment on its brutality. Fox at once saw his opportunity to attract the followers and lovers of the sporting life into the square ring. In 1880 he began to promote interest in a fight between Paddy Ryan and Joe Goss for the "Heavyweight Championship of America." It was a furtive, dishonest and raucous business. Goss was the "champion" recognized by the bettors. Ryan, called the "Collar City Giant" (Troy, New York), seemed a good butcher's block for a champ, as he sported calcified ears and brain and a game heart.

Actually, Fox had little interest in boxing or gambling. But since he had just added a sports section to his paper, he saw a chance to increase circulation by ordering his sports editor and some artists to cover the fight in flamboyant prose and truculent pictures. The first thing was to find a place for the fight. Outlawed in most of the United States, it was set for Canada, but British soldiers in red coats rushed the fighters and their unsavory entourage back across the border. Fox used all this to whet interest in the brawl.

At last, one June morning in 1880, on the turf near Collier's Station, West Virginia, the two fighters squared off with bare fists. The old London boxing rules were still in force. A round consisted of a knockdown, and when the fighter got up (if he could), another round began. While Fox's artists sketched and his writers reported, the bloody fight went on for an hour and twenty-four minutes, for a total of eighty-seven rounds.

The other papers, busy featuring the Garfield-Hancock contest for President of the United States, hardly covered the fight. *The Police Gazette* rushed out extra editions that sold out in the next four weeks. Four hundred thousand copies were printed and sold. From then on, *The Police Gazette* was sports-minded, and was read by nearly every gambler able to read. The paper became the sports authority on titles, bets and dates, and its "Answer to Correspondents" department was the settler of facts concerning sports events, crimes, dates and titles. Gamblers encouraged the reporting of contest races.

Fox was not one to miss a chance when it came along. He became the backer of Paddy Ryan, the "new champion," a backing that included a $5,000 offer for a fight with the "Boston Strong Boy," John L. Sullivan, whose drinking was matched by his ability to hammer opponents down to defeat. At times gamblers gave almost any odds on him as a favorite.

It was the Great Mulldoon who brought John L. to New York City to fight Steve Taylor in the cleared dining room of Harry Hill's popular resort. Sullivan won handsomely with an annihilating punch. The gamblers cheered. He was a fine figure of a man, and they clamored for him to fight Mr. Fox's own Paddy Ryan. Fox had developed a dislike of Sullivan so strong that it goaded him for years to find a man who could batter Sullivan to the canvas. It became an obsession with Fox, and its outgrowth was rewarding publicity. (He may also have lost money betting against John L.)

John Lawrence Sullivan was born in Roxbury, Massachusetts, in 1858. His five-foot-three father came from County Kerry, his five-foot-two, 200-pound mother from Athlone in County Westmeath. In his prime John was never the giant that legend made of him. He was five feet ten and a half and at his best fighting strength weighed 195 pounds. At the age of sixteen he is said to have pushed aside eight men who were trying to lift a derailed horse trolley back onto its track and did the job himself. Most likely the myth about his muscled body developed from his early years as a plumber and apprentice tinsmith. He was never a blacksmith, as some stories had it. He was handy with his temper and his fists, and when he lost jobs from bosses who didn't like to take a punch, John L. turned to semipro baseball, earning $100 a week. From baseball he went into the prize ring, in the old raw knuckles–ungloved days, when a round consisted of a knockdown and the three-minute round was not yet the rule. By all reports he had a popular uniqueness as a fighter. He hit hard and looked beautiful while doing it.

It all began the day Mr. Fox and his sports editor went to Harry Hill's place to have some of the resort's famous roast beef. The place was crowded, and Mr. Fox noticed a well-made young man who was the center of attention. Mr. Hill said, "It's that young fighter, J. L. Sullivan. He fought a fine brannigan here, in this very room, with young Steve Taylor, just two nights ago."

Mr. Fox said, "Tell Sullivan to come on over and see me." Sullivan told Hill, Mr. Fox's messenger, "You go tell that Mr. Fox if he wants to see John L. Sullivan to come over to my table. I'm here entertaining me friends now, and sure I don't intend to leave 'em."

Mr. Fox had not taken kindly to the rejection of his invitation. He decided to see if he could find a rival fighter to upset the Boston Strong Boy. Mr. Fox announced a stake of $5,000 to back Paddy Ryan against Sullivan. Fox ballyhooed the match, selling thousands of extras of his paper, and the gamblers did a fine business. The fight was to be on February 7, 1882, *if* a place could be found to stage it; most places had laws against prize fighting. It was finally held on the lawn in front of the Barnes Hotel in Mississippi City.

The Police Gazette gave eight pages to the fight, including information as to the fighting colors of the two men. Sullivan, it claimed, was un-American, since his colors had been made abroad. The *Gazette* insisted that they were not as attractive as the colors of the *Gazette*'s champion, Paddy Ryan, which the *Gazette* offered at $10 to $50. "Ryan's colors represent America, Ireland and New York. On white silk is a border of red, white and blue . . . in the center is an eagle standing on a globe . . . colored blue and dotted with stars. Beneath is the inscription: Paddy Ryan, Champion of America. The eagle holds a scroll with the inscription *Police Gazette,* New York, 1881. In the left-hand corner is an Irish harp, in the right-hand corner . . . an emblem of the Fenian Brotherhood. . . ."

Not too much was made of Sullivan's colors or that he was just as Irish as Paddy. As for the battle, it was Sullivan all the way. In eleven minutes of bare-fisted battering, Paddy went down and stayed there.

Soon Mr. Fox had new challengers: an Englishman, Tug Wilson; Herbert Slade, a New Zealand Maori; then another Englishman, Charlie Mitchell. All went down before Sullivan. Mr. Fox had spent $20,000 promoting anti-Sullivan fights, but it was money well spent, for it helped mightily the circulation of his paper. A return match with Mitchell was promoted, and Madison Square Garden was packed with nearly 14,000 people. In staggered Sullivan from the street, dead drunk. He held on to the ropes and said in the irrational, blurred tones of drunkenness: "Gents—hic—I am sure sick—hic—just not able to box t'night. . . . The doctor himself is here and this—hic—is the very first time I'm disappointing—hic—you. . . ."

The crowd did not take kindly to the speech, and Sullivan was assisted from the building amid boos, outraged cries and hisses. No money was returned by the promoters, but all bets were off. It didn't harm Sullivan's popularity, though people were still singing the song first heard in Tony Pastor's Music Hall:

> *The Fox may go to England*
> *And the Fox may go to France;*
> *To beat John L. he can go to hell,*
> *And still not have a chance!*

A diligent hunt for Sullivan killers ensued. In November 1884 Fox tried again with Alf Greenfield, who was so destroyed in the ring by Sullivan's blows, and bleeding so badly, that Police Captain Williams arrested both fighters for "not boxing but engaging in physical combat." In court Alf testified: "Sullivan, he's a good judge of the business . . . when I tried to hit 'im, 'e ducked 'is 'ead . . . I 'ad no ill-feelin', no ill-feelin' at all."

The judge looked at the battered Alf and turned to the Bostonian. He asked, "Were you angry during the exhibition, Mr. Sullivan?"

"No, Your Honor, I have not been angry in any of the exhibitions I have been in."

The jury returned the verdict: "Not guilty." It was a perfectly reasonable ruling: hit or be hit.

9

ROLL THEM DICE

Prehistoric graves have turned up dice of ivory, bear bones, stone and bronze. Dice like those used today were found in Egyptian tombs and in the ruins of Babylon. The playing of dice was popular in Greece and Rome, and dice were used throughout the Middle Ages. The game of hazards, considered by many to be the oldest dice game known, was popularized in the twelfth century during the siege of an Arab fortress by William of Tyre during the Crusades. While rules of the game and markings may have changed, it is still the sport of trying to make money by rolling some kind of combination of numbers.

The year 1798 is accepted as the one in which Bernard de Marigny introduced the game to polite French society. Dice games were introduced into North America by the French at New Orleans in the eighteenth century. When Americans, in 1804, began to expand New Orleans, de Marigny laid out a street which he named "Rue de Craps," now called Burgundy Street. There are legends that the game was named either after a Creole named Crapaud or the game called "crapauds," which was then shortened to "crapo," and eventually to "craps." By the 1830s, dice-shooting was as popular in Chicago as on the Delta. Anybody could carve a pair of dice from discarded soup bones (hence the term "rolling the bones"), and no elaborate setup was needed to play. Throwers didn't need tables, chips or wheels; any level bit of surface would do. The game was picked up by rich and poor alike, and soldiers played it during the Civil War.

The turn of the century saw crap-shooting admitted as a popular gambling game acceptable to gentlemen. However, the great gambling establishments run by Chicago gamblers did not include crap tables in their assortment of games of chance. The *Complete Hoyle* of 1914 admitted that crap-shooting was "replacing faro as the gambling game of America." Faro had begun to fade out before that; poker was to rival Chicago dice-shooting as the exciting game, but was docile compared to dice: no one prays out loud or sings for a pair or an ace.

What brought dice into nearly every levee dive was the returning soldier of the American Expeditionary Forces in France after World War I, and the million or so dice fiends from the army training camps near Chicago. The War to Make the World Safe for Democracy made the gambling young of America dedicated dice players, pushing aside faro, keno, euchre and three-card monte.

After the war dice playing became *the* game at Michigan Boulevard private parties of the rich. By 1918 every city gambling house had a dice table, or tables, as standard equipment, and gangsters were mostly in control, buying up the police, the city officials of Chicago and the judges. Jazz men were hired to play in Chicago roadhouses. (When the War Department closed the sporting houses of Storyville in New Orleans, the jazz players migrated north.) And most jazz players were crap shooters. It was the Negro jazz man south of the Loop who created the shooter's invocations as he talked to the dice as he rattled them close to his ear. "Come on, dice! Baby needs a new pair of shoes!" and "Seven brings me heaven!" and "I need nine, put it on the line!" or "Eighter from Decatur!" There were also obscene whispers to the bones. Preachers saw the mood of Ecclesiastes in the land. Dice *and* the Charleston.

It was possible, and still is, for either the player or the house's stick man to ring in a crooked pair of dice. Terms for crooked dice were "dispatchers," "plumbing the bones," or "loaded doctors." Chicago firms sold loaded and crooked dice openly through the mails. Loading was done by placing weights in corners of dice so they would usually fall showing numbers the player wanted.

For the professional Chicago dice gambler, loaded dice are usually sold in sets of nine: three sets to come up high, three sets to come up low, and three sets that are just ordinary dice. Dice do not always come up the way they are supposed to, but the odds on a pair of loaded dice coming up to please the tosser are very high. It is up to the thrower to use the highs, lows, or ordinary dice in a game the way he wants the drama to play. Another good combination for fast shooting and fast pickup is to have "specials"; one dice with two 1s, two 5s, and two 6s, and the other dice with two 3s, two 4s and two 5s. With this set in your hand, you can never crap out with a seven, and you roll until the point you're shooting for comes up. Of course you have to move too fast to allow anyone to examine those fixed dice. To throw sevens as your opening number and take the game you need a pair with one die all 4s, the *other* die *all* 3s. Trick dice can be bought from a catalogue. Before 1914, one Chicago dealer advertised his cheating devices for cards, marked cards, and dice, with price lists:

> Set loaded dice, best ivory, 9 dice, 3 high, 3 low, 3 square;
> Warranted sure, exact imitation of common dice . . . $5.00.
> Set 3 high or low dice . . . $2.50. 3 square to match . . .
> $1.00.

These are turn-of-the-century prices, of course.

Weighted spots are still being introduced into some dice to favor a seven, or to make a difficult number. Even with transparent dice, the loading can be hidden under certain of the dots. Many gambling games that catered to the rich Lake Shore sportsmen remained crooked. In honest play, theoretically the shooter and the fader have about the same odds and the same chance of winning. A gambling house would hardly be interested in fair odds.

One hears of some players who can palm, spin, and control dice to fall on certain numbers. If such expert tossers exist, they are few and far between. And such a player would soon be disposed of by the house. Some crooked dice when in play cannot be detected by the most expert crap shooter, not by sight or feel or throw.

"The best play at dice is to throw them away." So said an old wheel man and pit boss who once worked in gambling houses in Chicago and elsewhere. He explained: "Any gambling game can be rigged to trim the chump; any game has ways of giving the house the heavy advantage, an unfair one from the player's side of the table. Wheels in Chicago were rigged, dice loaded, cards marked, slot machines fixed. Even Uncle Sam is screwed, because the legal gambling joints outside of Chicago all skim off millions of dollars before they declare their take. There are bribes for federal payoffs, and for local cops and officials. There is *no* honest gambling; the house percentage is *always* against you. Play only for fun. Play if you enjoy the excitement."

10

GAMBLERS HALL OF FAME

I once interviewed Clarence Darrow, and among other matters we talked about was the American interest in heavy gambling at almost anything. "The American," said he, "is a gambler because all his life he hears how the nation was founded by people who took a chance. They gambled on killing off all the Indians; they bet they'd make it to Pike's Peak or bust. They gambled on finding water; on surviving Death Valley; on the vigilantes, the hired gunslingers, land sharks, the bankers' cold eyes and the blackleg lawyers deadlier than rattlesnakes. So the myth spread. Gambling was part of American get-up-and-go, the true beatific vision of holding four aces, or making seven six times in a row.

"Also, the average American is bored to death, living all the time in Thoreau's 'quiet desperation.' Cards, dice, the wheel give him the hope of beating the odds against his life. Gambling is deeply inbred in the Republic because of police and law corruption. Capone in his day had most of the police, the city fathers, and the courts in his pocket. To be honest was to be a fool in an imperfect world. Police take payoffs, judges do favors, politicians often split the loot with big-city bosses. The underworld as crime boss exists only because it pays off. And the best lawyers mostly don't work for the people. They protect the big gambler, the gambling hoodlums who own casinos, the bookie wires, the numbers games. Look always for the evil side of gambling as being protected by our lawmakers and law enforcers. Cynical? No. Go to the records."

I did. In the late nineteenth century, Bill Dovery was the New York chief of police. He was a close friend of the "Prince of

Gamblers," Frank Farrell. Farrell, under the chief's protection, set up a string of 300 poolrooms that were actually fronts for bookies taking illegal horse bets. He was publicly referred to as "King of the Poolroom Syndicate." His payoffs were not only to police but to prominent political figures in Tammany as well. State Senator Big Tim Sullivan and a gambler owned a share of the syndicate. He and Farrell got the franchise of the New York American League baseball team, the Highlanders (who later became the New York Yankees).

Farrell was a partner in the best and most luxurious gambling houses in the city, protected politically as well as by heavy metal doors. When in a reform wave District Attorney William Travers Jerome led a raid on Farrell's Thirty-third Street place, the bronze doors held off the raiders until blowtorches were brought in. By that time, of course, the society and political gamblers, along with all the tools of gambling, had been removed through a private passage.

Farrell had spent half a million dollars having the gambling establishment done over by the prime hedonist of the period, Stanford White. From 1895 to 1902 the patrons enjoyed losing fortunes in surroundings graced by Persian rugs, rare paintings of the Corot school, and fine wall hangings. The bronze door, White claimed, came from a doge's palace in Venice. Gamblers appreciated the food, which was rich and abundant. Diamond Jim Brady, one of those who had escaped during the D.A.'s raid by the secret passage, insisted that the place served the best steaks and broiled lobster in town. He would begin a meal, after gambling, with three dozen blue point oysters, a quart of *potage ambassadeur,* a whole roast chicken *demi deuil,* and two four-pound lobsters; for dessert he would polish off a cake.

While Diamond Jim and others were welcome to the Bronze Door, as Farrell's gambling house came to be known after the raid, the sight of George E. Smith brought no smiles. He was better known as "Pittsburgh Phil." Being small, not a cheerful type and not much of a speaker, he did not really enjoy his fame as a notoriously successful horse bettor who seemed to spook the bookmakers with an edge of malice in his winnings. At the various Eastern tracks he appeared to be an easygoing, not very interesting person. But the bookies knew better. Known as a man who paid up his losses, he would inspect the horses in the paddock, then casually walk past the bookmaker and lay a thousand here, five grand there. He would often bet $50,000 on a race.

Pittsburgh Phil had not an ounce of romance in his makeup concerning the sport of kings. When he owned a racing stable and found himself favoring his own horses in his betting, he sold out. He was considered one of the great handicappers of all times. He made big bets and won amazing sums, but when he owned a horse named Parvenue, he became cunning, and waited until the bookies were vulnerable. When he felt his steed was ready, he had friends place about $25,000 around in various bookie joints to keep the odds high. He was able to get high play at 40 to 1, and a low of 15 to 1. The audacity of his play was kept low key and, he hoped, secret.

However, a hassle over a scratched horse developed and all bets were off until the problem was solved. During the delay the bookies began to add up betting money and the odds put on Parvenue. When betting resumed, Phil's boys could not place money at the old odds. The best he could get was 12 to 1. Parvenue won, but paid only $45,000. Phil's dissatisfaction didn't show, but he continued to scheme.

He hired jockey Tod Sloan on a flat deal: he would give him $400 for every race he won. It didn't have to be Phil's horse— just a winner. Sloan really whipped up his brutes, and in one month Phil won $80,000 betting on horses Sloan rode.

Pittsburgh Phil believed in lucky streaks; when his losses were heavy, he bet lightly. When he felt Lady Luck riding on his shoulder, he plunged. Fixed races were rare, according to him. When two horses were the real favorites, he refrained from betting.

Phil was against touts, tout sheets, and newspaper handicappers. He believed that people were mistakenly impressed by newspaper handicappers, whose items were usually stale. Weather, betting odds, and even the condition of a high-strung animal could change the whole setup as the horses paraded before a race. "If handicappers were so goddamn sure of winners," Phil insisted, "they should play their winner choices and get rich, and not pick horses for newspaper readers with as many holes in their pants as the experts."

Pony Benny said he had worked for people who had known

Pittsburgh Phil. "He didn't just look at a track record, they told me. His daily bets were based on a study of wind, mud or dust on the track and the disposition of the jockey. Of course, often it was really the information he bought and paid for from jocks and stable grooms. He paid off, sometimes nearly a grand a day, to agents of jocks, trainers, and managers for information. Did he get feedbox info? He was the bettor with the inside data and he won a lot. There was no 'boat race,' or a jock ready to pull a nag on the last turn, that he didn't know about. Or what filly had a bad leg, or what gelding had a slightly pulled tendon. He may have looked dowdy and ordinary, but Pittsburgh Phil liked the good life and the flesh that went with it. He liked big dames, like most little guys do. It killed him, I heard. Still he left over two million dollars, and that's a miracle for a horse player."

Pittsburgh Phil ended in a North Carolina tuberculosis sanitarium. A journalist, Gray Gorham, reported that as Phil lay dying he asked his doctor:

"Doc, how long will I live?"

"About twenty-four hours."

"Bet you $10,000 I live longer than twenty-four hours."

The doctor, a gambler himself, wrote out a check and so did Phil. Twenty-four and a half hours later Phil smiled, closed his eyes, and died, the two checks clutched in his hand.

The Boss Gambler

He admitted he liked power, and he made use of it. Michael Cassius McDonald was born in 1839 near Chicago. In his prime he was a gambling-house owner, a politician in Chicago who allotted for cash the gambling rights to those wanting card and dice setups or sites for gambling houses. Mike would collect, promise protection, and pay the police and city officials their cut. Mike was boss of the Cook County Democratic party, an adviser to mayors Carter Harrison, Sr., and Harvey Colvin. The word was that Mike was the true boss of the city, ready to stomp into the ground anyone who opposed him.

And few did. For he who controlled the political scene owned Chicago.

Mike McDonald would do dishonest business with anyone without fear of the city's laws, courts, or police giving him trouble. The *Chicago Herald* properly identified him as a boss who never held office, but he ruled the city with an iron hand. He named the men who were to be candidates for election, he got them elected, and when they were in office they were merely his puppets. He ran saloons and gambling houses; he protected bunco steerers and confidence men and brace games of all kinds without hindrance.

He was only fifteen when he began a career as a train butcher (selling papers, fruit and candy en route), cheating the passengers, bracing suckers for card games on the train, and offering packages with "valuable prizes" which turned out to be trash. He worked the trains between Niagara Falls and Detroit and between New Orleans and Chicago. When war came, he signed a manifesto urging the Chicago Irish to fight for the Union. But he himself had better things to do than carry a rifle. With messianic zeal he organized bounty jumpers, those who enlisted and deserted many times to get the cash bounty for each enlistment. He made a wartime fortune as their agent.

Mike helped run a faro bank, and by 1867 he and con man Dan Oaks had their own gambling hall at 89 Dearborn Street. They ran rigged games; embezzlers on their way to ruin were their prey. In 1869, the assistant cashier of the Chicago Dock Company dropped $30,000 of his firm's money to Mike's cards. By a strange quirk of fate, Mike spent three months in jail for this—no one wanted to risk $60,000 bail on him. The trial was a joke. Mike brought witnesses who swore that he *always* ran an honest game, and besides, the debauched cashier had begged to get into the game; he had not been lured or enticed. After paying his legal sharks, Mike found he had nothing left to pay off the police to permit him to run his gambling house. He got used to being raided two or three times a week. For months he paid his fines, cementing his lifelong hatred of the police, who let him be if he paid graft but harassed him if he didn't.

After the Great Fire, Mike's luck turned for the better. He took on partners in one place, making $100,000 a year. Mike was an organizer. He brought together all the saloonkeepers to fight the Sunday closing law, forming them into a pressure group called, ironically, the People's Party, who backed for mayor Harvey D. Colvin, a womanizer and big-time bettor, and succeeded in getting him elected.

With the new mayor on a yoyo string manipulated by Mike McDonald, gambling houses flourished. Harry Varnell and the Hankin brothers, big gambling-house people, joined with Mike in 1885 to form a strong syndicate of bookmakers who controlled the betting at Chicago and Indiana race tracks.

With the mayor captive, Mike formed many partnerships. There was no terra incognita in Chicago gambling territory. One merger he joined with two sharpers to run a braced game in a big house called "The Store." A saloon took up the first floor; the gambling house occupied the second. There were rooms for rent on the third and fourth floors for private games or orgies or for cruising whores. Mary Noland McDonald, Mike's wife, was in charge here, and often Mike watched her, for he had been warned about Mary's eye for young men.

Roulette and faro wheels filled the gambling floor, and card sharks working for the house dealt seconds from packed decks or put in a cold deck. These experts at cheating dominated nearly every table. When, in 1873, The Store first opened for gambling, one of Mike's partners showed panic at the size and cost of the operation.

"Mike, we'll never get enough players to fill up the games."

"Don't you go worrying about that. There's a sucker born every minute." That remark joined American folk wisdom right then and there, as it was repeated around town. Mike's dice expert, Nick Hogan, had only one arm. The talk was, "If Nick had two arms, he'd have all the money in the world."

Mike soon dropped his partners; they lacked his drive and his sense of timing. The Store was the meeting place, the club, of the city officials, ward bosses, and the more prominent criminals with a sense of class. The saying was, "Don't bother goin' to City Hall for anything—go to Mike's office at The Store; that's the *real* City Hall . . ."

Mike had a way of humoring the public. Twice a year reporters were invited to see the police make a traditional raid on The Store, break up some old tables and wheels, and arrest six or eight croupiers and dealers. All were freed after paying small fines. Now all was clear for six more months. The press got a headline story, and naïve people nodded and said, "We're cleaning them out."

There were, of course, honest police, and Mike McDonald

made their lives hell when he could, with his political power. Mayor Carter Harrison, Sr., in 1879, had by chance appointed an honest superintendent of police, Simon O'Donnell, who felt that McDonald was not above the law. In 1880 the chief set off a real raid at The Store. For this he was busted to captain; he never again held any position of power.

Mike had his own man appointed chief of police, one William J. McGarigle, who pulled some fancy swindles against the city for Mike, selling them chalk and water as a new kind of paint preservative for the courthouse. Mike collected nearly $128,000 before the swindle was discovered. McGarigle had to run to Canada, but Mike was never prosecuted.

Police raids usually did not venture above the second story of The Store. On one occasion, when a raid included the rooming-house section, Mike's wife, Mary, shot a policeman. Mike was eventually forced to tone down his activities. With $2 million of his fortune, like the later Mafia and Cosa Nostra he went into legit businesses, retaining his position as the Democratic party's chief. He owned a newspaper, the *Chicago Globe*, for two years and was treasurer of the company that built Chicago's first elevated railroad, the Lake Street line. As the city was a big buyer of sand, stone and gravel, he bought a Lemont quarry. Selling to the city at high prices, with kickbacks and markups, showed him that gambling with rigged gear wasn't the only way to make easy money.

As for McDonald's wife, the story is well worth retelling in all its strange manifestations. A few months after the McDonalds moved into a new house, Mary disappeared. Mike McDonald told friends that his wife had run off with a minstrel singer, Billy Arlington, who had come to Chicago to play in black face with *Emerson's Minstrels*. Mike traced his wife and her paramour to the Palace Hotel in San Francisco. There, Mary greeted him with, "Don't shoot, for God's sake; it's all my fault! Take me back, for the love of God!" Mike brought her back home. However, in 1889 she vanished again, this time with a young priest with whom she had knelt in prayer in the chapel of the McDonald mansion. They ran away to Paris, where they lived together for six years. Then the burden of his fall from grace into carnal sin came to Father Moysant and he went into a monastery.

Mary McDonald came back to Chicago to run a boarding-house, as before.

Mike, feeling betrayed by the church, had smashed the family altar and renounced Catholicism and divorced Mary. In 1898, when he was sixty-six years of age, he married a Jewish girl of twenty-three whom he had seen in the chorus line of a show. Dora Feldman was the ex-wife of a baseball player named Sam Barclay. Mike, infatuated, became a Jewish convert and married Dora under the prescribed canopy.

But Mike had no luck with wives. He built Dora a splendid house on Drexel Boulevard, but she also proved unfaithful, and left his bed and board for a commercial artist named Webster Guerin. She was madly in love with him, but, for reasons unknown, in February of 1907 she shot and killed him.

This was too much for Mike. He took to his bed, called in a priest, and was again received into the faith, saying that Mary McDonald was his "only true wife" in the sight of God and the Pope. He died anointed, with Mary at his side. Mary, however, got none of his estate. Dora Feldman McDonald got one-third of his fortune and $40,000 to pay for her lawyer's fees for the impending murder trial. She was acquitted in 1908.

Eadweard Muybridge's Running Horse Pictures

Watching a trotter pace, the cognoscenti of horseflesh see a beautiful motion, but sportsmen were also interested in how race horses run. This led to arguments and bets. Some were sure there was just a moment—one moment—when a running horse had all four hoofs off the track. Ridiculous, said others. But look at the famous paintings of horses by masters—of race track scenes and running horses. The argument was that painters had invented movement that did not exist. In fact, those old sporting prints and paintings of horses running with all four hoofs off the ground—the forelegs up in the air and the hind legs also—were in no way realistic but a mere convention that one lazy artist copied from another.

American sportsmen gave this serious thought. Among them was Governor Leland Stanford of California, who, with Huntington, Crocker and Hopkins, had swung some huge railroad swindles, and all had become multimillionaires. Along with a desire to be governor, Stanford wanted winning horses, so he set up a breeding farm to propagate the species with fine horses, and planted a few hundred acres in carrots for his thoroughbreds. His racing stable was impressive. With fellow breeders at leisure moments of horse talk, the argument often came up over the unprovable deceit that at various gaits at full speed a horse had all four feet off the ground. In 1872 Stanford, his patience at an end, said to a couple of fellow horse lovers, "I'll bet $25,000 a horse *does*."

The bet was taken, though some felt it was merely the indulgence of a very rich man. But it was up to Stanford to prove it. He decided to do it with the camera. The man he picked for the job was a forty-five-year-old Englishman, Eadweard Muybridge, a San Francisco photographer who had done camera work for the U.S. Coast Survey in Alaska. He owned a huge box camera and used the wet glass-plate process. (This was before the flexible dry film strip had been invented.)

Muybridge went to Sacramento to take pictures of the galloping gait of the Stanford horses. The best shutter speed he could get on his camera was one-twelfth of a second, which was much too slow to reveal anything but a blur.

Muybridge began to look around for some method of catching on his plates a clearer image of a running horse. But the reality of domestic life suddenly replaced science. In October of 1874, Muybridge's experiments were rudely cut off by the discovery that his young wife was having an affair with a Major Harry Larkyn, employed at times on a San Francisco newspaper. Harry was a handsome, woman-loving sportsman. The gay life of the town knew him in his smart cheviot overcoat and silk hat. He was rumored to be the younger son of a noble English family.

The affair came to Muybridge's attention while his wife and newborn child were visiting friends in Oregon. Muybridge was late in paying the midwife, a Mrs. Susan Smith, her bill of $100 for delivering the baby. Muybridge, annoyed, may have protested the high fee in a day when doctors made house calls for a dollar. Spitefully Mrs. Smith told him the truth: that Larkyn was his wife's lover and they had used Mrs. Smith's house as a secret love nest after the baby was born. She showed the husband letters Mrs. Muybridge had written containing unmistakable proof of the relationship. Worst of all, there was a picture of the baby with the name "Harry" written on the back. Imagine the shock to Muybridge, a middle-aged husband, deceived by a young wife.

On October 17 Muybridge armed himself with a revolver and took the ferry to Calistoga, where he had learned the major was taking the sulphur waters at the foot of Mount St. Helena.

It had been a favorite spot for Major Harry Larkyn to carry on the affair with Mrs. Muybridge in tranquil safety while Eadweard was taking pictures of the Stanford horses. Later it came out that Mrs. Muybridge had gone to Oregon without telling the major, and he, mad with passion, was hunting her as he himself was being hunted. He had even placed personals in the newspaper columns trying to find her.

That night at eleven a hack driver from a livery stable delivered the outraged and armed husband at the Yellow Jack mine, where the major was spending the night. The photographer stood in front of the main house and called out for the major to show himself.

Major Larkyn came to the door. He couldn't see who was calling him in the dark. Muybridge yelled, "My name is Muybridge! Here is a message from my wife!" He fired, and the major, clutching his chest, staggered backward. He died almost at once.

Muybridge went into the house to make sure his responsibility for the deed was final. Then he gave himself up and was lodged in the jail at Napa City. Locally it was a sensational case. Though neither man was rich or famous, it was a murder trial involving a menage of three, and that always drew a good house. The liaison and the murder were fully exploited by the local press.

Napa City courthouse was the scene of the trial on February 3, 1875. It lasted only two days. Justice was swifter in the 1870s, and an urgent expectancy permitted no waste of taxpayers' money.

Without needless ramifications, Muybridge's lawyer at first tried to establish a defense of temporary insanity, claiming his client had suffered a head injury in 1860 in a stagecoach accident. The case had been settled for $2,500. Wort W. Pendegast was defending Muybridge, and he was expected to bring a little drama into the case. He was from Kentucky, a lean and fancy speaker who had studied the ranting Shakespearean actors of the day. He had a voice that could go from deep church-organ notes to delicate bell tones. He pleaded "the unwritten law"— the biological, religious defense of a husband's manhood.

Wort W. was an expert at courtroom oratory when he had a thin case. He began the defense of Muybridge's action as *above* the law, as a God-given right to drill at close range any man who tampered with his client's wife. His closing speech is a good example of its style:

"I cannot ask you to send this man forth to family and home—he has none. Across the arch of his fireplace where once were written the words 'Home — Wife — Child — Content and Peace,' there now appears as a substitute for all, in black letters, placed there by the destroyer, the single awful word 'Desolation.' But I do ask you to send him forth free; let him take up the thread of his broken life and resume that profession on which his genius has shed so much luster, the profession which is now his only love. Let him go forth into the green fields, by the bright waters, through the beautiful valleys and up and down the swelling coast, and in the active work of securing shadows of their beauty by the magic of art, he may gain surcease of sorrow, and pass on to his end in comparative composure . . ."

The jury left Wort W.'s exploitation of California landscape and his plea for a life to consider their verdict. They could not agree, having eleven "Not guilty" and one holdout for "Guilty." The man who voted guilty was W. T. Commary, who rejected the notion of unwritten law. The jury foreman, knowing that Commary had a pretty young wife and that she was alone while Commary was on jury duty, took Commary aside and said, "Bill, I'm a-going to pray to God that while you're locked up here in this jury room some son of a bitch fucks your wife!"

The foreman knelt down in prayer. Commary, shaken at last by that grim picture, said, "Sam, let's take another ballot."

The verdict made headlines:

The Napa *Daily Register*. Saturday, Feb. 6, 1875.
NOT GUILTY.
End of the Muybridge Trial.

Brilliant Speech of Senator Pendegast.
The Prisoner Overpowered with Emotion.
Muybridge was brought in. It was:
We the jury find the defendant not guilty.

On hearing his acquittal, Mr. Muybridge was so over-come with emotion as to fall into a paroxysm similar to that which had seized him on the memorable 17th of October when he had heard of his wife's infidelity. He fell upon Mr. Pendegast and wept and went into convulsions. He was removed to the offices of his counsel, and Dr. Boynton was sent for. By the time of that gentleman's arrival, however, he had so far recovered as to be out of the need of medical aid, and rapidly regained his wonted composure.

He is now a free man and has received the congratula-tions of a multitude of friends. He leaves tonight for San Francisco, where so confident was he of acquittal that he had an engagement to dine with a friend tomorrow . . .

Commary hurried home to see if his wife had remained faithful and not succumbed to the hired man. Muybridge went out of the courtroom a free man. Of Mrs. Muybridge and little Harry, no further record exists.

Muybridge also vanished into some derelict despair. His life turned sour. He is supposed to have spent the next five years in some backcountry ranch owned by Stanford. What we do know is that at the end of his exile he was back at the Stanford breeding farm, being urged by Stanford to get that picture of the horse with its four legs off the ground. The bettors were pushing him to pay off the $25,000. The bet was becoming a tedious joke in horse circles.

There was better material for Muybridge to work with now, superior photographic plates; and while some of his new pic-tures *might* show horses with all their legs off the ground, Stanford and his bettors were not satisfied. There was still no clear image of the desired moment.

Stanford suggested that Muybridge use a whole battery of cameras, cost no object, to catch a moving horse in a series of pictures as it passed. Muybridge set up a row of cameras to snap the pictures, with strings stretched across the path of the running horse. But the strings upset the horse. As writer Leigh Hunt put it, "The horse appears to be content with as few ideas as a domestic animal can well have . . ."

Stanford got John D. Isaacs, a young man from his railroad engineering department, to help. The camera shutters were now made to snap shut by heavy rubber bands at one-thousandth of a second. Twenty-four cameras took pictures as the horse passed by, the cameras set off by a series of electrical connections contrived by Isaacs. And soon there was the proof Stanford needed: horses with *all four legs off the ground* while passing in a gallop. It had cost him $40,000 to win a $25,000 bet. He never regretted it.

The pictures proved that artists of the past had wrongly depicted the running horse. For Muybridge they brought fame. He never married again. Instead, he passed himself off as a bachelor in his years of glory and honors, with a chest full of medals. His series of pictures were brought to the attention of Thomas A. Edison and most likely had a great deal to do with Edison's production of the first motion pictures: the passing of a film strip with a continued series of developing action or subject through a lens with a strong light behind it.

Today, every American track photographs the finish of every race by stop-action photography developed from Eadweard Muybridge's work with his cameras. John D. Isaacs, who invented the electric shutter device that made it all work, is hardly remembered.

The Son of The Great Chicago Fire

Many historians believe that Kate O'Leary kept a cow that kicked over the lamp that caused the Great Chicago Fire. She also had a son James.

"Big Jim" O'Leary, who became a millionaire, had a long life as a famous gambler. Even as a youngster he made contacts fast. He became a handyman for Mike McDonald and his friends, and served "Silver Bill" Riley, who was the first to take horse bets exclusively. Silver Bill was a pious man about most things but condoned betting on horse races because it was for "improving the breed." He was against alcohol and card-playing. He thought them a disgrace to God's grand plan, as also were smoking and cursing. He did not permit minors to gamble on his premises.

After a few years, Big Jim left Silver Bill and entered the bigtime. By the 1890s he had a share of John Condon's gambling house, and when John went blind, they still continued the partnership. The partners went into a gambling syndicate located twenty-three miles from Chicago, at Long Beach, Indiana. It was so far out that it failed to attract local interest, and the two big-city gamblers lost their investment and all enthusiasm for country life.

Back in Chicago, on South Halstead Street, Big Jim settled near the stockyards. He began to operate in a solid fashion, forming a strong syndicate of bookies, poolrooms and hand-books with other gamblers. In the end Big Jim, by force of character and what we today call clout, controlled much of all the gambling and betting on the South Side.

Big Jim was the tough boss-man of 600 bookies and pool-rooms. In 1904 he established a floating poolroom aboard the steamer *City of Traverse*. How the few who only wanted to play pool were able to control the billiard balls in the dipping lake tide was a wonder. But this was the first gambling ship in America. It made an afternoon sailing from the South Chicago docks of the Illinois Central, carrying at least a thousand sportsmen and horse handicappers around the lake until the day's racing results were in. Wireless, a novelty in private hands in those days, sent the betting odds and winners out to the waiting lakeborne players.

But the police began to arrest the passengers when the boat docked. They also learned to scramble the wireless messages. The last lake trip of the *City of Traverse* was made in May of 1907. It was infiltrated by eighteen Chicago detectives and seven journalists, for only forty-two authentic bettors aboard.

Big Jim O'Leary's unique quality of leadership remained on land. His gambling-house headquarters on South Halstead had a fancy layout: a Turkish bath, a fine restaurant, a bowling alley, and a splendid billiard room. All the while, constantly changing blackboards were under observation. They listed the betting odds and the result of every major horse race in Canada and the United States.

One could bet on more than horse races with Big Jim: he'd give or take odds on wrestling, boxing, football, baseball, and election results. If someone wanted to get in on the weather or the harvest figures, Big Jim was game for those too. He won $10,000 betting on eighteen consecutive days of rain during the month of May.

He took no chances of the premises being molested, for the place was, he said, police proof, fireproof and bombproof, with its iron-reinforced heavy oak doors, steel plates set in the walls, and rooms lined with zinc-covered timbers. When the Gamblers' War of 1907, a civil war for control of territory among the various gamblers, broke out, attempts were made to plant bombs at Big Jim's place. The police, in their attacks on the place, used axes and sledgehammers to break in when it was politically necessary to stage a spectacular raid for the press. But Big Jim usually received timely warning of such raids; on one occasion he filled his hollow walls with red pepper. When the police axes cut through the zinc sheeting, the invaders were blinded by the pepper, and most had to be hospitalized. Defense for Big Jim was more than just the usual facile optimism of gamblers.

By 1911, Big Jim O'Leary was ready to retire. "I never paid a dollar for protection," he bragged. "I could have had all kinds of it, but let me tell you something. Protection that you purchase ain't worth nothing to you. A man who will sell himself ain't worth an honest man's dime. The police is for sale, but I don't want none of them."

This was nonsense. There were times when he like everyone else paid for protection, and things ran smoothly; times when reform for a while made things tough, and periods when he, the city officials and the police didn't agree as to the cost of the fix.

On the West Side, while Big Jim was rising to his prime, other combinations were taking over gambling. Almost up to the end of the nineteenth century, the floozies, the brothels, the gambling houses, and the Irish shebeens (home stills) were in the hands of native-born Protestant stock, Irish Catholics, Jews, and Negroes. Italians were as yet still involved within their own ethnic group, preying on them through the *Black Hand*. But with Johnny Gazzola among the pioneers, the Italians were to move into the mainstream of the Chicago underworld. In crime there was no permanence.

The Loop vice was still held by the Celts: Tom McGinnis, John and Pat O'Malley, Alderman Hinky Dink Kenna, and Bathhouse John Coughlin; gamblers paid off, as did the whores and con men.

The North Side was Mont Tennes's territory, aided by "Hot Stove" Jimmy Quinn, victim of the popular jest, "Jim Quinn, he'd steal a red-hot stove . . ." By 1910 Hot Stove was mostly devoting himself to selling protection—for card games and his own "permits" at $100 to sell whisky. His political muscle for his deeds was Barney Gorgan, a West Side Democratic boss.

Tennes ran gambling on the North Side, where he controlled several hundred bookie joints and was the kingpin in Chicago race track bookmaking. The Illinois Crime Survey gave him a detailed study in one of their published reports: "He was avowedly a real estate man, for a period the owner of a cash register company, and for more than a score of years the proprietor of the General News Bureau, controlling the wires for the gathering and dispensing of race track news in Chicago and principal parts of the United States. Repeated exposés have always found him in control of strings of handbooks and gambling houses in Chicago . . ."

He bought the Payne Telegraph Service of Cincinnati for $300 a day and wired it to poolrooms and bookmakers, each of whom paid $50 to $100. He also got half of their total receipts, out of which Tennes paid half the losses. Tennes controlled every gambling joint in Chicago, for they could not operate without the telegraph service he alone could furnish. The Loop and the South Side syndicates declared war.

In June of 1907, while Tennes was promenading peacefully with his wife, he was set upon by sluggers and beaten. Bombs were planted at places owned by him, and five bombs were set off among his biggest rivals, Jim O'Leary among them. Oddly, some officials were stone deaf. With bombs going off within hearing range, Chief of Police George M. Shippy stated that "there is no gambling worthy of the name in existence here at the present time . . ."

If you can't beat 'em, join 'em, Tennes figured. *Then* take them from the inside. He went to make peace with the other gamblers. The combine worked fine with Mont, by 1909 the ruler of the race track business. He extended his special friendship deeper into the police department and got their happy nod as they counted their payoffs and stood by as he took over the city's biggest dice games, busiest roulette wheels and poker setups. Carter Harrison, Jr., matching his father's record, had just been reelected mayor for the fifth time in 1911 with the help of the vice districts, and the lid was off the city. Hotels ran big dice and card games openly; fifty gambling joints were active in the Loop, taking the marks for their rolls.

Mont Tennes's syndicate had a fair set of rules for payment for every kind of protection fee: Poolrooms, 40 to 50 percent of win; roulette, 40 percent of win; faro, 50 percent of win; craps, 60 percent of win; poker and other games, 50 percent house share.

Mont was most likely the first sanguine crime boss to take nationwide control of many criminal interests. He was the Daniel Boone of big crime, a pioneer of the methods the Capone mob and today's Mafia families were to use with such success, from Vegas to drugs.

In 1910 Mont had set up his own General News Bureau for getting results on horse races and betting odds, sending the old Payne Service into outer darkness. Ninety pool joints as a group in Chicago alone paid him $3,000 a week. He controlled race betting in many states and Canada and bought so many police departments across the country that his gangs could use shotguns and dynamite on any who tried to muscle in on Mont's organizations. His income was said to be several million a year, with no Internal Revenue to plague him. Our modern income tax didn't begin to bother the nation until 1913.

Tennes was investigated right into the 1920s, but he was indicted only once, and he beat that rap. When he retired (the Goo Goos, a Good Government reform movement, had closed 200 of his bookie joints that paid him a yearly profit of $364,000 a year), he sold most of his interests in his horse wire service to the Annenbergs.

Gambling in the East was usually done in the best gambling houses with more decorum, but there were also many popular gambling setups for the man or woman of the lower classes. If the West had few laws against gambling, they were merely winked at. The East did have laws that made gambling illegal, but there were always city officials and police who would look the other way if their pockets were filled. Some even owned shares in protected gambling houses.

One of the best reports on conditions in New York City is included in a detailed description by James D. McCable, Jr., in the book *Lights and Shadows of New York Life* (1872):

> In spite of the fact that games of chance for money are prohibited by the laws of the State of New York, there is no

city in the Union in which they are carried on to a greater extent than in the Metropolis. There are about 200 gambling houses proper in the city, and from 350 to 400 lottery offices, policy shops, and places where gambling is carried on with more or less regularity. About 2,500 persons are known to the police as professional gamblers. Some of the establishments are conducted with great secrecy. Others are carried on with perfect openness, and are as well known as any place of legitimate business in the city. The police, for reasons best known to themselves, decline to execute the laws against them, and they conduct their career from year to year without molestation.

Ninety-five of the gambling houses of the city are classed as "Faro Banks." Faro is the principal game, but there are applicances for others. Faro is emphatically an American game and is preferred by amateurs because of its supposed fairness. An experienced gambler, however, does not need to be told that the game offers as many chances for cheating as any others that are played. It has attained its highest development in New York.

The gambling houses of New York are usually divided into three classes: First and Second Class, and Day Houses. The First-Class Houses are few in number. There are probably not more than half a dozen in all, if as many. In these houses the playing is fair—that is, cheating is never resorted to. In its internal arrangements the house is magnificent. The furniture, carpets, and all its appointments are superb. Choice paintings and works of art are scattered through the rooms in truly regal profusion.

The servants attached to the place are generally negroes of the better class. They are well trained, many of them having been brought up as the *valets* or butlers of the Southern gentry, and answer better for such places than whites, inasmuch as they are quiet, uncommunicative, attentive and respectful. One of these men is always in charge of the front door, and visitors are admitted with caution, it being highly desirable to admit only the nominally respectable. The best known houses are those of Morrissey, in Twenty-fourth street, and Ransom's and Chamberlain's, in Twenty-fifth street. Chamberlain's is, perhaps, the most palatial and the best conducted establishment in the country.

The house is a magnificent brownstone mansion, not far from Broadway. Ascending the broad stone steps and ringing the bell, the visitor is ushered into the hall by the man in charge of the door, who is selected with great care. An attentive colored servant takes his hat and overcoat, and throws open the door of the drawing rooms.

The guests consist of the most distinguished men in the city and country. Chamberlain says frankly he does not care to receive visitors who are possessed of limited incomes and to whom losses would bring misfortune. His visitors are chiefly men who are wealthy and who can afford to lose, or whose high social or political stations make them welcome guests. You may see at his table Governors, Senators, members of Congress and of Legislatures, generals, judges, lawyers, bankers, merchants, great operators in Wall Street, famous actors and authors, journalists, artists—in short, all grades of men who have attained eminence or won wealth in their callings. The early part of the evening is almost exclusively devoted to social enjoyment, and there is very little gambling until after supper, which is served about half-past eleven, after the theatres have closed.

Then the back parlor is the centre of attraction. There is a roulette table on the eastern side of this apartment, said to be the handsomest piece of furniture in the Union. At the opposite side is a large sideboard bountifully provided with liquor and cigars. The faro table stands across the room at the southern end, and is the most popular resort of the guests, though some of the other games find their votaries in other parts of the room.

The table upon which faro is played is not unlike an ordinary dining table with rounded corners. At the middle of one side, the place generally occupied by the head of a family, the dealer sits in a space of about three square feet, which has been fashioned in from the table. The surface is covered with tightly drawn green ladies' cloth. The thirteen suit cards of a whist pack are inlaid upon the surface in two rows, with the odd card placed at the round of the letter U. The dealer has a full pack, which he shuffles, then inserts in a silver box with an open face.

The playing is conducted largely by means of checks on the National banks of the city, men seldom carrying money about their persons. Here Mr. Chamberlain has to use his wits. A check given for gaming purposes is not valid in law. Therefore it is necessary to know his man—to be sure of his wealth, to be certain of his credit.

Next to the First-Class Houses come the Second-Class Houses, or "Hells," as they are called in the city. These lie principally along Broadway and the side streets leading from it, and in the Bowery. They are numerous, and are the most frequented by strangers. They are neither as elegantly furnished, nor as exclusive as to their guests as the First-Class Houses. Anyone may visit them, and they keep a regular force of runners, or "ropers in," for the purpose of enticing strangers within their walls. They are located over stores, as a general rule, and the Broadway establishments usually have a number of flashily dressed, vulgar-looking men about their doors in the daytime, who are insufferably rude to ladies passing by.

Faro is the usual game played at these houses, but it is a very different game from that which goes on under the supervision of John Chamberlain. In gambler's parlance, it is called a "skin game." In plain English it means that the bank sets out to win the player's money by deliberate and premeditated fraud. A common trick is to use sanded cards, or cards with their surfaces roughened, so that two, by being handled in a certain way, will adhere and fall as one card. Again, the dealer will so arrange his cards as to be sure of the exact order in which they will come out. He can thus pull out one card, or two at a time, as the "necessities of the bank" may require. Frequently no tally is kept of the game, and the player is unable to tell how many turns have been made—whether the full number or less. Even if the fraud is discovered, the visitor will find it a serious matter to attempt to expose it. The slightest effort at resistance will ensure an assault, and the guest is either beaten and thrown into the street, or he is robbed and murdered, and his body thrown into the river.

Many persons coming to the city yield to the temptation to visit these places, merely to see them. They intend to lose only a dollar or two as the price of the exhibition. Such men voluntarily seek the danger which threatens them. Nine out of ten who go there merely through curiosity lose all their money. The fascination of the game, however, has now become so great that day gambling houses have been opened in the lower part of the city. These are located on Broadway, below Fulton street, and in one or two other streets within the immediate neighborhood of Wall Street.

Square games are rarely played in these houses. The victim is generally fleeced. Men who gamble in stocks, curbstone brokers, and others, vainly endeavor to make good a part of their losses at these places. They are simply unsuccessful. Clerks, office boys and others who can spend but a few minutes and lose only a few dollars at a time, are constantly seen in these hells. The aggregate of these slight winnings by the bank is very great in the course of the day.

It is not necessary to speak of the evils of gambling, of

the effect of the vice upon society. I have merely to de-
scribe the practice as it prevails here. New York is full of
the wrecks it has made. Respectable and wealthy families
there are by the score whose means have been squandered
on the green cloth. There are widows and orphans here
whose husbands and fathers have been driven into suicide
by gambling losses. The state prisons hold men whose good
names have been blasted, and whose souls have been
stained with crime in consequence of the vice. Yet the evil is
suffered to grow, and no honest effort is made to check it.

Legendary dice shooters may have existed or been invented
by historians of the sport. Two actual great crap shooters were
Nick the Greek and Arnold Rothstein. The last time I saw Nick,
old, broke, and down on his luck, he still spoke of the great
games he played for thousands of dollars with Arnold Rothstein.

"He beat me a lot. Maybe because he had a bigger stack of
money. Yes, I dropped the biggest roll ever seen in a crap game
in the United States, playing with Arnie."

He wouldn't tell me how much, but the opinion among those
close to the gambling grapevine put Nick's loss to Arnold
Rothstein at $600,000 in one night.

That part of the population that never held a pair of dice or a
card hand can be lured into public gambling without becoming
aware of what they are doing, as in the case of the "Bank Night"
games during the Great Depression. To lure patrons into the
motion picture theaters, raffle numbers were printed on each
ticket, and prizes were given after a drawing of lucky numbers.
Everything from pots to groceries was given away on Bank
Night. In one case an offer was made of a "real live baby." It
turned out to be a suckling piglet, but it drew crowds. The lure
of Bank Night was so great that people did not choose the film
they wanted to see but patronized the theater that offered the
biggest prize.

Gambling masked as public welfare was often effective, creating in some a manic euphoria. The Irish Sweepstakes tickets
brought in millions to aid Irish hospitals. State lotteries are now
gaining favor to help reduce taxes. They do add revenues; but
no matter how much tax money or revenue a state collects, it
will find ways of spending it.

The poor and the middle class mostly see nothing wrong in slot machines. When the majority of us think of slot machines, or "one-armed bandits," we think of Las Vegas, Reno, and the Chicago mobs of the 1920s that placed them about in various roadhouses (and shady businesses controlled by organized crime). Actually they date back to 1895, when they were perfected by some unsung Edison of levers and cogs as a way of creating miserly odds against the handle puller. Early forms were designed to produce poker hands on spinning reels. On the "Little Gem," for a nickel one could try to turn up a royal flush to pay five dollars, or a straight flush to get two-fifty. However, as most machines had a suit missing, the odds were often 3,000 to one to hit a royal flush. The "Hi-Lo" was also popular with draw poker players. If a group wanted to play together, there was the "Jockey," using two or three machines connected for cozy twisting of the iron arms.

Losing money could be a very satisfying passion till one comes to wars. Soldiers find soldiering to consist of lots of dull training, boredom in camp or field duty, and dangerous short periods of deadly peril that could lead to injury or death. For the periods of boredom, from the American Revolution through Vietnam, gambling was the most popular form of recreation.

Gates and Rothstein

Some claim that Bet-a-Million Gates was the most bizarre gambler America produced. He has certainly presented us with many legends about his bets. He appeared to move in a world of roles, not realities. One August day in 1902, at the Saratoga track, he lost $400,000 in an afternoon's betting. Dining at the Club House, Canfield's gambling establishment, that night, he went in to play faro and lost $150,000. Asking for an extension of the limits of stakes to $10,000, he sat down to win $300,000 by three in the morning. It remains the biggest faro game in gambling history.

Gates had a simple explanation for his peculiar habit of betting huge sums on almost anything. "For me there's no fun in just betting a few thousand . . . I want to put down enough to hurt the other feller if he loses, and enough to hurt me if I lose."

He was addicted to no-limit poker and to the highest sums

bet at a race track. He insisted on dollar-a-point bridge. He was eccentric about the type of wager he'd take on. He would bet on how many flies would alight on a lump of damp sugar in an hour. If some stranger butted into a card game and asked to sit in, Gates liked to stagger him by the size of the stakes. Once, when a stranger put down $500 and asked for a stack of chips, Gates said to the dealer, "Give the gent *a* chip."

Gates liked a good session of four to six days of poker. At the old Waldorf-Astoria Hotel, with half a dozen sporting millionaires, he played with $1,000 bets. He showed no indication of self-pity or pain when he lost; he expressed glee when he won.

The biggest poker game, according to the *New York Herald*, was one in which Gates played, with a million dollars on the table. Levi Z. Leiter, the wheat speculator and partner of Marshall Field, bluffed Gates with only a pair, to take in a pot of $80,000.

Gates would bet on election returns. When William McKinley beat William Jennings Bryan for the presidency in 1896, Gates was betting in the lobby of the Hoffman House. Half a million dollars was laid out in bets on how the vote would go for the GOP in various states. Gates excused himself from time to time to go "to the gents'." Actually, he rushed over to the party headquarters nearby to check returns. He won $200,000 betting on McKinley.

Horse-racing odds seemed so strange when Gates was betting that it was assumed by many that the races were fixed. No such evidence was ever produced. However, Gates was warned by the New York State Betting Commission that if he continued to place his huge bets he would be barred from the tracks. He took his grandiose wagers elsewhere.

One last word about John W. "Bet-a-Million" Gates. Besides barbed wire, wheat speculations and his gambling, he ran a brokerage house with his son Charles in the Waldorf-Astoria—Harris, Gates & Co. He was a big plunger on Wall Street. As a side issue he would bet with anyone on how much a certain stock would lose or gain. In the panic of 1907 he took huge losses in the market, and finally gave it up. He repeated a well-known saying about stock-market dealings: "Sometimes the bulls win, sometimes the bears; the hogs, never." He went back to the steel business and recovered much of his losses.

Like a reformed courtesan who finds God in old age, he

WIN OR LOSE / 166

appeared in 1909 before a meeting of preachers of the Southern Methodist Church in Texas and gave the assembled ministers some advice. "Don't gamble, play cards, bet on horses, speculate in wheat or on the stock exchange, and don't shirk honest labor." There is no record that he ever did such labor. He died two years later at the age of fifty-six. The *New York Herald* wrote of him and his millionaire fellow gamblers: "They set so hot a pace . . . few could be found able and willing to follow them."

The gambling urge seems to have been inherited by his son. In 1910, Charles, to celebrate his recovery from an appendicitis operation, lost $40,000 at faro and roulette in a gambling house on West 46th Street, run by the notorious Arnold Rothstein.

Rothstein had the composure of a church deacon when he was in a tight corner. His reflexes were fast, and as with most professionals he had the endurance to play through long nights in succession. He never drank, and seemed able to control his hair-trigger temper until a desire to win or crush an opponent took possession of him. In his youth, he was one of the great pool hustlers of his time, exhibiting cool skill and perfect muscle control combined with a sharpshooter's eye. In 1909 he played a thirty-two-hour game against the champion pool player of the Philadelphia Racquet Club, winning $6,000 in side bets.

Known as "The Brain," Rothstein was always available to hold and place bets of any amount. He seems to have been trusted as fairly honest (for a gambler); actually he dealt with the underworld as a crime backer and fence. He expressed himself publicly when August Belmont refused to admit him to the Belmont race track because his bets paid off too well.

"Most of the human race are dubs and dumbbells. They have rotten judgment and no brains, and when you learn how to do things and how to size people up and dope out methods for yourself, they jump to the conclusion that you are crooked."

Rothstein went to see Belmont, and he was again permitted to attend the Belmont track, and he continued to bet heavily. His masterpiece, however, was the rigging of the 1919 World Series.

Baseball fans accept Abner Doubleday as the inventor or the popularizer of the American game of baseball. Its true forerunner was the old game of rounders. By 1786, as "baseball" it was tough enough to be banned at Princeton. From 1820 to 1833 it was known in Eastern cities as "Town Ball." In 1845, in New York City, Alexander Cartwright set down the basic rules that were to be followed by players from then on. The next year the first game of record by his rules was played in Hoboken, New Jersey, the "New York Nine" defeating the "Knickerbockers" 23 to 1 in four innings. The first professional team appeared in 1869 as the Cincinnati Red Stockings. From such beginnings the big leagues emerged into an affluent business to the delight of gamblers. By 1919 baseball was taking in millions of dollars at the gate. That was the year a cabal of gamblers rigged a World Series.

The World Series opened that year in Cincinnati on October 1 on a sizzler of a day. The city was decked in bunting, with bands playing, as it anticipated its first World Series game. The Reds were heroes. Seats for the first two games were all gone, and ticket speculators were scalping the public at $50 a pair. The town was jumping; hotels were packed, whisky flasks were everywhere, and kegs of beer foamed in private suites.

The crowds arrived early at Redland Park. More than 30,000 fans packed the stands, chomped peanuts, guzzled pop, devoured hot dogs. The fans were proud of the team that had won the right to play in a World Series, but few had much hope of beating the powerful Chicago White Sox.

When the umpire yelled "Play ball!" the idea that a scheme was afoot to throw the Series occurred to none of them.

To understand how all this came about, let us begin with a bookmaker named Joseph Sullivan, known as "Sport" Sullivan. Three weeks before the opening game, he was at the Hotel Buckminster in Boston, calling on Chick Gandil, the White Sox first baseman. Chick had played pro ball for fourteen years. He was thirty-one, and in a few years he'd be out of big-time baseball.

Chick had a proposition for Sullivan. He could persuade enough of his pals on the team to throw the Series to the Reds, who were expected to lose. "We want $80,000," he said. Sullivan remained poker-faced. He said he would think it over. He didn't mind breaking the law, he told Chick, but fixing a World Series was something to think about!

Chick Gandil had been brooding for some time. Charlie

Comiskey, owner of the White Sox, was a mean and greedy man. Charlie had designed Comiskey Park for his team's games. Most of his stars got less than $6,000 a year, and pro baseball was like slave labor, under contracts that favored the owners. Players on other teams not nearly as good as the White Sox often got $12,000 a season. There were no pensions, and the owner allowed the men only three dollars for meals on the road.

Chick had put the idea of throwing the Series to his buddy Eddie Cicotte, the pitcher. Eddie had money troubles, a heavy mortgage on his farm in Michigan, and a family that liked to live well.

One night, as the Pullman car took the team to Boston, Eddie Cicotte agreed. For $10,000, the gamblers' fix of the Series was settled.

The White Sox sell-outs insisted on the cash in advance. Chick agreed. Another pitcher was needed: Eddie Cicotte and Lefty Williams would probably pitch the five out of nine games the Series would most likely run. In came Swede Risberg and Fred McMullin. Now to convince Buck Weaver, "Shoeless Joe" Jackson, and Happy Felsch. That would do it.

On September 21, 1919, the chosen eight were in Chick Gandil's room at the Ansonia, talking things over. Chick explained that Sport Sullivan would get them the $80,000. They would be paid off before the first game. As to what games would be thrown, that depended on how the gamblers wanted to juggle the odds.

Eddie Cicotte had been promised, in 1917, a bonus of $10,000 if he won thirty games. But Charlie Comiskey had Eddie benched when the player came close to that payoff figure. He also had promised fine bonuses to the team if they won the pennant that year. He paid off with a case of cheap champagne for the whole team.

Sullivan and his friends, after failing to raise the payoff money, said there was only one man who had the loot and might back the fix: Arnold Rothstein.

Rothstein ran politically protected gambling houses. At Saratoga he spent over $100,000 converting a mansion into a plush gambling house. Fortunes were lost there by Harry Sinclair, the oil man; Charlie Stoneham, owner of the New

York Giants; Sam Rosoff, who built subways and took care of the Tammany boys in turn; and even Nick the Greek. Rothstein was said to be a millionaire a few times over from his gambling ventures. But he was eager for bigger gains and newer angles.

He was told of a possible fix in the coming World Series. He was at the Jamaica race track when two of Sullivan's friends approached him with the idea. Rothstein shook his head. "I don't think it will work." In the end, however, Rothstein promised the bribe money.

Rothstein was going to work with Sport Sullivan as his contact with the boys. The players would get $40,000 up front. The second $40,000 would be in the safe of the Hotel Congress in Chicago. If the boys carried on as they should, it was there to pay them off. He had other things to do, like getting down all the bets he could, particularly very big bets on the Cincinnati Reds to win the 1919 Series.

Rothstein let his pigeons know that he was making book on the Series. He got his pal Harry F. Sinclair to bet $90,000 at good odds on the White Sox. Another pigeon was Nick the Greek, whom Rothstein had taken for $250,000 in dice and cards the year before. Nick was broke, but he felt he could touch Rothstein for a loan. Rothstein said, "Why not?" and gave him $25,000, then offered him a "sure-thing" tip. "Put it on the Cincinnati Reds for the Series."

In all, Rothstein put out $270,000 on the Reds. He had a million or so more to bet, but felt, at that stage of the fix, that it would work out all the way in his favor. He didn't want to go in too far.

A go-between cheated the ballplayers out of $30,000 in bribes; he gave Gandil only a $10,000 down payment. "The odds are dropping . . . has one of your players leaked something out?"

The players had agreed to throw the first two games by errors, dropped balls, bad fielding, and easy pitches.

The day of the game, the betting was heavy. The Cincinnati bettors were backing their team, and the even-money betting held. The day was hot, the crowd wild; and the ball game was, as planned, a disaster for the White Sox. The Reds won the first game of the Series 9 to 1.

The boys said no more games would be thrown unless the rest of the money was on the line. However, they were in the noose. To collect, they had to go through with the deal. The odds of 8 to 5 against the White Sox were now 5 to 4, and Rothstein was worried. It was too easy.

The boys stayed fixed, in hopes of the sight of money. They lost the second game to the Reds, 4 to 2.

Rumors spread. Sportswriters like Ring Lardner took them seriously. He put it to Cicotte: "How come the first two games were so lousy?"

Cicotte replied, "I was just off form." Next game, Cincinnati edged out the White Sox 2–0.

Chick Gandil counted $20,000 in new $1,000 bills that some faceless man had silently delivered to him. He divided up what had been collected: $5,000 each to Swede Risberg, Hal Flesch, Lefty Williams and Shoeless Joe Jackson. Cicotte already had $10,000 from the first payoff.

In the end, a World Series of absurdities and senseless bad taste was successfully rigged. Gamblers made millions; the public lost millions; and baseball was never again the pure and honest American game.

In time, after an investigation by a grand jury, eight ballplayers were indicted. Most of the ballplayers involved testified. Some confessed. It made front-page headlines:

EIGHT WHITE SOX PLAYERS ARE INDICTED
ON CHARGES OF FIXING 1919 WORLD SERIES:
Cicotte got $10,000 and Jackson $5,000.

TWO OF PLAYERS CONFESS.
Cicotte and Jackson tell of their work
in throwing games to Cincinnati.

Rothstein was called to testify. The twelve decent and simple men of the jury, still believing in the good clean game, came in with their verdict. A cheer went up. The ballplayers were all found not guilty.

A defense attorney said with a straight face, "The verdict is a complete vindication of the most mistreated ballplayers in history."

The *New York Times* commented: "The Chicago White Sox are

once more whiter than snow. A jury has said that they are not guilty, so that settles that. The Court instructed the jury to determine whether the defendants intended to defraud the public and others and not merely to throw ball games. To the lay mind, this sounds very much like asking whether the defendant intended to murder his victim or merely to cut his head off."

The ballplayers who were found not guilty went on to play ball in outlaw or semi-pro clubs for a few years. The one line from the whole affair that entered American folklore was spoken after the first grand jury hearing, after Shoeless Joe Jackson had made a full confession. As Jackson departed from the grand jury room, a small boy tagged after him, clutching his sleeve.

"Say it ain't so, Joe!" he pleaded. "Say it ain't so!"

"Kid, I'm afraid it is."

Rothstein got off Scot-free for his rigging of the baseball series. He continued to play in high-stake poker games and to attend horse races as a heavy bettor.

Whatever his system on the track was, in 1921 he won $800,000 at Aqueduct on a horse that appeared on the track as a last-minute entry and at huge odds. On the first Dempsey-Tunney fight, he admitted to half a million in winnings.

But, as often happens to gamblers, he died broke. By the end of 1928, either Rothstein's luck had turned or his skills had deserted him. He had lost $340,000 in a high-stake spade game (cutting a deck: the holder of the highest spade was the winner) and was welshing on paying off most of it. He claimed he had been in a crooked game. There were many such disastrous sessions, and his horses were riding out of the money.

He usually played cards with half a dozen big-time gamblers in a floating game run by a man named O'Reilly. It was to these hard characters that he lost the $340,000. He offered an IOU, insisting, "You'll have to wait. I'm Rothstein. That name ought to be good for the money."

A week later, his provocative claim of a crooked game being disallowed, the winners began to lean on him, hard. A Chicago hit man was reportedly in town to collect the money or kill him. Certain cops whom he had bribed warned Rothstein. He shook his head. "I'm not going to pay off a red cent. That goes for the gamblers and the gorillas. If they're looking for me, I'll be at Lindy's."

In the 1920s Lindy's on Broadway was a hangout for gamblers. Rothstein was having coffee with friends there on a cool November night. He was called to the phone and returned to tell his friends it was a sore loser, George McManus, who demanded his $51,000 winnings, and that McManus wanted to settle the debt and make peace between Rothstein and the other gamblers, at the Park Central Hotel. No one close to the event cared to talk of what happened after Rothstein left.

An hour before midnight, Rothstein was found near the hotel's service entrance with a .38-caliber slug in his stomach and $6,500 in his billfold. He was taken to the Polyclinic Hospital. True to the code of the underworld, he gave his name but nothing else.

George McManus and three others were tried for the murder of Arnold Rothstein. The jury failed to convict, and a directed verdict of acquittal was asked for and received.

Rothstein died on Election Day, with bets on Herbert Hoover that would have paid him half a million dollars. His departure from the world, however, voided all his winning wagers.

11

TWENTIETH-CENTURY GAMBLING

"Truth is," said the Palm Beach sportsman, a gentleman listed in the *Social Register,* as we sipped mint juleps, "we here always considered Miami Beach a sort of slovenly tramp who somehow got into the wrong part of town. I'm not being facetious, but her ideas of gambling never had the class of our Beach Club."

This comment expresses better than any survey the attitude of Palm Beach toward its more noisy middle-class neighbor to the south.

The sportsman lifted his second julep into the balmy Florida air. "To Colonel Edward Riley Bradley, who ran the Beach Club and introduced respectable wives and sweethearts to gambling."

There are older people still around, mostly insulated by the invulnerability of class and money, who remember the Colonel and the Beach Club in Palm Beach.

It had begun with Henry Morrison Flagler and his railroad, the first to run from the North to Florida. He built up the land around the railway, with here and there a hotel, a church, and certain places where gentlemen could handle cards or bet on the wheel. In 1894 his progress reached Palm Beach, where he built the Royal Poinciana Hotel and added the Royal Poinciana Chapel and the Beach Club.

Flagler was a man who hired the best. For his gambling club he chose a man who had risen to importance as a professional gambler. Edward Riley Bradley was no silver-spoon product of "The 400" (defined as those worthy of being in exclusive New York Society) or member of the Astor or Vanderbilt set. He was born into a poor Irish worker's family in the Pennsylvania steel-mill country. At thirteen he toiled on the end of a steel puddler's rod, running pig iron. After a year of this he ran away, heading west, as did most runaways. During the 1870s he herded cattle, mined, raised horses, became a skilled gambler, played frontier poker, and served as a scout in the Indian wars of the Great Plains. Mostly, he learned to keep his head clear in a lusty, imperfect world.

"The Colonel used to tell my father," said the julep drinker, "that he was in the campaigns against Apaches, and he was with the horse soldiers who captured old Geronimo. If anyone doubted him, he was ready to bet he was there. Perhaps he was; nobody ever tried to prove he wasn't. What can be proved was that after the Indian troubles he became a professional gambler. He told some senator holding one of those damn investigating sessions, 'Yes, I am a gambler.'

"My father remembers him as a bookie in Little Rock and Memphis. He was a smart bookie, more than likely, or the bettors were dumb. But he made a lot of money and began to work the tracks around Chicago and St. Louis, and then in Maryland and New York. He began to own horses, and eventually bought a hotel in Chicago. He moved to Kentucky, where he had his own stable, Idle Hour Farms. Would you believe his horses won the Kentucky Derby? Four winners in the Churchill Downs Kentucky Derby.

"Bradley in Kentucky saw how well Canfield and others were doing with fashionable gambling casinos. He gave up taking horse bets and established himself with gambling houses well protected by political power in Long Beach [New Jersey] and Rockaway [Long Island]. He took to carrying a cane with a meerschaum handle and gold ferrule.

"Moving to Florida, he and a brother ran the Bacchus Club, a Flagler enterprise in St. Augustine. Then he took the job of casino manager at the Beach Club in Palm Beach.

"It was not much of a place, originally. No fountains, no ornate grill work or mottled, colored marble interior. It was a white house of frame construction on Main Street and Lake Worth, set up as 'a gambling establishment for gentlemen only.' Its charter insisted it was run for 'games of amusement as the management and members may from time to time agree upon.'

This 1879 print shows serious women gamblers turning their full attention to cards. *Ross collection*

LEFT: Leland Stanford bet a fortune that a running horse had all four legs off the ground at the same time. *Ross collection*

RIGHT: Diamond Jim Brady lived a good life worth the money.

It was said that she picked winning horses with a hat pin, but won as often as most handicappers.   *Author's collection*

No longer standing, the Grand Union Hotel was the favorite hangout for Saratoga's gambling set.   *Ross collection*

Canfield's Saratoga—the most famous gambling house in the nation in 1889.   *Author's collection*

A race-track scene about a hundred years ago when the costumes of visitors were gayer.   *Author's collection*

An 1874 print of a proper pacer making a run for it in a harness-racing meet.   *Author's collection*

Arnold Rothstein fixed the
World Series of 1919.
Ross collection

The Belmont Stakes
and the Belmont race-
track are named after
their founder August
Belmont. Two of his
horses placed first
and second in the
Futurity Stakes
in 1880.
Author's collection

Taking the turn at Aqueduct. In a close race, the jockeys ride well over the horses' necks. *Courtesy of the New York Racing Association*

A California newspaper ad advocating legal dog racing and track betting. *Author's collection*

The greyhound is an intriguing blend of grace, power, and speed. Born to run, this skillful performer inspired man 5,000 years ago to create a sport that has emerged into the 20th century more exciting and entertaining than ever.

Las Vegas in 1906 was a railroad supply station with no hope of being anything but a desert outpost. *Private collection*

Part of an ad for a book that claims to reveal all about blackjack. *Author's collection*

ADVERTISING SUPPLEMENT TO THE LOS ANGELES TIMES

MAKE EVERY CASINO IN THE WORLD YOUR UNLIMITED, PRIVATE BANK ACCOUNT!
The skilled Blackjack player can travel the world—free!

If you ever intended to step inside a gambling casino then reading this book, **HOW TO WIN AT WEEKEND BLACKJACK by Stanley Roberts, is a must. Your fortune, your ego and your personal welfare are at stake.**

Casino owners all over the world have been taking money from the gambling public for years. Preying upon human frailties, emotions, inadequacies and plain ignorance, these operators have been separating people from their money . . . and making them like it. Yes, to most people who vacation at a gambling resort winning is only a faint hope. They expect to lose . . . and they do. **But they don't have to!!!**

Gambling Casinos make their money on games of CHANCE by paying LESS than the correct odds on EVERY bet you make. This is called the house "edge" or "vigorish." Unlike the other casino banked games, such as Craps, Roulette, Keno and the Slots, **Blackjack or "21" is not a game of chance,** but a game of SKILL. In spite of this the house still collects its edge in this game because better than 99% of those who play know very little about the game. The game survives on *public ignorance.*

LET OTHERS MAKE DEPOSITS WHILE YOU MAKE WITHDRAWALS

● The Dealers . . . how and why they may cheat . . . how they cheat the house.
● Players who cheat and how they do it.
● Bankrolling your play . . . how much you need . . . where to get it . . .
● A Super Bonus section on how to collect an additional $50 per day FREE – EVERY DAY . . . These are but a few of the facts you will learn that will make YOU a WINNER every time you play.

WE'LL MAKE YOU AN OFFER YOU CAN'T REFUSE
We are going to make you an offer that every person who will ever enter a gambling casino again must accept. We are going to give you **MORE THAN DOUBLE YOUR MONEY BACK** even though you'll love the book. You will virtually be getting this book FREE. Through this offer you will actually get back more CASH than you sent us . . . With your order we will give you certificates worth $120 for your next Las Vegas trip. They include $24 in CASH, $32 in Lucky Bucks, plus drinks, souvenirs and 8 meals. These bonuses are supplied by other businesses who promote Las Vegas casinos. Casinos will not know you have our book.

★ A Super Special 3 day/2 night Las Vegas Bonus, A FREE DELUXE ROOM, is sent to all orders received within ten days.

ABOUT THE AUTHOR
The author, Stanley Roberts, is a licensed Architect, Real Estate Broker and a City Planning Consultant. With the aid of a computer, he figured out how to beat the tables in Las Vegas to raise the capital to build his own buildings. Now, *successfully engaged in three businesses, which earn several times the $500 a day practical limit for a professional Blackjack player, he has released his secrets for public use.*

Nevada has no state or inheritance taxes. Its share of the gambling play keeps it going. Note the legs of the guard at the top of the photo—he watches the play, looking for cheaters.

Printed with permission of Harrah's Club

"The Colonel—a title hardly relating to his war record as a lonely scout against the men of the plains—insisted that evening clothes be the ticket of admission to the club, and no one younger than twenty-five was allowed on the premises. Drunks were not passed on to the hazard games and roulette tables. No women were allowed to play at the tables, nor were the 'natives,' meaning local Floridians—servants, crackers, rednecks and poor whites. The Colonel did not show a profit after a year, and seeing the eager interest in gambling shown by the society matrons and their daughters, he opened the play to them. It was the salvation of the Beach Club; often the females were its heaviest plungers. "Well, you see, lonely rich widows and divorcees often grab gambling like a barracuda grabs a baited hook. The accepted ones moved to Palm Beach.

"With success, a funny thing happened. Old man Flagler got 'the call.' Yes, to save his soul, he turned against gambling and tried to force the Colonel to give up the Beach Club. Well, the Colonel was a charmer, but a hard man to remove. He must have had an ironclad agreement with Flagler. My father always insisted the Colonel was offered nearly half a million dollars to get out of town. Well, maybe it was a little less. But Colonel Bradley just stood pat, and the two men really went at it hot and heavy. Why, Flagler even hired hell-fire preachers to cry out from the Royal Poinciana Chapel that gambling was the road to hell, the ruin of the young, the curse of the aged in their last years.

"Bradley prospered and moved to a new place. What made the Colonel a success besides that Celtic charm? Well, he ran an honest place, and if any house man—he paid them like fifty dollars a day plus keep—ever tried anything not right on his own, the Colonel booted him out. Then, too, the club had some great chefs. He'd pay them $25,000 to $30,000 a season, and you never ate such gumbos and crab bisques. The way to a gambler's wallet is often through his stomach. My father was nearly ruined by coquilles Saint Jacques and hazard.

"Hazard is a kind of chuck-a-luck game. The Colonel felt he wanted a bit more action than that, and in 1923 he set up chemin-de-fer tables. Lord, that paid off! About three million the first year. I was just out of Princeton then, and in 1928 it was a pleasure to come to the club and see all the superbly gowned ladies and the men in evening clothes, and the barmen mixing those horse's necks, gin fizzes and sidecars. I'd meet big players: plungers like a Whitney, a Studebaker, a Sinclair, an Astor, a Vanderbilt. One man lost $200,000 in a season. And Palm Beach season is really three months, while the blizzards blow up North. But the heavy losers never made any trouble. No one ever committed suicide. There was a real robbery attempt—I mean with guns and masks. A sensation. Now you can't walk downtown without suspecting a mugger.

"Poker at the club was for the richest of Palm Beach residents. Select groups would set up a poker session, and a chip could cost $5,000 or $10,000. John Cosden, a man who got control of a lot of oil wells, came to Palm Beach and gambled for big stakes. In one hand at poker he pulled in nearly $900,000. You didn't have to fear being waylaid or the club being raided. The city fathers, of course, didn't make waves, and the Colonel always had eighteen or twenty Pinkertons around, mixing with the guests. The preachers could preach and the bluenoses howl, but the Colonel stayed open and was well liked. Of course he had what you call the PR sense. He laid out money for charity. When a storm knocked out churches, he paid the damage—Catholic, Protestant or whatever.

"He owned the two local newspapers, the *Post* and the *Times*, and the reporting was about sun and sand, parties, and names in the *Social Register*. Women liked to see their names and their pictures in hostess gowns in the paper. Palm Beach was one of the few places outside of Monte, in those days, where society could play cards, bet $10,000, $50,000 on a hand."

Actually, the Colonel never had an easy time of it at those periods when reform elements complained of gambling. Back in 1915, the Colonel and his brother were jailed for running a gambling house. However, the grand jury took no action, and the Bradleys went free. In 1937 a Florida governor vowed to end the reign of gambling in Florida. The Colonel just stayed open and was never even touched. Political speechmaking was a farce to Florida voters.

Pictures of the Colonel show him to have been a solid-looking man with a gleam in his introspective eye. He had built his own church [St. Edwards] and was a pious member of his congregation. He bred splendid horses at the Idle Hour Farms, and he enjoyed watching the Bradley racing colors in action. He raced at Saratoga, at Belmont and in Maryland. At Saratoga his friends would join him at his elaborate dinners and watch the trainers and exercise boys work the Bradley thoroughbreds.

But, every season, he was back in Palm Beach at the club by January. The papers insisted that Palm Beach was popular not for its sunshine or society or hotels; Bradley's club was the attraction.

But he was mortal and old. Colonel Edward Riley Bradley died in 1946.

"And that ended it," said the sportsman. "He left the damnedest will you ever read. The Beach Club was to be torn down, and all the gambling tables, wheels, chips—all the stuff—were to be barged out a couple of miles and dumped into the ocean. The club site became a public park, fully deeded by the Colonel. I suppose under it all was a sense of middle-class morality."

The Idle Hour Farm was later sold for $2,500,000. Gambling still goes on in Palm Beach. And of course there are places where horse bets are taken. But it isn't the same, according to those who remember the Colonel.

Closest rival to Las Vegas and Reno, and with a longer history of gambling, is Miami Beach. Some claim that Ponce de Leon sailed into Biscayne Bay in 1513, betting that a fountain of youth existed someplace near Miami. Later, Spanish missionaries fought the insect life. In the early 1800s there was a military post nearby, called Fort Dallas.

Miami came into bloom in 1870, when a man named Henry B. Lum appeared and found some Tekesta Indians in possession as squatters. Lum saw the Miami site as just the place for planting a coconut grove. He set out nearly half a million coconuts. But rabbits, deer and raccoons ate the young trees. The nut gamble was a failure. Only a few families moved into the beach area, to a lonely life of bucolic simplicity. The place stagnated until 1890, when the flamboyant Henry Morrison Flagler began building that rail line southward, stocking it with hotels along the route. Reaching Palm Beach in 1895, Flagler went nearly a hundred miles farther south, to Miami. The rest is the history of boom times and busts, speculators and land salesmen. By 1912 there was a bridge from Miami to the sand spit, Miami Beach, and by the 1920s the great land boom was on.

Little gambling was done in the early days, just small bets on yacht races, lawn games and private card games. Then in the late 1920s Al Capone moved into Miami. The first gambling house in Miami was run by two men named McCloud and Meyer, at their Beach and Tennis Club. It featured no outdoor sports, but did have Helen Morgan singing, usually seated on a piano, while the gambling went on. It was "a class joint," as the partners put it, featuring gourmet food and tropical *Gemüt-lichkeit*. One had to have a bank roll to get in. The partners expanded their operations to other gambling places called the Embassy Club and the Brook Club. Capone had a share of many enterprises and hotels where gambling was the main activity. His was often as much as a quarter share of the take. He tried to muscle in to the Villa Venice and the Deauville Casino. There was talk of Chicago-style warfare. Those who refused Capone's demands brought in their own gunmen to protect their interests. The sheriff's office was enormously profitable; it cost one gambling-house owner $1,000 a week to keep the sheriff's men off his back. The local law had an insatiable appetite for graft.

In the 1930s Miami Beach became an early Las Vegas for tourists, show folk, and the mob. Clubs featured stars like Jack Benny, Sophie Tucker, and Eddie Cantor. Capone, physically and mentally debilitated in the late 1930s, was no longer a factor in competition, and men like Frank Nitti, Meyer Lansky, and Frank Costello controlled the Florida gambling interests. Race tracks opened; dog tracks were set up. It was clear, as Westbrook Pegler wrote, that one could "buy local officials, state legislators and other politicians. . . . Race track lobbyists openly haunted the legislature, and men . . . placed themselves under obligation to racketeers."

Despite the Depression, by 1931 Joseph E. Widener had built up the busted Hialeah race track into big time, with flamingos decorating the track's lagoons. Tropical Park, another track, also expanded into a great success for a time, and the pari-mutuel law was passed to make the business of betting a valued source of revenue. But Tropical Park went broke, and the mob moved in. The track then set a record for crooked racing. In 1941 the state stepped in and threatened to recall its racing license. The mob sold out to a syndicate, the American To-talizer Corporation.

Dog racing flourished around Miami Beach. The dogs

chased electric hares. The Miami Beach Kennel Club (the word "club" covered a multitude of projects in the South, some of them shady), the Biscayne Kennel Club, the East Flagler, and the Hollywood Dog Track brought in about $12 million a year in state taxes.

I asked Alex Lateal, with twenty years' experience in dog racing, how to pick a winner. "Listen, them mutts have about as much class as a trash-food joint's hamburger on a bun, as far as I can see. They used to fix them in the old days, give some favorite hound a heavy meal, or give a winner-to-be a hot enema. But today they just let the mutts chase the electric bunny. Most of the union-pension crowd and Social Security folk put in two bits each to buy a two-dollar ticket. Who picks the hound? There's a regular meeting on the choice. Every Tom, Dick and Harry has a favorite. It keeps them hopping and lively. There was a breeder here a couple years ago, had a greyhound he named Moshe Dayan, and all the older *shul* crowd bet heavy on him. The dog lost, and one of the bettors is said to have protested, 'It was a swindle. That dog was a ringer; he was not circumcised, even.' "

The older pension and Social Security crowd from the retirement hotels don't attend the jai-alai games very often. The odds are made on a *quiniela* wheel. Shapely Cuban girls move about taking bets and paying off right on the fronton court. In the *quiniela* bet, two post positions are selected, and to win they must finish either first and second or second and first. "It's a kind of hard and fast handball off the walls," Alex told me. "The players are usually Basques and exiled Cubans still crying about how rich they were in Havana. It's no small-time sport. There are half a dozen games in the district. The Miami jai-alai fronton court is right at the Miami Airport. It can attract nearly a thousand people a night. Bets sometimes run to $400,000 a night."

The state, in a three-month period of jai-alai, takes in over $15,000 in taxes. The horse races, of course, make this look small, paying the state about $45 million a year.

The jai-alai players are professionals, the heroes of the huge Cuban refugee colonies in Miami and Miami Beach. Gregorio Solozabal, a Basque, plays part-time and also runs a food shop featuring Latin delicacies.

"I play good," he says, "but I play not for money, which is

good to have, but for the crowd. The women I like; the ladies like the players. We move like the ballet, they say. And why not? It's good to see our bodies. So when they come with the fat old men, the women have eyes for us. They tell the men who are playing how to bet the *quiniela*. Yes, we made too many friends with gamblers. You understand, we sent money back to the Basque nation underground to free us from Spain. So we all are helped by American gambling to win our freedom."

In 1950 Senator Estes Kefauver came to Miami with his special crime investigation committee. He found that the 200 or more bookmakers had been forced into an organization by four mob men. The S & G Syndicate controlled the gambling setups, the bets, and the payoff. Kefauver wanted to know what S & G stood for, and was told, "Stop and Go." The method the S & G gang set up to drive out-of-town gambling-house operators and bookies into their arms was to connect with the Miami Beach City Council, then send detectives out to warn hotels and others leasing to the out-of-towners that they must deal with the S & G. One local sheriff, on a salary of $7,500, was banking $70,000 a year.

By the middle of the 1940s, the S & G mob was making over $20 million a year, with profits running into the millions for the clubs. Later, shops and hotels permitted S & G bookies to take bets on the premises. The payoffs grew even bigger. A deputy sheriff could collect $50,000 a year in protection grease, as it was called.

Other outsiders came in with heavy muscle and opened gambling casinos—the Club Bohemie, Colonial Inn, Island Club, and others. Citizens worried over heavy investments in real estate and assorted businesses formed, in 1947, "The Secret Six." They hired an ex-FBI man to seek out evidence on the S & G clique—its horse parlors, numbers-game control, and other illegal doings. This led to a Miami Crime Commission and news accounts of crime running rampant in Florida. But the S & G continued to flourish, until heirs of the Chicago mob came down and cut off their wire service. The S & G saw the light, and the Chicago invaders took over a good share of the setup. There was no more interruption of bookie service; it was like a big-business merger.

Kefauver exposed the fact that the Boca Raton, the Roney

Plaza and the Hollywood Beach Hotel had extremely profitable bookie concessions connected with such individuals as Meyer Lansky and Joe Adonis. Poker, roulette, blackjack and dice were available to one and all.

A pit man, Morrie Brown, a former Lansky associate who now spends his time fishing, remembers the great days and the scandals when payoff investigations reached right into the Florida governor's mansion: "It was like opening a rat's nest when the rackets were exposed in City Hall—lawsuits, arrests, indictments of the city fathers. It led—a trail of $100 bills— right into the capitol at Tallahassee. The old fat sheriffs ran with the loot, and new sheriffs got in. Old Meyer Lansky, fast as a fox with a chicken, got all his gambling gear together and rushed over to Havana, where they lasted until Castro came in. Then the mob moved to Vegas. The IRS grabbed up anything they could for unpaid income taxes. Oh, not all the big crime boys left; the Mafiosi still got the big homes down here. Sure, you can play blackjack, toss dice, go for roulette all over the county. But you want action, I'll give you sixteen addresses right outa my head right now."

While some of the mob went into respectable enterprises in Miami as a coverup, gambling continued in Miami Beach. The *Miami Herald* reported that almost every racket known to man was operating. As Polly Redford reveals in her book, *Billion Dollar Sandbar*, the newspaper's investigators found "gambling, prostitution . . . jewel snatches . . . protection, extortion, etc. Syndicate gangsters owned major hotels, restaurants, night-clubs, and were heavy investors in service industries. . . ."

In Las Vegas there were problems, even if gambling was legal and supported the state. No one admitted how deep the criminal element, the Mafia and others, was inside the big Nevada casinos. But efforts were made to seek them out. In March 1976, having gotten information on past dealings with interests linked to Meyer Lansky, Nevada authorities acted to make the corporate owner of Caesar's Palace and the Thunderbird accountable for its future conduct. The Nevada Gaming Commission made Caesar's World, Inc., of Los Angeles, the publicly traded parent firm of the two Las Vegas hotel-casinos, follow strict regulations regarding loans to persons of unsavory reputation.

A controlling shareholder of Caesar's World reportedly was warned in 1972 by Nevada gaming commissioners about his association with men linked in business with criminals.

Harrah's Place

Not all gambling casinos are run by the Mafia or their stooges, as the public suspects, or by hard characters with shady pasts. Out in the open is William Fisk Harrah, a man in his sixties, who runs Harrah's Club in Reno.

Harrah is the big man of the Reno-Tahoe gambling establishments, and his idea of fun is to increase the tempo of the game. His place is the only one of its kind listed on the New York Stock Exchange. Harrah's income increases annually. His 1975 revenues of $127.8 million, for a net profit of $10.6 million, was 16 percent over the previous year.

Bill Harrah did not come out of a ghetto. His father, an Iowa lawyer, owned buildings in Venice, California. John Harrah converted one structure into a bingo parlor. Bill, then a twenty-year-old sophomore at UCLA, quit school to help run the place. The boy was critical of the operation. His father said, "Can you do better?"

"Yes," said Bill, who then bought him out for $500 and soon netted $10,000 at the game. Bingo in Venice became a target for law enforcement, while Nevada made a bid for tourists by legalizing gambling. Bill moved to Reno, paid $2,000 to open a bingo parlor, and failed. He tried again, this time adding dice, roulette, and card games. That was the proper combination; he added slot machines and pretty girl dealers. He saw that atmosphere, lights, color, and a "good time" setting increased trade—and the lure of gambling. He added bells and lights on slot machines. Every jackpot became a celebration, and he advertised his payoffs as very generous.

He improved his club's setting and its hired hands, put his dealer through a good training course, got a Hollywood designer to dress them, and allowed no smoking, drinking or chewing gum on duty. General Motors or U. S. Steel could not have found a better manager for their corporations than William Harrah.

When Las Vegas began to hire big stars for its stage shows, Harrah's had to follow. Bill went whole hog to please stars, as

Las Vegas did. He paid big salaries, offered servant-staffed guest lodging, boats, and chauffeur-driven cars.

He has been married six times (twice to his first wife). The present Mrs. Harrah, half his age, is a blue-eyed ash-blonde, a former cocktail waitress. They live on a 162-acre spread, Rancharrah, in Reno. Their home, guarded by a security force, has a patio for outdoor entertaining and a small lake with swans.

Rules for gambling in Reno closely follow those for Las Vegas. If they heeded advice from habitual gamblers, casino owners, pit men and blackjack dealers, the tourists and small gamblers would know they have little chance of winning in the long run.

After I had interviewed some fifty gamblers and casino managers, their advice could be boiled down to this: Gamble if you like, but be aware that the chances are against you. If you are playing with small stakes for the fun of it, fine. If you are an average citizen, most likely you are lured by hope. If you don't know the odds, the sense of counting cards, or the dice table sideline betting, it's best to start with an amount you can afford to lose. If, after a few hands or rolls or wheel spins, you're ahead, put half of your winnings away in your pocket and play with the rest. If your luck holds, keep pulling half back every three or four plays. Then play until you lose the rest, which you will.

But what about those who exist for serious gambling—the addicts, the trapped? For the lucky or unlucky, the advice is: Study your game and know the house cut. Research the betting odds at dice, the wheel, or cards. Serious gambling takes special knowledge, a cool temperament, the ability to fight off wild hunches, and, most important, a real sense of when to quit.

Do casino owners and managers follow their own advice? Hardly ever. I have heard stories from them of their own misfortunes at various other casinos. Often they were the victims of their own percentages, and they were usually addicted to the games. Casino owners involved in gambling move around to gaming tables about town, and with disastrous results. In Reno one casino owner had a streak of luck and won $40,000 at dice in an hour. After a few weeks he was half a million dollars ahead. A couple of months later he was flat broke.

12

HORSE-RACING PRIMER

Next to numbers, horse racing is the most popular form of big-money gambling in America. But unlike numbers, betting on horses is usually legal. In its legal form, pari-mutuel betting at the track takes in about $6 billion a year, with sixty million or more people attending the races every year. There are about 6,500 racing days a year in the United States, and sixty or so major races.

On a good day a popular big track can handle $3.5 million in pari-mutuel betting. Most Americans have had some apprehensive acquaintance with the tracks.

How much is bet illegally through bookies, horse rooms, and by friendly wagers on special horses and on races like the Kentucky Derby, the Preakness, or the Belmont Stakes? Four times as much as at the tracks, some say. No one really knows.

Race tracks offer an attractive atmosphere, often good food, open air, and well-landscaped space. One meets all kinds of people, from kooks to desperate system players, two-dollar hunch bettors who use a pin to stab blindly at a program, to skilled handicappers who have been up all night "scientifically" picking the best horse and listing the betting odds.

Mostly, a day at a track is just waiting. Not much more than twenty-five minutes of actual racing occurs. Yet it can take four hours to prove you can't trust past records or tout sheets. Actually, most horse bettors hardly ever go to the track. Instead, they bet with their bookies, and follow the results on radio or television.

The bettor's dream is to win on a long shot. (Favorites win about 35 percent of the time and pay meager odds.) The odds are set according to how the bettors' money favors a horse, and can change right up to post time—and actually *after* the race, when the totalizator goes to work with mathematics and computers.

Horse races are run to make a lot of money for the track and its stockholders. The track takes a fat cut off the top on every ticket sold, and the state tax, too, is considerable. Regardless of which horse wins, the track and state do well. The track's usual cut is about 18 percent. It also takes the nickels and pennies, the odd coins called "breakage." It adds up. A winner often drops his winnings back at the ticket window, and each time he does, 18 percent is taken off as "vigorish." With entrance fee, food and drink, parking, and purchase of racing sheets and programs, the average bettor usually is lucky to break even after a day at the track. However, there are winners, and—who knows?—you may be the lucky one.

Do all horse players die broke? They don't die rich or live on winnings at the track. I've known many big horse bettors. All those I've met have lost fortunes at the track, but most didn't die broke. But it was their occupations, not the track, that saved them from penury.

Barry X is a classic example of a horse player's destiny. He was one of the top screenwriters at a big Valley studio. Barry had a wife and three children, a beautiful large house, two Cadillacs, and a job at the studio that earned him $1,500 a week (this was in the 1940s). He was the best horse handicapper in Southern California. He would sit up nights working out form sheets based on records and past performances of horses and jockeys. When he came to the studio on race day, his predictions of race results would be eagerly sought by all. He was persuasive and his enthusiasm was contagious.

In the afternoon as many of the top studio people as could manage it would go to the track, betting according to Barry's form sheets. They usually made money and often hit big. But Barry? He would go over his form sheets, make changes here and there, and rework his sheets before he put down his own bets. Sometimes he won, but usually he lost; the final doubts and changes upset his night's careful work. He was like a master painter who spoiled the outcome with a few added brush strokes.

When the season opened at Del Mar near San Diego, Barry would load the family into one of the Caddies and stay at the track until the season was over. He often lost a great deal. He slowly sank into a morass of doubt about his abilities. When television hit the film industry a severe blow in the 1950s and the studio system began to limp, Barry was laid off. Desperate, he turned to his ability to pick horses. Within two years he was bankrupt. He ended his days in a sanitarium. No one had more knowledge of horse racing or handicapping than Barry, yet there was the fatal flaw of doubt about his own·skills.   .

Horse racing came originally from England. The American colonies were betting on the ponies in 1665, at the "Newmarket Course" in Hempstead, Long Island, named after the famous English track. The first imported race horse arrived around 1730. George Washington loved horse races, and while tracks arose in Kentucky, Maryland and Virginia, this was mule racing on a grass track. In 1823 someone decided that track rails were needed. The Union Course on Long Island was the first with a dirt track, and it is said that over 50,000 people showed up opening day and bet a million dollars. While the first stake race (a winner's purse) was run in Canada, the Travelers Stakes at Saratoga Springs was the first in the United States. Betting was between gentlemen and sports. Pari-mutuel betting didn't come in until 1871, at Jerome Park in New York.

Horse racing was usual at country fairs and at gypsy tracks, with horses and riders not of the first rank. Honesty was not part of the game; fixed races and crooked jockeys and trainers were common.

The first stud book had come out in 1793, in an attempt to improve the breed and keep records of sorts. A horse named Byerly Turk was shipped over in 1685 at stud. He and the Darley Arabian and the Godolphin Barb are supposed to be the ancestors of every thoroughbred racing today. Man o' War, Equipoise, Sarazen, Sea Biscuit, and Discovery all go back to one of these three horses. Their relatives are running today at the four great tracks, Aqueduct and Belmont in the East, Hollywood and Santa Anita in the Far West. In the South there are Tropical Park, Hialeah, and Gulfstream; Maryland has Pimlico and Bodie; and around Chicago are the ovals of Arlington, Sportsman, and Washington Park.

Best known is the running of the Kentucky Derby and the

wild circus of Derby Week at Churchill Downs. There is also Keeneland, with its loyal followers.

In 1942 the Thoroughbred Racing Association came into being to bring order to the nation's tracks. It was sorely needed. There had been talk of "boat rides" (fixed races agreed on by the jockeys), pulled horses, doping, ringers, and the use of the battery (a pole attached to a storage battery that shocked a horse to excitement just before it came out on the track). Every track employee, worker and official, was fingerprinted. Horses are now tattooed on the inner lip for identification. Urine tests are made to see whether the horse has been drugged or jogged by some injection or jolting mixture.

A blacklist exists of people around racing with a suspect history. There is a great deal of money in racing to be preyed on and exploited.

Is horse racing honest today? It's as honest as any event where millions are bet to win or lose, where syndicates own horses, and where millions can be made if the horse that wins can be manipulated by professional gamblers. If the public backs a particular favorite and the bookies see big losses, sometimes that horse loses. What of inside information? There are whispers; there is gossip about a boat ride by track folk, and that jockeys have fifty-dollar tickets in their boots; often the judges wonder whether a favored horse wasn't pulled (held back) by a jock making a turn, or whether an owner hadn't ordered a jockey *not* to try that day. The track officials and horse owners are always apprehensive of such talk.

There have been scandal-hinting investigations. But the government and the state get huge incomes from horse racing, and they frown on inconclusive investigations. The towns where the tracks are built also prosper. And at every state capital, every track has powerful lobbyists loaded with cash to see that new laws favor the tracks.

Breeding horses is big business. Birthing little racing horses out of matched pairs can bring the price of a sire or a brood mare of famous winning lines up to nearly a million dollars. Breeders are a tightly cohesive group; they do not make figures easily available. There are about 1,600 breeding farms, many of them in Kentucky, and there are at least 17,000 foals dropped each year. Stud fees can begin at $1,000 and go up to $50,000 or even $80,000. The average fee for a horse in the top ten would be around $30,000. Man o' War was bred twenty-five times a year for twenty-two years. Today, with artificial insemination, his sperm could serve a couple of hundred mares a year.

As the cost of a great sire goes up, syndicates are formed which own shares in the horse's breeding abilities. In 1955 Nashua was syndicated at a million dollars, a record for that time. Nijinsky was a syndicate choice at nearly $4.5 million. Owning racing stables is risky and costly, and few really know how to pick trainers, horses and jockeys, and how to decide when to race. Some people used their stables for social status rather than as a scientific enterprise in running horseflesh for profit. One can have no precise point of view toward horse owners; it's an exciting, debilitating and costly hobby.

The role of the jockey creates cults, and a jockey with a winning record is in great demand. Horse owners and some jocks I have interviewed do not agree that this is to the good. The jockey is overrated when it comes to winning races, most believe. "A winning race is only as good as the horse is. Of course, you don't put a blind, one-armed kid on a horse. But it's the horse that should get the credit—say 85 to 90 percent for a winning race. A jock of experience and a little guts helps maybe 10 to 15 percent. In a close finish, naturally, that's a help. Don't ever bet the jock; bet the horse's record."

Billy Pearson, the famous art-loving jockey, didn't agree. "The horse," he says, "is the dumbest, craziest animal alive. He has no sense at all. He'll run into a brick wall if it's there, without turning off. In a fire, if you lead him out of the stable, the dumb bastard will go right back inside to get barbecued. Even the great ones, Count Fleet, Man o' War, Whirlaway, were no smarter than some nag going to be made into Alpo dog food, which is where a lot of ace horses end up."

Jocks do a lot of things the judges watch out for. They crowd each other into and sometimes over the rail. (Pearson once broke almost every bone in his body when he was dumped over the rail.) They also often take their whips to each other, slashing away, all control lost, as in the 1933 Kentucky Derby, when the jocks on Broker's Tip and Head Play held a whip duel, to the amazement of thousands.

Putting down jockeys doesn't detract from the fact that there are great riders whose record of winners is amazing, even if the best jockey usually wins only one out of every five races.

For some gamblers, the important thing in a jockey is his small size. An underfed nine-year-old boy is a perfect specimen, Billy Pearson insists. Diet, steam baths, and other measures are taken to keep the weight down. Pearson often drank a bottle of Pluto Water, a popular physic, the night before a race.

Pearson admits he rode some odd races in Mexico for a fat general who carried a pearl-handled pistol in full view. On one occasion the general chased Pearson, gun aimed, after he had lost a race that should have been won. Betting on Mexican races can be hazardous; often, only suckers bet.

Betting fever has produced some records on the track. Bet-a-Million Gates is supposed to have been the biggest horse bettor of all time. He never actually bet a million on one race or on one day, but he did bet millions, and sometimes he won— and often he lost. Payne Whitney lost half a million, some say, in a series of four races, yet ended with $15,000 in winnings. Arnold Rothstein, who rigged the 1919 World Series, won $800,000 at Aqueduct in 1921. A Chinese tong leader in San Francisco, Little Pete (Fung Jing Toy), fixed horse races after the Gold Rush days. He would bet $9,000 a day. He won $100,000 in two months at the Bay District and Ingleside tracks. When the races were turning honest, he quit.

Horses win when they are ready to win—when the track is right and it's the right race against horses they can beat. There is no blunted power of ability and determination, for of course the owner and trainer decide to let the horse extend itself. There have been cases where horses were held back in early races to build up the odds, then entered in a race to win at favorable odds.

Many people come to the track convinced that some races are fixed, that there is feed-box information of a "boat ride," and that there are people who *know* and will pass the secret on to you if you'll buy a ticket for them when you buy your own. These individuals, who are called touts or hangers-on, claim to have inside information. They sometimes pick a winner by chance, but rarely. As "Pony Benny," whom I knew, put it: "Still, it only costs me time and a quick con. Besides, you can only con some klutz who feels he's getting illegal information."

The big money usually goes to off-track bettors. Most betting is done outside the law, off the track, for there is a certain pleasure in challenging respectability. The pari-mutuel system of track betting was developed to try to stem bookie activities. It began in 1864, when a man in Paris put together the first system, now done by the American totalizator with complex computer tapes electrically controlled. Odds are figured by the machine every minute and a half. The system was begun in the United States in the early 1870s. Bookies were against it, and it did not receive sanction on the New York track until 1913. The state government favored the system, as it gave a fair count for tax purposes. However, it ruined a bettor's chance to seek good odds at the track. Bookies in those days gave better odds than the tote board.

Losers sometimes try to doctor a losing ticket to look like a winner. Fake tickets have also been printed and tried out at a busy pay-out window. Such tricks are in vain. There are quick tests that show up the phonies. "Sheer nonsense," said Pony Benny, "is this legend of delaying a wire service to get a mark to bet on a race already run. That is why the movie *The Sting* is crap." The old horse player grimaced. "No hoodlum boss, like in the picture, would fall for such a lousy gimmick as the Redford and Newman setup. He'd see through them crooks in a minute. He'd smell a fake horse room before he was halfway across the doorway. Also, you can't place a half million dollars in cash just before a race. No legit bookie room would touch it. The bookmaker would need time to lay it off across the country with other horse rooms or the syndicate, to spread the money 'round in case of a win."

Pony Benny is certain the track drives bettors to bookies. "It takes up a fat percentage off the top right away, in the cut and taxes. So the odds paid are not the true odds; they don't pay off on five-cent units, neither. They pile up a lot of breakage, which they keep. A $400 winner loses twenty dollars in some setups."

As for special services and "winners today" sheets, *The Daily Racing Form* is really the only bettor's bible. It lists a lot of information that puts a bettor wise as to weight, conditions, breeding, past records and jockey. Benny's advice (and I got it from many others) is: don't go for a sure-thing system, or "daily winners" sold outside the track. There are helpful systems but no sure things. For a system to aid you, you must have common sense and judgment. It's better to read a handicapper going on information.

Look for a good horse that hasn't really been trying, and bet him in his next few races. He may be getting ready to be let out. Do this by studying the record information. There is also the good horse that always runs a good race and wins many of them. Is the horse jumpy? Does he act up? A horse to bet is one that has often finished second. That's a horse to watch. Favorites at slim odds win one out of every three or four races, so betting on the second favorite horse is a good idea. But remember, it's always a gamble.

Pony Benny admitted there is something nice to say about newspaper handicappers. "If you find in four or five newspapers that handicappers have agreed on some of the horses to win, place and show, it's a good bet. The men are not all dummies, and many know how to handicap and weight their choices."

The most expensive gambling of all is racing your own horse and seeing the jocks wearing your stable's colors. While most owners of racing stables are professionals, there are many others who have turned some of their income into the buying and racing of horse breeds. The Warner brothers, Louis B. Mayer, Elizabeth Arden, Bing Crosby, and various others have owned race horses. Cold, coherent facts on the problems of ownership are no barriers to horse lovers.

Of all the professions, doctors seem to have a gambling streak stronger than most. They are big investors in oil-well stocks of the more risky sort. I have known two who owned race horses.

One medical man I know has raised horses for years. "Yes, I had a stable for ten years," he told me when I asked him about his experiences in owning race horses. "I see too much of the human body. Horses are more beautiful. I was always a bettor at Hollywood Park and at Santa Anita. Then I got this bug in my head: how would it be to have my horse carrying my colors? I decided on blue and gold before I bought my first horse in a claiming race. What did I know about owning horses? Only what I'd picked up from other owners—a lot of talk with men and women who had stables, and that adds up to very little. And the advice? Worthless!

"I decided to buy my second horse, a yearling, at auction.

There are auctions of colts and fillies all over the country, but the yearlings selected by the Keeneland Association and the Fasig-Tipton Company pick the best. They are sold at Keeneland, Kentucky, and at Saratoga, New York. I decided on Saratoga, as I was going east for a medical convention at the time. I found dealers a tough-fibered, pugnacious lot.

"The auctions are fair and well managed. You can buy a colt with a fair blood line for $10,000. But for a really good horse, $40,000 is not too much. Some have sold for around $800,000. So you see, it's no game for everyday horse lovers. I bought a filly at $20,000 and got stable space, along with a trainer who moonlighted for me, and we began to go over the jockey books. I had old H———, a crusty old track expert, with me. I should have gone for a $50,000 yearling, but I didn't always buy the best.

"I also watched the sales advertised in *The Thoroughbred Record* and *The Blood Horse*. So I picked up two more horses— yearlings. You feed and train for a year before they're two years old and permitted to race. Believe me, it's easier raising three kids. Raising race horses is as expensive as brain surgery, let me tell you.

"I bought my best gelding at a claiming race. That's when you can claim any horse in the race for the price he's entered by the owner. I got the gelding at $17,000. I saw him run before I claimed him, and he looked good. Never a great champion, you understand, but he won some good races for me. Almost enough to pay his cost and keep.

"I never went into syndicates, in which you buy shares in a horse. You can buy a share today of some great blood-line horse for $50,000 to $100,000 a share, lesser lines for $20,000. I never could figure out how fair or honest it was. Mostly, syndicates bank on making profits for stud fees, and I wasn't interested in breeding horses: I was mainly concerned with feeding them and paying the veterinarians. Those birds are as greedy as Beverly Hills specialists.

"Yes, I raced my own stable for about ten years. I have some pictures of myself with a sweating horse and some old race programs. My accountant, another horse bettor, worked it out for me. Taking a hundred average race horses, the animal costs from 30 to 40 percent more to keep than it earns, and that doesn't take into account what you paid for the nag originally. I never owned a really headline horse. They cost up to $250,000. Even with them, their owners usually only break even. They go in for the sport and the thrill of it. The big payoff comes to the real gambler, taking losses of maybe half a million a year, but with an eye on the big races that in a lucky season may bring him a million or a million and a half. As for me, I vacillated between dreams and facts. Then I got out. I had my costs as tax losses on my income-tax returns, of course. I was getting in too deep. I opened up a nice little gold mine instead—a private hospital. You want to buy some racing colors, let me know."

I interviewed several other owners of race horses, past and present: lawyers, merchants, wholesalers, a woman who owned a dozen beauty parlors, another who had a fancy chain of quick food shops. All had huge incomes and wanted excitement. Some said they were breaking even "and hoping." Most admitted it was a very costly hobby. All, however, enjoyed racing, the excitement of seeing their colors on a rider making the turn at the three-quarter pole. Said the beauty parlor woman, "I've gambled on human inconsistency: three husbands, all losers. Now I find nothing is as stirring as watching your horse make a try for the finish line, coming in by two lengths. There's no man around today who can give me the same charge. Sad, isn't it?"

One of the oldest horse-racing gambling ploys is the use of a "ringer"—the fast horse entered under a new name, or producing a slow horse in workouts and then switching to a fast horse under the same name for a big race. All this is done to get heavy odds. The scheme goes back to colonial days. It has been rare in recent times, thanks to the tattooing of a number on each horse's inner lip and to other vigilant track procedures. But it is still sometimes tried for a big killing. In February 1976 a British court case involved builder Tony Murphy and race-horse trainer Anthony Collins, who were fined $2,000 each for conspiring to defraud bookmakers.

It began on the day a four-year-old chestnut gelding was sent from Dublin to Collins's stables in Scotland. Documents on the trip across the Irish Sea identified the horse as Gay Future. The animal, in fact, was not the real Gay Future.

Poor training gallops made it certain that the real Gay Future would get heavy odds when he raced in England. In August, the genuine Gay Future arrived from Dublin. The gelding was secretly transferred to one of Collins's mobile vans on a lonely road, and the switch was made.

The plotters had formed a syndicate and recruited a small army of bettors to place three-horse parlays on Gay Future and two other horses trained by Collins. The other two horses would be withdrawn from the race so that all the bets would go only on Gay Future. The syndicate placed small bets of $10 to $20 at gambling shops all over London. More than $8,000 had been wagered when a betting-shop official took notice of the money pouring in. Bookmakers stopped accepting bets and tried to lay off the wagers to drive the starting price down.

Gay Future won the race by fifteen lengths, at ten to one. However, Scotland Yard detectives had noticed the arrival of the group of Irishmen and feared they were IRA guerrillas. The police assigned a special agent to watch the group and soon learned of the scheme. The syndicate collected $12,000 before bookmakers stopped payment and started the inquiry that led to the disclosure of the plot.

As for the real Gay Future, he fell and broke his neck in a race on the day the trial started.

People who are not professional horse owners sometimes buy a share in a promising thoroughbred, and sometimes they are lucky. "Take a horse called Telly's Pop," said Telly Savalas. "Two years ago, I paid $3,000 for a half share in a horse nobody wanted. I named him Telly's Pop, and something happened, baby." Telly's gelding, which he owns with Howard W. Koch, finished in the money in all of his seven races on West Coast tracks, winning $300,000 and an invitation to the Kentucky Derby. Telly had competition from Hollywood horse owner Rod Steiger, who paid $50,000 for half ownership of a bay colt named Stained Glass. At Santa Anita in December 1975 Steiger's steed outran Savalas's by a length and a half. "We beat him. We can beat him anytime," said Steiger.

It should be noticed that both Savalas and Steiger are new to ownership of race horses. One season's luck doesn't make a permanent stable. A five- to eight-year period, most horsemen agree, is the true breaking time for owning a stable. By that time the stable will show whether it's making a profit or breaking even. Most celebrities, after a few years of rising losses, drop out of running their own colors.

Harness Racing

Not all racing fans are involved with a jockey *on* a horse. Many prefer harness racing, where a driver is perched behind the horse, on a two-wheeled seat called a sulky. However, betting continues as the attraction for most harness-racing fans. There are, judging by admission charges, about thirty-two million people a year who watch standard bred horses in harness racing.

It all began as a country sport, with natives on dirt roads racing their horse-drawn buggies against one another, often with their best girls at their sides. In time this was formalized as a sport, in which the rules are different; but to the harness-racing buff the sight of a great trotter or pacer pulling the sulky, with its two bike-sized wheels, around a track makes it all worthwhile. The horse is not permitted to run, canter or gallop. He can only trot or pace. If he breaks away from these two forms, the horse must go to the outside, and his driver then tries to get him back into the prescribed gait. The moments lost are added to the horse's time from start to finish line.

What is the official gait? At all times, a pacer's right hind leg and right foreleg must be moving in the same direction; the left legs must also move together. Most pacers wear a harness on their legs so they can't change the step. A trotter does it all differently. The left foreleg moves with the right hind leg, and the right hind leg with the left foreleg, and no leg harness is used. Some watchers like the trotters; others prefer the pacers. Both styles make harness racing a pleasure reminiscent of a time that is past. The betting is about the same as in races run with jockeys up.

The Kentucky Derby of harness racing is the Hambletonian at Du Quoin, Illinois, and the Fox Stake at Indianapolis. Other famous tracks for the sport are at Bay Meadows, California; Washington Park, Illinois; Scarborough Downs, Maine; Pompano Park, Florida; Blue Bonnets, Canada; Suffolk Downs, Maine; and Saratoga Harness, New York.

As the harness-racing horse carries no weight on its back, the drivers can be heavier and older than jockeys. In fact, great drivers like Farrington, Marsh and Pletcher often weighed up to 190 pounds. Their average age at their best was in the forties.

Position is important in a race. A start at the rail is a great advantage; coming around on a wide turn, it's a time saver. In betting on harness racing, the feed-yard "experts" say to bet on the driver. His record and the position are what matters. The closer to the rail, the better chance you have to win.

The most exciting races are run on a mile track. But not all tracks are mile lengths. There are half-mile and even shorter lengths. Short tracks call for lots of turns. The horse on the outside, called "parked out," is covering more ground, which can add seconds to the run. Also, on the outside there is the added danger of accidents.

The half-mile in harness racing is usually run in two minutes. Two minutes four seconds is about the average. Two minutes seven seconds is a slow horse. Harness racing is big business, but the other kind makes more money (and more losers).

Pari-mutuel betting brings in the biggest gambling take in the nation. It makes all of Nevada's figures seem small. Harland B. Adams, an expert on gambling, states that the Hollywood Park race track in California pays the state more money than all the casinos in Las Vegas and Reno pay Nevada. Add that sum to bets placed illegally with bookies, and you probably have sums close to what the Pentagon spends on its war toys. New York City opened off-track centers to take in huge profits. Right now it is estimated that $15 billion a year is bet illegally on horses throughout the country.

Gambler's Digest claims that gambling is America's biggest industry. "It surpasses the combined total volume of the 75 largest industrial organizations . . . including General Motors, U.S. Steel, and all the oil companies."

The average citizen should bet small amounts and avoid touts and systems. For those who want to become expert handicappers I recommend the following books by Tom Ainsie: *Scientific Handicapping* and *Science in Betting*. But the best part of horse racing is the enjoyment of the finely turned-out horses, the color of silks, the fresh air, and the excited crowds watching the inconsistencies of chance.

13

POKER

Poker bears out Talleyrand's remark: "Language was given us to conceal thoughts. . . ." Poker—where conversation shields the handful of cards—has become the rich man's high-stake game, played with men of his own position in a military-industrial society in control of the big money, including professional gamblers as partners. The French called their version *poque*, with the cry *"Je poque d'un jeton,"* or, "One chip to begin betting." And the answer, even in English, was to say, "I *poque* against you."

By 1836, poker was called a "favorite game of cards of the South and West." Gentlemen, cowpokes, the gamblers of Bret Harte's best stories of Yerba Buena, the Chinese, and even madams and sporting visitors like Oscar Wilde, all helped to make poker *the* high-stake card game, to the delight of those holding a good hand. Fabulous poker games and fantastic amounts of money won or lost became legend. Cheaters were often hanged higher than Haman or were gunned down at once.

One of the first truly solid endurance contests at poker took place in 1873 in McDonald's Tavern, Atlantic County, New Jersey. Four rich natives of the state, Silas Daniels, James Howe, John Strange and Hosea Brockway, tired of deer hunting, sat down to a friendly game of poker. The opening bet was $1,000, and the play never got below $50. They played for seventy hours, and when they counted up, they found that none of the players was out much beyond twenty-five dollars. Consequently, there were no smothered grievances or ruined households.

A classic poker tournament was the Austin, Texas, game started on the night of June 15, 1853. Two rich planters and ruthless poker players, Major Danielson and Old Man Morgan, sat down, and for a couple of hours the play went first one way, then the other. When both drew good hands, the betting went up, and play went on all night. When the inn's rooster crowed at dawn, the players agreed to do away with limits. From then on, pausing only to eat, answer nature, and arrange for more cash loans on their plantation holdings, they played on, day after day, week on week. Soon people were keeping score by the month. The game became an institution, then a tradition. It was famous, notorious, and a great crowd collector. The town boomed; stagecoach and railroads extended their lines; new hotels went up.

The Civil War came, and the two old men still played on. The carpetbaggers and the other horrors of Reconstruction took over around them, and still the play went on. For seventeen years it continued. In 1870, the first decks of cards used were sent to the vaults of the National Bank of Austin as precious Texan relics. The two poker players died almost at the same moment. They had appointed their eldest surviving sons to carry on. Five years passed; one son went mad, and the other died in a train wreck.

It would appear that perhaps it was a stunt, a publicity gimmick to boom the town, since the rules of continuous play had been relaxed to permit one of the players to be away long enough to meet his death by steam engine. But Texans remain unamused by those who see it all as a farce.

In the West, cards were dealt to the left in a poker game, so, it was claimed, a man could reach for his pistol with his shooting hand if he suspected cheating. To mark the dealers in turn, a knife, usually with a buckhorn handle, was placed in front of the dealer. When the dealer passed the deck to the next man, that player could pass his chance, and so the term "passing the buck" was created. Flushes were introduced into the game before straights. Two hands that couldn't be beaten were four aces, and four kings and an ace. They were as solid as Bible morality.

The Civil War gave the game its final form of stud. Stud was played with open cards, and is said to have been named for a bettor who put up a stud stallion in a Western game. One historian gives the stallion story to Ohio after the Civil War.

Cheating at cards began almost as soon as the first playing card was drawn. Sometimes the results of a play were so amazing that it seemed no one would have dared to cheat in that manner. The New York Blossom Club, a Tammany hangout, produced a classic example. In a poker game there, a Washington, D.C. fat cat, General Schenck, who in the past had dealt cards to Daniel Webster, Henry Clay and other famous phrase makers, sat in on a game at the Blossom Club with three Tammany boyos: Isaac Oliver, Jake Sharp, and Richard Flannigan, with Oliver dealing. The betting was heavy. Each stared deadpan into the growing pot. When they laid down their cards, *each* showed a straight flush, from three to seven. For years poker players talked about it: Did Oliver, who was no real card handler, stack the cards? Was the shuffle a fraud? Or was it just that millionth or zillionth chance that came up in that game at the Blossom Club, one of the most famous hands in poker?

"Stripping" (shaving the edge of some high cards, to make them slightly narrower) was an easy cheating device. There was also signaling by a confederate standing near, signaling with various gestures such as a touch of a tie or coat lapel, but all this would succeed only with new players. Sometimes a mirror was hidden in a smoker's pipe to enable a player to read his neighbor's cards. "Holdouts" were extra cards produced by wires, springs and clamps planted in vest, coat or sleeve. "Bottom dealing" was dealing special stacked cards to the player who was to win, while making it appear that the dealing was from the top. Bottom dealing requires a great amount of coolness and nerve, which is possessed by perhaps one person in a million. Many people who didn't have that skill tried it anyway, and died over a poker table or were ridden out of town on a rail, in tar and feathers.

A fingernail or a pinpoint set in a ring could mark a deck's high cards to be read from the back. This was "blazing scratch paper." Hand marking before the game couldn't fool a real pro. So stamped marked cards were produced, the code being some part of the pattern printed on the back of the card, which denoted its value. Soon big-city printers were selling stamped cards. The best ones, easy to put into play even against gamblers, were legitimate cards from respected manufacturers.

These were sold to printers with the backs blank. But for minute changes, the marked patterns added were the same designs used by legitimate printers. In the business of making money, a convenient morality prevails.

Sometimes a man sold a marked deck to one gambler and the code to another in the same game. Such deviousness has sent many a cheater to the grave.

It was easy to introduce the marked cards into a game by bribing steamboat bartenders, sometimes cutting the card seller in for a piece of the take. Calling for a fresh deck of sealed cards (resealed, actually) didn't prevent the pigeon's being plucked.

Modern times introduced electric cheating devices. The most recent scandal took place at the Friars' Club in Beverly Hills, an organization supposed to be a club for actors but loaded with lawyers, businessmen and others of no clearly defined theater background. In the card room of the club, holes had been bored through ceiling rafters, telephoto lenses were set up over the card tables, and electrically controlled radio signals were sent to certain players through devices concealed on their persons, informing the cheaters what cards were held by the other players. The cheaters took them for a few million dollars.

When the cheaters were brought to trial after exposure, one of the defense lawyers was found to have stolen grand jury texts that were not for his eyes. He also committed perjury when he denied that the stolen records were in his hands. The whole matter could have caused him to be disbarred, but it was hushed up with a minor fine. Justice makes many futile pilgrimages in gambling cases.

There are various schools of thought about poker. Is it a game of chance or skill? Or is it a study in character, in which a player can influence another to play the right or wrong card? How much depends on the human factor and how much is pure gambling? Some claim psychological forces enter into the game. The shift of a chair, the blink of an eye, the throb of a vein in the neck—all have been cited as making it less a game of chance than one might suppose. Philosophers of cards have spoken of free will prevailing over fate or chance. It has been put by Nick the Greek as "not what is going on, but what someone *thinks* is going on."

It is said that bluffing is the important factor in the game, that the character of the players very often decides the winner. At times the value of the cards depends on what the player thinks the cards are worth. Basically, poker is a game played for gain.

It is one game where a bad hand can be played, sometimes to win over a better hand, by bluffing. Losses, too, can be controlled by the discipline dictated by a skilled player. Playing with the same people, knowing their faces, their stares, and little tics and muscle habits, makes the game much more interesting. Here the strengths and weaknesses of the people one faces come into play.

What of possible hands and possible odds? Someone with a computer has calculated that there are 2,598,960 dealt hands in draw poker, using the fifty-two-card deck, as follows:

Straight flush	40	(or once in 64,974 hands)
Four of a kind	624	(or once in 4,165 hands)
Full house	3,744	(or once in 694 hands)
Flush	5,108	(or once in 509 hands)
Straight	10,200	(or once in 255 hands)
Three of a kind	54,912	(or once in 47 hands)
Two pairs	123,552	(or once in 21 hands)
One pair	1,098,240	(or almost once in 2 hands)
Other hands	1,302,540	(or once in 2 hands)

In poker you hope to get a certain combination of cards. To win you have to come up with the highest hand in the game, each player being dealt five cards. In draw poker, you can throw out cards that don't make winning combinations and call for others. You bet on the value of your hand against the other players' cards.

There are various kinds of poker, draw and stud being the most popular. But all are based on high cards and their combinations. Players have devoted their lives to poker, seeing it as a theatrical and even messianic experience.

Gin rummy calls for drawing cards that add up to three or four of a kind, to make sequences. You knock when you think you have the advantage.

For a detailed explanation of card-playing rules and procedures, the best books are *The Complete Illustrated Guide to Gambling*, by Alan Wykes (Doubleday, 1964), and *Hoyle's Standard Games*—any edition will also contain the rules of casino, hearts, euchre, pinochle, red dog, backgammon, acey-deucy (varieties of backgammon), and cribbage (played with a scoring board).

Since 1970, America's professional poker players have gathered each year in Las Vegas for what can be called the Professional Poker Players' Olympics. The press has played up the event and glorified the winner. There is only one winner each year, and he can carry off close to $300,000.

In 1976, Adrian Doyle "Texas Dolly" Brunson won $220,000 as world champion of poker in a thirty-two-hour session at Binion's Horseshoe Club. "Nothing much to it," said he. "You just sit down at a table once a year with a few of your best friends—and fight for your life." Twenty-one other players had backed the play with $10,000 each to enter the final match of the World Series of Poker, and each lost.

Texas Dolly added, "I'm sure glad poker isn't like that all the time. It was rough. Still, you can't beat the wages. . . ."

Texas Dolly's winnings, added to the $90,250 he won in a preliminary deuce-seven match, less the $10,000 entrance fee, totaled $300,250.

The ante went to $500, and then it had an opening pot of $1,000. In the game, $25,000 pots were common, as were $500 chips. In high-stake poker there is no second place—only one winner. Some amateurs had been eliminated early. Three-time champion John Moss had tapped out after two hours, followed by "Treetop" Jack Strauss and Bob Hooks. Two newcomers, Bobby Baldwin of Dallas and Tom Huffenagel of Schwenksville, Pennsylvania, in their first championship game, surprised the pros by holding big money on the first day of play.

Big names in professional poker had fallen away in defeat: Amarillo Slim, 1973 champion Pug Pearson, Tahoe Andrew, Cadillac Jack Grimm, and Roger Van Arsdale. All had bad runs of cards.

Of course, the matches had to be listed as "social events." The reason for calling it a "social event" is a federal law that makes it a crime to cross a state line for illegal gambling. Years ago professional gamblers traveled from state to state, and if local authorities winked at the law, the game was played. Federal law now prohibits such interstate poker movement, professional or not. Any meeting of poker pros must be held in a state like Nevada, where the game is legal. Hold-em (a center-table game akin to seven-card stud) is the poker played. In Hold-em, each player gets two cards face down; then five cards are dealt face up on the table. A player's hand consists of the best five-card holding he can make from all seven.

"Texas Dolly" Doyle Brunson is no wall-eyed, high-heeled Texas redneck off a steer ranch. Unlike most of the great poker players, he holds a master's degree in education administration and was a star college basketball player and mile runner. He is bald, wears glasses and, unlike oldtime gamblers in their lace shirts and diamonds, he dresses informally, without jacket or tie.

On another level, a deck of cards could decide elections and recall history. In June of 1976, Robert Pittman won a seat on the city council in Show Low, Arizona, by drawing the deuce of clubs at high noon. To settle a tie between Pittman and Mayor David Foil in an election, the community of 2,100 re-enacted the game that gave the town its name. In 1876, Marion Clark and Colonel Coryden Cooley decided to dissolve their business partnership. Clark took up a deck of cards: "Show a low card and the ranch is yours." Colonel Cooley turned up the deuce of clubs, and later named the town after the Show Low Ranch.

Speaking of names of towns in connection with gambling, we recall that Bret Harte wrote of a fictional mining camp called Poker Flat. However, you can find quite a number of real towns in the United States to remind you of games you might have played: How about Winner, South Dakota, or Roulette, Pennsylvania? For luck, take Luckey, Ohio—and four towns named Horseshoe (Idaho, Kentucky, North Carolina, West Virginia). Watch out for Crook, Colorado, and Crooks, South Dakota. Perhaps you need a Clubb (Montana), a Spade (Texas), or Harts, West Virginia? Diamonds are plentiful—there are nine throughout the United States. Prefer to Deal (New Jersey)? Then have a King (Arkansas, Kentucky, North Carolina, Texas, and Wisconsin), a Jack (Alabama, Missouri), a Queen (Pennsylvania), or Queens (Kentucky, New York, West Virginia). If you are rolling dice, Elevenpoint (Arkansas) is a good throw; or Sixes (Oregon). Take a Chance (Alabama, Maryland, Kentucky, South Dakota, Virginia) on the Money (Mississippi), depending on the Odds (Kentucky). The game is either High (Iowa) or Lowe (North Carolina), but what is more important, let's have Fair Play (Colorado).

14

THE CHINESE CONNECTION

San Francisco has the largest settlement in America of people of Chinese descent. While Chinatown appears on the surface to be given over to eating places, curio shops with gaudy imitations of art, and "ivory," usually made of beef bones, the city has a deeply ingrained West Coast gambling aura, going back to the Gold Rush of '49. By the 1970s a rebel generation of street gangs and numbers pushers had evolved. Today there is a social pecking order, with Chinese bankers and merchants on top and workers in shops and factories on the bottom. Gambling still plays a big part in the life of Chinatown, with poker, dice and roulette.

Los Angeles also has a large Chinatown, which once occupied the area now taken over by the Union Station. The "new" Chinatown moved a few blocks away and still has back rooms of gamblers huddled over cards or dice. In the early 1970s there was a scandal in City Hall when a Los Angeles government official was accused of accepting protection money from Chinatown gamblers. However, no indictment was handed down.

Hundreds of thousands of Chinese were true settlers and makers of Western history. The Chinese came from Foochow, Swatow, and Canton, from Shanghai, Amoy, and Harbin, from the dried-out fields of central China. They were to dig the right-of-ways, clear sagebrush, blow up mountains, lay the iron rails through the California passes, and set out the railroad ties. And they gambled wildly.

In time they formed settlements in every large Western city, particularly San Francisco. They set up laundries and eating places, worked hard, and kept their private rites to themselves. They were not the simple, polite people they seemed to be. They were fantastic gamblers, losing fortunes at fan-tan (a lotto setup played with colored discs) and other games.

The Chinese made a vital, clever, solid group of citizens. They formed hongs for trading, and tongs, with hatchet men, for continual warfare among themselves over control of business enterprises, opium, and gambling.

The Chinese came to California early; two months after gold was found in 1848, the ship *Eagle* landed at Yerba Buena Cove with three Chinese, a girl and two men. In one year in the early fifties, 10,000 Orientals came in. By 1852 the state had an Oriental population of 22,000; twenty years later there were nearly 80,000 Orientals, almost half of whom settled in San Francisco. Exclusion acts in 1882 and again in 1888 eventually stopped entry of Chinese.

Reported a newspaper: "One meets natives of the Celestial empire, and subjects of the uncle to the moon, with their long-plaited queues or tails, very wide pantaloons bagging behind, and curiously formed head coverings—some resembling inverted soup plates, and others fitting as close to the scalp as the scalp does to the Celestial cranium it covers."

And the Chinese would just say, "No savvy" or "*Dweibuchi*" (pardon).

They lived on the upper section of Sacramento Street and all of Dupont (Grant Avenue today). The section was about seven blocks long and three blocks wide, and it swallowed thousands of Chinese a year. A nineteenth-century survey shows 30,000 living in a dozen square blocks in nearly 16,000 sleeping bunks, and they gambled as hard as they worked.

The first Chinese buildings in San Francisco came from China in sections and were erected on muddy land, lanes and alleys. Fires soon took their toll, and the buildings that followed were shacks, gambling huts, and store fronts. The original Chinatown was a crazy-quilt of cheap buildings and crowded living among piled-up bundles and boxes. The fire of 1906 was a blessing in a way, for it caused the erection of the modern Chinese section of the city, with all its dragon fronts and Peking red color.

A wine merchant's daybook of the early 1900s describes the gambling scene. "Chinese gamble on anything. Took party of Newport folk from the East to the heel of Sacramento Street. All a row of gambling establishments. Went to Lee's. Much kowtowing, bland smiles. Smoke thick, voices shrill. Chinese not at all silent and solemn. Lust for gambling on many faces. Fan Tan and poker most popular. Chinese drinks interesting. But drunk warm."

The Chinese was often a madman at the gambling table. Savings and fortunes changed hands over tables to the click of fan-tan gear. The *Annals of San Francisco* (1855) tells of gambling rooms which offered music. ". . . There is an orchestra of five or six native musicians, who produce such extraordinary sounds from their curiously shaped instruments as severely torture the white man to listen to. Occasionally a songster adds his howl or shriek to the excruciating harmony. . . . Heaven has ordered it, no doubt, for wise purposes, that the windy chaos is pleasant to the auricular nerves of the natives. Occasionally a few white men will venture into these places and gaze with mingled contempt and wonder upon the grave, melancholy, strange faces of the gamblers and their curious mode of playing. . . . There seems to be only one game [fan-tan] in vogue. A heap of brass counters is displayed on the plain, mat-covered table, and the banker with a long, slender stick picks and counts them out one by one, while the stakers gaze with intense interest on the process."

King of the early Chinese gambling world (in partnership with the white political despotism that ran the city) was a Chinese called Little Pete, born Fung Jing Toy in Canton in 1865. He was brought to this country at the age of five and was a delivery boy for a Chinese shoemaker. At twenty-one Little Pete was making shoes himself under the name of J. C. Peters & Co. This was merely the front of a skilled and wily mind that soon pervaded the city. He expanded into gambling dives, opium dens, and investments in Chinese girls. He seized power in the Sum Yop tong. He hijacked assets of other mobs on a grand scale, seizing property from the Sue Top tong. This led to bloody gang wars, with *boo how doy* hatchet men.

If Little Pete was Mr. Big in Chinatown, then the man to team up with to boss gambling was the white Mr. Big of San Francisco, Christopher A. Buckley, the city's political dictator. For twenty years Buckley held the city in his grip, encouraging gambling. Amazingly, Buckley was blind. He had come to the coast in 1862, and in five years he *was* the Democratic party, lock, stock and ballot box.

Chinatown was Little Pete's by royal Buckley grant. He collected fees from all enterprises: all legitimate shops, as well as gambling and opium emporiums, had to pay a percentage of their earnings to Little Pete. Those who welshed were soon raided by the police.

Little Pete was a traditionalist. He wore a long shiny queue and spent hours having it combed, washed, oiled and braided. As a true gambling lord he never did any killing himself, leaving such duties to his mob. As a family man, he led a wholly respectable life. His wife and two children made their home in a three-story house on Washington Street. It was claimed that he could not read or write Chinese; translators and interpreters helped him carry on his city-wide control of his countrymen. He was a spic-and-span dandy, given to sporting a dozen large gold watches and diamonds of all sizes.

Little Pete liked gambling—if the odds favored him. When he turned to horse racing, he saw no reason not to expect the running of the nags at Bay District and Ingleside to continue his luck. He bet on the average $8,000 to $9,000 a day, and always seemed to win. In two months he was ahead $100,000. The stewards of the Pacific Coast Jockey Club became suspicious. Horses became ill and collapsed; good jockeys lost easy races; somehow odds and breeding and form charts of splendid horses had no meaning.

Detectives followed jockeys to the offices of J. C. Peters & Co. Soon it was proved that Little Pete bribed riders, trainers and others to drug or poison the horses he wanted out of the running when he was betting on a fixed horse with the big odds. Jockeys were ruled off the turf or suspended in the resulting scandal. Little Pete retired from the sport of kings a big winner.

The other tongs figured if they couldn't lick Little Pete, they might join forces against his Sum Yop tong. Thirteen tongs got together and sent out the hatchet men, the *boo how doy*, to earn a reward of $3,000 for one man's life in Chinatown.

But it was not going to be easy to collect. Little Pete lived and slept in a room without a window, behind a barred steel door with a savage dog leashed to each doorknob. Under his tailored suit he wore a long coat of chain mail. A piece of curved steel shielded his head. His person was guarded at all daytime hours by half a dozen Chinese hatchet men, and an inner cordon of three white thugs was within reach to keep Little Pete safe from harm. At the rear of this armored group was Little Pete's valet, carrying a case of the boss's jewelry and his toilet kit of cosmetic needs.

For months the killers, professional and apprentice, tried to sneak past the guards around Little Pete, but failed. Then down from the mountains in January 1897 came two young gold hunters, Lem Jung and Chew Tin Gop. They had pokes filled with gold and were out to celebrate in Chinatown before shipping home to China to end their days as rich men.

Lem and Chew were members of the Suey Sing tong, and they listened with interest to the talk of the reward for killing a man they had never heard of. Lem said, "There is no reason why we should not earn this money." Chew agreed.

The two made their move on the night of the Chinese New Year, January 23. There was a barbershop on Washington Street, and here Little Pete was having his usual tonsure. He had carelessly sent his bodyguard away to do some errands while the barber had him bending over a washbasin, the first step of the two-hour ritual of plaiting his queue.

Into the shop walked Lem Jung and Chew Tin Gop. No one knows whether they had planned their move or had just been lucky enough to stumble on Little Pete alone, his head under a flow of water, his back to them. Lem moved quickly. Elbowing the barber aside, he gripped Little Pete by the hair. Chew Tin Gop remained on guard at the door.

Lem pushed the nose of a .45 revolver between Little Pete's naked spine and the coat of mail. Five times he pressed the trigger, sending slugs into Little Pete's body.

The killers walked out into the noisy New Year's night to collect their reward. They slipped home to China. Nothing more is known of their lives after their last great gamble.

The wars of New York's Chinatown from 1900 to 1925 created a great deal more interest than killings. The cloying musical notes of slowly played "Chinatown, My Chinatown" brought to the minds of New Yorkers a miniature city within their own larger boundaries, a city of incense-scented little shops and crimson-painted surfaces decorated with dragons, inhabited by mysterious people. They were believed to be smoking opium, sexually enslaving white girls, and serving up exotic dishes such as bird's-nest soup, shark's fins and 100-year-old eggs. They also offered food unknown in China: chow mein and chop suey.

Actually, the district around Mott Street was merely the enclave of one more minority that had settled in New York. New York's Chinese, besides laundering and cooking, lived off tourists. New Yorkers saw Chinatown—Pell Street and Mott Street, the color and smells of Doyers Street—as an exotic, spine-tingling district. Actually, the twentieth-century New York Chinatown was for a long time the battleground of the tongs for the control of the section's gambling, drugs, trade in women, and the honest merchandising and tourism.

The tongs, like chow mein, were popular in America. They grew out of the thousands of coolies imported to help build the Western railroad. At first they were protective groups organized against the mobs of Western racial bigots, and in time they became power clans controlling the gambling and other business in the Chinese communities across the nation.

By 1900, the Chinese in New York were a prosperous community. The first Chinese person to settle in New York was Ah Ken, in 1858. The most powerful enemy was the Hearst press, which whipped up the "Yellow Peril" scare, warning of murderous millions coming from Asia to seize America and the world.

Actually, behind the restaurants, laundries, and stores full of dried duck and strange vegetables, there was an active world of gambling in fan-tan, *pi gow*, and even poker. *Gow* (opium), too, was a relaxing addiction after facing the white devils all day in trade. White and Oriental slave girls were also available in rooms along Doyer, Pell, and Mott streets. But much of the atmosphere of dope and slave girls was created for the tourists. The district was crowded, and by the turn of the century at least 250 Chinese gambling houses were busy, and one could smoke opium in maybe as many or more places.

They all operated with New York police protection. The Chinese owner paid eighteen to twenty dollars a week to the cops. He also gave a share of the take to the Gamblers' Union, as well as something to the tongs for protection.

The twentieth century came to its first East Coast tong war because the On Leong tong controlled most of the gambling and vice in New York, while the Hip Song was a weak organization working only the fringe of Chinatown. Power came to the On Leongs because their boss, Tom Lee, had votes for Tammany on election day. Chinese votes, if few, could be repeated often. The city expected no Judeo-Christian moral values from its Chinese.

As the mayor of Chinatown, Tom Lee held a nonelective "office," and Tammany saw to it that he became a deputy sheriff of New York County. Lee was a huge man, with two bodyguards and a chain-mail shirt. His rival, Wong Get, didn't matter. He had no pigtail—only a smart Broadway haircut and a dude's outfit.

As with all absolute rulers, there were always new rivals, and in 1900, a man named Mock Duck appeared in Chinatown. He was a fat fellow, ironic, mean, fond of *she-juploong-har* (lobster) and *yew toe* (fish gut). He too wore the mail shirt and carried two Colt .45s and a razor-sharp short-handled hatchet. He was as ready for a shootout as Bat Masterson, Doc Holliday or the Earps. But unlike them, he had the bad habit of closing his eyes, sitting down on his heels and firing in the general direction of any On Leongs within range. He usually missed.

Mock Duck also had a shrew of a wife. She was known to slap and kick him down Pell Street if she caught him nested away with some younger girl. Mock Duck's gambling fixation went beyond the wild surge of recklessness in most Chinese. He'd bet on the number of pips in an apple, on horses, or on American games of dice and cards.

A Hip Sung man, he joined forces with the dude Wong Get and began to recruit and train *boo how doy*. He then went to Tom Lee and demanded to be cut in on half of all the gambling rights in Chinatown. If not, there would be trouble. Lee is said to have replied, *"Ni syihwan cha, ma?* You care for tea?"

Lee felt no fear of the rival Hip Sungs, but his attitude changed when two of his tong died in a mysterious fire in the tong's dorm on Pell Street. In return, On Leong killers went out with their hatchets and chopped up a Hip Sung member. The big tong war, the first in New York, was on. The Brothers group joined the Mock Duck gang, and Tom Lee was the main target. He was followed and shot at.

Mock Duck, with the mind of an economist, decided to get Tom Lee where it hurt. Mock Duck went to the white anti-Tammany reformers and revealed where all the gambling houses, opium dens, and whorehouses of the On Leongs were located (of course the police, as their protectors, already knew). After the On Leong's places were raided and closed, Mock Duck and Wong Get took over the premises and ran them for the Hip Sungs and, naturally, for themselves. It wasn't all profit; the police continued to be paid off, and new *boo how doys* had to be imported to replace the dead, for the tong wars lasted until 1906.

The city of New York had had enough. Visitors didn't enjoy stepping over hatchet-chopped bodies. A judge of the Court of General Sessions called for a peace conference of the tong leaders. Terms were worked out. The On Leongs would hold on to Mott Street as their fief, and the Hip Sungs would boss their section. As for Pell Street, it would be open country, a sort of buffer zone free of weapons. This led to feasting and revelry at the Port Arthur Restaurant in Chatham Square. It is said that Tom Lee downed over a hundred saucers of rice wine at the celebration.

A week later the war was on again, with each side claiming the other had fired the first shot. The judge called for help from the Chinese government, which used the simple method of arresting fifty of the threatening tongmen's close relatives in China and threatening to let their heads fall to the great sword if the tongs didn't make up at once. This forced peace lasted until 1909.

Mock Duck had an adopted daughter, Ha Oi, born of a white mother. When he was discovered with a relative deep in an opium daze, Ha Oi was taken from him. He sorrowed, went to court, lost, and left town on a gambling spree. He won thousands of dollars, adorned himself with large diamonds, and sported a wardrobe that called for three to four changes of outfits a day. When he returned, the tong wars warmed up, and while he was known to have killed or caused people to be killed, he himself managed to escape revenge. However, the day came when three On Leongs caught him walking down Pell Street, and they went into the firing-squad position, hugging the ground, eyes shut, blazing away. Amazingly, Mock Duck was only wounded. After a few weeks in the hospital, he was ready for a Chinese Gettysburg. It was a time of great knifings. The New York press loved to write up the tong wars. Business in Chinatown, between bloodshed, was good. One enterprising eating-place owner and fake opium-den dramatist even put out chicken blood in front of his place to show where two On Leongs had died.

Mock Dock was brought to court, but the evidence against him as a gang leader was weak (or, as some suspected, the police were seeing that key witnesses remained mute). Mock Duck was sent to Sing Sing for a few years for operating a gambling game. Once free of prison, he decided, so he told the press, that he was finished with gambling, with tongs and with rivalry. Afterward he was to proclaim himself a citizen of Brooklyn, happy in his comforts there, and he said that Chinatown would see him no more.

As the price of peace, the On Leongs demanded that the Hip Sungs, in abject humiliation, present them with a Chinese flag, ten thousand packets of good-sized firecrackers, and a large roast pig.

So the war continued, and no pig was roasted, no firecrackers presented. By 1910 the Chinese ambassador to Washington had been brought into the situation. A committee of forty Chinatown citizens was set up, and peace seemed again in sight. But in 1912 someone saw the need for a new tong of young, active hot bloods, and the Kim Lan Wui Saw tong, the newest in town, was ready. It offered to take on both the older On Leongs and Hip Sungs in a bloody power struggle. It was only the Chinese government's threat to use the official ax on the necks of relatives back in the old country that brought a new peace treaty.

The next tong war in New York broke out in 1924, induced by the good old Occidental-style embezzlement of funds. A few months of war followed. It seems to have been fought by a Chinese expeditionary force, for the dead were mostly among the restaurant workers and laundry men in Brooklyn and the Bronx.

Later, the hatchet men were fazed out and modern Capone-type weapons brought in. The young gangs were modeled on New York's Mafia rather than on the fairly respectable tongs' *boo how doys,* now all grown old. The Chinese Merchants' Association members became pin wearers of the Rotary, Lions, and the Elks. And, of course, the popularity of Chinese food prevailed.

The Politician and the Bettor

In a large city like New York, illegal gambling exists because it is often protected by police and city officials. The political figure who corrupts the power that controls gambling is perfectly embodied by a turn-of-the-century figure, State Senator Timothy Sullivan, head of the Gambling Commission. A big chief of Tammany, often called dishonorable and dishonest, he was as well-loved a character in the history of that organization as ever graced its ways. Big Tim took boodle, as graft was then called, from gamblers, whores and madams. People were quick to point out that he was "a darlin' man; never smoked, never touched a drop, and liked the card games." In Washington, where he served the party in Congress, he was said to be the champion poker player of that august body.

He saw to it that the syndicate, through its poolrooms, controlled the bookies and took protection money from gambling houses. It came to a good sum. The *New York Times* stated that "more than $3,095,000 is paid every year . . . for the protection afforded them by the police and other powers." Poolrooms paid out $1.5 million, gambling houses $500,000 a year. Floating crap games shelled out nearly $1 million a year.

Frank Farrell, the syndicate boss with an insatiable appetite, didn't see why people should be denied a little fun with cards or horse bets. He saw no grave delinquencies in what he did. "Isn't the city prosperous? Was money ever so plentiful as now? Why are we attacked in this manner? Didn't the people endorse us in the last election? I believe in the rule of the majority . . . and New York has said there should be an open town."

Reformers set up a ticket of proper candidates to drive corrupt officials from power. Dr. Charles Henry Parkhurst of the

Madison Square Presbyterian Church made a name for himself. "They are a lying, perjured, rum-soaked and libidinous lot," he stated. He headed the Society for the Prevention of Crime and was adept at getting attention. There was scandal when two of his undercover agents were found to be in the pay of the gambling syndicate. They were warning the gambling houses when raids were due.

In 1901 a reform ticket was elected in New York, and for a time some of the gambling houses were closed. But as a letter writer remarked in a newspaper, "Throw the rogues in; it will take them four years to turn dishonest, and then we can elect a new set. Gambling will go on." It did.

Tammany and the gamblers' syndicate recovered, and in later years were able to point out that President Cleveland and President Harding played poker and weren't ashamed to admit it. Cordell Hull, later Secretary of State, was proud of his record as a colonel and poker player during the Spanish-American war; he had won many a pot in his company on payday.

Popular songs and poems encouraged the idea of gambling as being manly and solidly American. Years earlier, Stephen Foster had written "Camptown Races," about the man who "bet on the bay."

By the end of the century, some Americans were singing of the women being as addicted as the men:

> *She bets on the horses*
> *And all the race courses . . .*
> *Each day all the papers*
> *Give space to her capers;*
> *She glories in poker,*
> *At billiards she's a corker,*
> *This up-to-date girl of mine. . . .*

There were songs like "Poker Love," "The Racing Game," "Rufus, Throw Dem Dice," and "Gamble on Me." From across the sea came "The Man Who Broke the Bank at Monte Carlo." In the popular theater, gambling was applauded in musicals like *Guys and Dolls*. Harrison Floy in *High Button Shoes* is a flim-flam man and bunco artist. *Porgy and Bess* also glorifies the gambler Sportin' Life.

Just as Prohibition failed because the public felt it was an unfair law that couldn't be enforced anyway, so gambling has continued to be looked upon by many as a popular pleasure for the sporting set and for those ordinary folk who feel a bet on a horse now and then makes life a bit more exciting and perhaps, with a little bit of luck, more rewarding.

For the bookmaker who sets up shop illegally, protection from the law is a must. Odds-On Harry, who ran a fairly prosperous bookie joint in Chicago, figured out his costs in taking bets during the 1930s. "I had me this back room behind a tailor shop off the Loop. I paid $200 a month rent. I laid on $150 a month to the cops and the ward boss, and—would you believe it?—to a reform group. I had six guys on the payroll, handling the wire service and the six phones, and I had to slip the phone company boys half a C note from time to time not to yank the phones. But I'd do in eight months, a year maybe, $60,000 above the nut [costs of doing business], and I'd take bets, be open to take wagers on, say, 8,500 races a year. On maybe fifty tracks. Did I cheat the bettors? I didn't want a leg broken. Some bookies screw the horse players. Of course the fixers often double-crossed themselves. How do you really make a fixed race a science? At most it's like, say, an art."

Harry described that art. You can throw a horse off his natural stride by giving him "wobble shoes"—heavy shoes and light shoes mixed up on different legs; the horse is not used to running with mixed weights. Or the jock can hold a horse back a few seconds at the gate. Some stables overfeed the animal just before the race so he's running on a full stomach. Or they run him into a sweat the night before the race. Double-wrapping helps the jockey (winding the reins twice around his hands so he has the pressure to pull the horse up). Arranging to lock or pocket the favorite consists of either keeping the favorite crowded and not able to run free, or a jockey locking boots with the jockey on the favorite. Can't the judges see it? "Sometimes. Sometimes they don't look closely."

Since saliva tests, the old needle or foo-foo dust drugging is rare. A horse can still be made into a drug addict; then, in an important race, the horse's shot of narcotic can be withheld, which makes him sluggish.

On certain tracks a small battery under the saddle could be turned on to give the horse an electric shock. But this too seems to have had its day. However, there is talk of horses being given some really hard shocks with a storage battery before a race. Brash sophistication finds new methods as the old are discarded.

However, the biggest damage to the bettor is done by bookmakers. Pierre V. Lorillard, the cigarette king who built Tuxedo Park, blamed them for the low esteem in which racing is often held. "I am very much opposed to bookmakers because they rob the public and rob owners of horses . . . rascals who would be fit subjects for prison when their profitable trade of robbing the public on the race course is at an end." This came from a man whose horse Iroquois won the English Derby, the only horse from this side of the Atlantic ever to do so.

Horse players and owners in the higher brackets tended to get together in spas: Saratoga, French Lick, Indiana. French Lick at one time was the most lawless of the spas, running wide-open poker games. It was controlled by Boss Tom Taggart, chairman of the Democratic National Committee that nominated William Jennings Bryan—a nongambler, a drinker of grape juice—for President.

By the turn of the century, the mecca of gamblers, the Monte Carlo of the Middle West, was Hot Springs, Arkansas. It was notorious as the most crooked place of high-stake amusements: pinochle, poker, dice, horses, and slot machines rigged to return 90 percent to the house. In 1910 a reform governor was elected, and Hot Springs was temporarily closed.

Many of the gamblers' terms for dice came from these spas. Those most familiar are:

Boxcars: two sixes
Snake eyes: one and one
Crap: two and one
Little Joe from Kokomo: add up to four
Natural: first throw a seven or eleven, a win
Crap out: seven out after the opening roll
Making a pass: winning by rolling the first number thrown
Fade: to cover the shooter's bet

15

A SHORT COURSE IN BETTING

CASINO POKER:

This is played legally in Gardena, California, near L.A., and is favored by housewives and old ladies with blue-rinsed hair. There are six licensed poker parlors of this type in the United States. The Herbert Group runs the Gardena Club and the Horse Shoe Club. These are open all week except Wednesdays. On Sunday they open at noon for the returning churchgoers who like to play cards. No liquor is served. It's all rather subdued, like a middle-class funeral parlor. While whole families play, there is a rule forbidding children and adults to play at the same table. The clubs collect a fee for the use of the table.

BASEBALL BETTING:

Betting on baseball through bookmakers is said to reach nearly $4 billion a season. Personal betting at bars, in the office, or among friends is estimated to raise the number to $15 billion a season. The odds and handicapping for the bookies is done in Las Vegas. Somehow the odds seem set so that betting either team comes out about even.

There are private office pools based on runs scored or on innings that decide a game. There are also professional cards for betting, usually run by the Mafia or a local mob. These cost from a dollar up, and one wins or loses on the runs scored by half a dozen teams. It's illegal, of course, but very popular. The card operators take as much as 80 percent for themselves. The cards are sold everywhere—pool halls, newsstands, dry-cleaning stores, drug stores, even door to door. A little store can make $600 a week on its cut of 10 percent for selling the cards.

In factories, a card handler can make $30,000 to $60,000 a year. It is estimated that $4 billion a year is collected by the card operators. Office bettors used to be mostly men, but today, women are betting nearly as much.

FOOTBALL:

Office gambling works like the baseball pool, but with a greater use of the postal service. You make contact with someone who will mail you a weekly ticket that you fill in with your choices. Payment, if you win, comes back by mail. Europe is wild about this kind of pool play on soccer. The odds are decided according to who is playing and the amount of money being wagered. American operators work mostly on the point edge. It's based on what teams are playing and their records. And so the odds, or points, are decided. Bookmakers do a land-office business in football betting. When college football was the big attraction, weekend betting on thirty-five college games could bring out $65 million in bets. On pro football, the amount runs as high as in baseball, perhaps higher. To most Americans, sport is a spectator sport.

Do gamblers reach football players to get them to shave points? There have been such rumors, but nothing has been proved. The first hint of such scandal was in 1963. Five Detroit Lions put up $50 each to bet on the Green Bay Packers to take the NFL crown that season. The players were fined $5,000 each, the club $2,000. Of course, in football the weather and injuries often upset the best-points style of betting.

BASKETBALL:

This sport has been the most prone to gossip that it is a fixed game for gamblers who like to have a sure thing going. Officials have a way of favoring the local team, so that some bettors in evenly matched games put their money on the home team. There were more fixed basketball games a few years ago than games that were on the level, some believe. People are still leery of pro basketball because of this. It's a fast, wonderful game, and people like to bet on it. Bookmakers will take the play and the point system. It's all in favor of the bookmaker. Of course, you can bet on a total score rather than on win or lose.

HOCKEY:

In Canada, it has been estimated that gambling money amounting to $30 million a year changes hands. It's less than that in the United States, but the figures are growing. Bookmakers say that a lot of betting on hockey is done during the game by buffs. Few Americans as yet know the fine points of the game; they just have a liking for fast action and lots of body slamming. The wise ones told me not to bet on a team that's touted to be ahead by two goals or more. This is known as "the spread line," and it puts bad percentages against you.

BOXING:

This has been called the most crooked of all sports to bet on. And as gangster and mob interests have entered boxing, the wise should stay away from what looks like a dive or a carry. Muhammad Ali, for a time, made boxing only show business. The gamblers had to take bets on rounds, and in what round, with the time figured to the second sometimes, the fight would end.

The first big money in boxing was brought in by Tex Rickard (formerly of Alaska in the Klondike Gold-Rush days), who became the fight promoter in the classic age of Jack Dempsey, Gene Tunney, Max Baer and Joe Louis. Most boxing fans think the sport has deteriorated into publicity shows with odd-ball characters. Boxing, which started with the Romans, who fought with lead-studded gloves, was from the beginning a betting game. In the seventeenth century, the British went in for bare-knuckle bouts. These were so bloody and bone-crushing that in the 1860s the Marquis of Queensberry rules were adopted; somewhat modified, they are in force today. In America, boxing has sometimes been looked upon by minorities as fighting one's way out of the ghetto. The Irish took up the fight in the square ring. John L. Sullivan and James Corbett, betting favorites, led the Irish. Then it was the Jews' turn, with such fighters as Benny Lennard and Battling Levinsky. As the material lot of the Irish and the Jews improved, the black fighters came forward, often controlled by gamblers. The best was Jack Johnson, the first Negro world champion. He was so resented by the bigots that for years bettors hunted for a "White Hope."

Johnson, labeled a Mann Act violator, went abroad, struggled and sported, and then took a dive to Jess Willard in Havana. Since the rise of the great black fighter—Joe Louis, Sugar Ray Robinson and Muhammad Ali—the black boxer has been on top. The first Ali-Frazier fight brought in $20 million for closed-circuit TV rights. The fighters divided nearly $3 million. However, the push now comes from the Puerto Ricans and Mexican-Americans wanting a chance at the fame and money.

Boxing for gamblers was at a low ebb, Pony Benny said. "When Ali refused to serve in the Vietnam war, betting on boxing dropped from $500 million to about $10 million. Also, odds makers used their own knowledge and ways of setting up odds. Sometimes they guessed wrong.

A gambler I know advises: "Smart bettors follow the rule: Always bet on the champion, because he's picked his opponent; he's wiser in the ring. It's a big-money setup to remain champion; he isn't going to pick out the toughest man right off. Ali made the boxing business into a theater exhibition rather than a real contest. Oddly enough, the greater the clowning, the bigger the take, thanks to closed-circuit television. Betting rules for the gambler in fairly honest bouts are: Don't back a man who has had nearly fifty fights getting there. Don't put your money on a bleeder; the crowd and the ring official have a way of stopping such a fight. Don't back flatfooted fighters. Contests are often won by a pair of legs, not fists. A fighter who has rested too long between bouts is a good man to bet against. Remember, a fighter slows up with age, as do his reflexes. Boxing today is sure a changeover from a real contest to a circus show. So betting should be done only for the fun of it. The game has dropped off into just showtime."

Playing Cards
Manufacturing cards used for pleasure or for gambling is a large industry. The U.S. Playing Card Company of Cincinnati is a giant, run by Andrew Luther, Jr., and it is not just king card maker of the United States. The company is the world's largest manufacturer of playing cards and has developed a world market, particularly in the Far East. The plant supplies cards to four out of every five American households and distributes to more than a hundred nations. Far East sales now rival those of

Las Vegas in volume. In Las Vegas, a deck is used until some-one asks for a change. In Macao, a Portuguese island off Hong Kong, a deck is used once or twice, and then destroyed. Chinese are superstitious gamblers; a fresh deck is always in demand.

While business abroad prospers, growth on the home front moves on. "Frankly, if our best client quit us tomorrow, we could survive very easily," said Luther. The company has a work force of 1,000 employees and twenty-five presses. One press produces 20,000 decks an hour, twenty-four hours a day. Plastic-coated cards are on the market, but most gamblers do not use them.

Luther insists that the base of the business is the everyday guy who plays gin rummy and the family that can't afford to go out. "It's still the cheapest form of entertainment going. Most businesses fall off when the economy suffers. Ours gets better."

The most popular cards are the Bicycle and Bee lines, which have been used for almost a century.

A good part of the firm's sales comes from special custom designs and made-to-order signature cards for individuals or firms. Years ago they made a deck for Winston Churchill. They have also made special decks for Presidents Eisenhower and Nixon. United States astronauts who circled the moon had fireproof cards. Presidential jets are stocked with decks carrying the Chief Executive's seal. These often are "borrowed" and never seen again.

The company offers fifty varieties, including Braille cards. The company doesn't make trick or marked decks. They notify the FBI and the Nevada Gambling Commission when someone tries to order them. As Charlie Ross told us, "Good card mark-ers exist. Cards are easy to mark. Use pin pricks or dots, or shade a bit of a pattern. Special eyeglasses can pick up colors invisible to the ordinary eye. The only danger is in getting killed if you use them."

16

BINGO

Defending the Catholic Church's big money-raiser, bingo, an official archdiocesan newspaper of the Church, *The Advocate,* wrote in 1953: "It is not gambling but the abuse of gambling that involves an immoral act." After long years of effort, bingo games (very like Las Vegas keno and other forms of lottery that resemble it) are now legal in more than a dozen states. The bingo amendment of New York in 1957 passed by about 650,000 votes.

Historically, bingo is a derivative of the ancient Italian game of lottery. The first Italian immigrants brought it to this country. Here it caught on quickly, so that by the turn of the century it was respectable in churches, clubs, and fraternal orders, and had become a weekly or semiweekly event before movies became full-length features. Bingo is now prevalent everywhere.

Some $2.5 billion a year is spent buying bingo cards. In the most popular form of the game, a player buys a card, usually for two dollars. The card has boxes numbered 1 to 75 in five rows, with five numbers in each row. Every card therefore holds twenty-five numbers, and the combinations on the cards are all different. Numbers are drawn from a bowl or a cage; as the number is called out, the player covers or marks on his or her card each number that is called. (Generally, it's a woman's game in many churches.) The winner is the first player in the room to cover five numbers in a row, up and down, across, or diagonally.

In Illinois, bingo has been legalized since 1971. "Bingo in Illinois is big business," admitted Illinois Revenue Director Robert H. Allphin. The state gets 10 percent of the take from bingo games. That produced $7.2 million during 1975, 25 percent more than in the previous year. Money spent on bingo in Illinois is more than $70 million annually, and it keeps increasing. "We're not aware of infiltration by criminal elements," said Allphin. "Investigators, it is hoped, are keeping the game clean and seeing that the state gets 10 percent off the top."

There is no commercial bingo. Games are run only by state-licensed religious, charitable, fraternal, veterans', educational or labor groups. Only unpaid volunteers are used to run games.

In 1976 California proposed that bingo be legalized statewide, with the proceeds to go to charitable causes, and neither the state, counties, or cities collecting any revenue. The cities and counties would charge a license fee for playing. The proposition was passed by a huge majority.

The game is usually honest, but secular groups have had scandals. The person who picks the numbers can palm a set of winning numbers, with a confederate holding a card with matching numbers. Certain cards can be given to certain players, and the bowl or cage will contain *only* those numbers for a quick win. The Church sees bingo as being as natural as conjugal rights and denies vehemently that it is habit-forming and that it creates gamblers who go on to cards, dice, or horses. Others claim that, since the payoffs in bingo are small, many who enjoy games of chance move on to forms of gambling where the winner gets a bigger percentage.

Raffles are a spin-off from bingo in which an organization puts up a car, clothes, kitchenware, sporting goods, or similar items. Books of coupons are sold with numbers that may later be drawn to win. The drawing held for the lucky number winners can be a gala affair.

The raffle is often a swindle. Many organizations never even have a drawing, or the prizes are not the ones shown. Shills win many of the big prizes, which are returned to the merchants. Even so moral a publication as *Reader's Digest* was accused by some of failing to deliver the winnings in a prize coupon contest.

In California, McDonald's held a contest for autos and other prizes. Students using a computer at Cal Tech made a shambles of the scheme by sending in thousands of computerized listings.

The students won most of the prizes, and the chain owners had to put out an extra set of prizes for less-creative citizens.

Contests for cash or other prizes held by publishers, newspapers, and manufacturers in which one sends in a slogan or finishes some awesome praise of a product in twenty-five words or less are as chancy as any pick-a-winner gamble. On television game shows the winning of products or cash is regarded as earnings, and the winner has to pay federal, state and city taxes on them.

National Lotteries

During World War II bills were introduced in Congress for national lotteries to help the war effort and pay for part of the general slaughter and the consumption of national resources. None of these bills became law. But the government did see gambling as part of a soldier's life, something to keep G.I. Joe from becoming antisocial. As a "comforting item" the quartermaster depot bought nearly a million pairs of dice, and the PX furnished soldiers with over 50 million decks of cards in one year. Figures as to how much money was wagered in Army and Navy wartime gambling are hard to come by. One figure given me (unofficially) by someone close to the Pentagon was $300 million a month, and nearly $80 million of that went to professional gambling tricksters, dice and card manipulators, some of whom enlisted simply to run games and bilk soldiers and sailors.

The war leaders themselves did not mind gambling. Churchill would bet on horse races and the Oxford-Cambridge boat races. In 1944 General Eisenhower bet his staff five pounds that the Allied armies would cross the German frontier by Christmas. As he admitted publicly, "They didn't, and I lost." Lord Mountbatten was an avid bridge player, but didn't want it known that he gambled.

Eisenhower was a poker player. Asked about the odds on getting three of a kind and a pair of jacks in a game, he said, "I'd say about 1 in 1,082,900. Any mathematician will prove I'm completely wrong. . . . Don't count on doing it in a pinch." General Patton bet on polo games, but during the war he traveled only with his hunting dogs, not his ponies. Franklin D. Roosevelt liked a big bet. He played bridge enthusiastically, for good stakes, and always bet on Harvard in the Yale-Harvard football games.

The race tracks also did their bit during World War II. The New York State Racing Commission raised $3 million. A small New Hampshire track raised $80,000. (A PX sergeant told me a lot of race horses ended up as steak in officers' mess, "as prime Kansas steer.")

The war accelerated gambling, and Nevada had a licensing system under the control of sheriffs and county boards. But the war brought in the Mafia, and it was able to get many of the sheriffs and boards to listen to reason and feel the roll of bills offered them. Because of this, in 1945 Nevada made gambling the job of Nevada's State Tax Commission. It could cancel licenses; however, the mobs pressed in anyway with dummy fronts and hidden interests in many of the big hotels. They had come out of the war with millions made in the black market on sugar, tires and war contracts. They needed a place to dump their loot; gambling casinos offered them the opportunity.

All through the war the gambling patrons did not care who owned what. Across the nation, gambling went on at fever pitch. One slot-machine loser pasted on a robber robot the message:

IN CASE OF AIR RAID STAND BY THIS MACHINE.
NOBODY HAS HIT IT YET.

But hope springs eternal in slot-machine addicts. As one gray-haired old lady playing a paper cup of half-dollars told me in Miami Beach, "It's my exercise."

The gambling of ordinary citizens went on after the war. It is almost impossible to pass a day without seeing gambling promoted on TV or in the newspapers. For several years I kept a scrapbook on the subject. Here are a few items.

One of Britain's bookmaking firms announced in 1976 that it lowered the odds against a visit from outer space to 40 to 1 following a rush of bets from Southern California. It had been 100 to 1 with Ladbroke and Co. Ltd until the bets started pouring in. The long shot was shortened to the new mark, and the firm stands to lose $500,000 if someone does drop in from outer space.

Mrs. Ruth Norman is the bettor who staked $8,000 to $10,000 on the belief that alien landings will take place this year, so said Ladbroke's oddsmaker, Ronald Pollard. Mrs. Norman is a leader of the Unarius (Universal Articulate Interdenominational Understanding of Science), an educational foundation in El Cajon, California.

FOUR ILLINOIS CITY OFFICIALS ACCUSED OF CORRUPTION. The police chief, an administrative assistant to the mayor, the director of public safety, and a police lieutenant were charged with official corruption. Chief ——, forty, and Safety Director ——, sixty-eight, were arrested on charges of official misconduct on allegations of condoning, permitting and protecting gambling operations, according to St. Clair County officials. L ——, fifty-seven, assistant to Mayor William E. Mason, and Police Det. J ——, fifty, were arrested on charges of accepting money to protect gambling.

"You've got to be kidding. It's unbelievable," said Kenneth Householder, fifty-eight, a bachelor and architect for the city of San Francisco. He had just learned he had won the $800,000 super prize in the Irish Sweepstakes. "I don't know what you do with money like that." Somewhere in the Internal Revenue Service there had to be an agent calculating what Householder could do "with money like that."

In the 1970s about two dozen states were working on some kind of a state lottery, or beginning to talk of it. Federal law prevents the mailing or advertising of legal lotteries out of the state, as well as the shipping of tickets or winnings. For all that, the state lotteries, impervious to morality or the risk of creating whole generations of compulsive gamblers, do bring in cash. New York sold about $25 million worth of lottery tickets a year in the 1970s. New Hampshire sold about $5 million worth.

Thirteen states now have legal lotteries. Nine states have prizes of $1 million each. *The National Observer* reported in August 1976 that 160 persons had gambled and won $1 million in state lotteries. Usually the million is paid out at $50,000 a year for 20 years, or for life, for the reason that heavy taxes on the winnings would be disastrous, and often the million dollars paid out in cash, all at once, could have an adverse effect on an individual's life and on his or her family.

Dr. H. Roy Kaplan, sociologist at Pitzer College, Claremont, California, has spent time interviewing thirty-four of the lottery-winning millionaires. "They were extremely hostile, for the most part," he said. "Once you win, it's open season on you. . . . There was an overwhelming feeling that money isn't as much as they thought it would be. But I haven't met anybody who, despite the adversities, would conclude that it wasn't worth it and give the money back."

The best guess is that $75 billion a year is bet in gambling in the United States. This does *not* include playing the stock market. However, as Richard Ney, stockbroker and author, stated in *The Wall Street Journal,* "Investors lose and the house (stockbrokers) wins in the greatest gambling casinos in the world—Wall Street."

Outside of Wall Street, the biggest betting centers, mostly in illegal wagers, are Lexington, Kentucky; Dayton, Ohio; New York City; New Orleans; San Francisco; and Tijuana, Mexico. Havana used to be important, before Castro took over. Dice players seem to have the most fun. At least they are the most vocal.

The question I was asked more than any other about dice play is whether a shooter can control honest dice. Long-time crap shooters usually answered, "Most likely, if it's the blanket roll" (when the dice play is on a thick blanket). Charlie Ross agreed: "An expert handler tossing onto a thick blanket can control the numbers coming up by the hold and release of the dice, at least enough times to give him great odds."

On November 4, 1976, Americans not only elected Jimmy Carter President of the United States, but they read in headlines: 4 STATES APPROVE GAMBLING INITIATIVES; *Sweepstakes, Lottery, Casinos OKd, but Delaware Rejects Slot Machines.*

Delaware rejected an initiative that would have permitted slot machines, whereas other states approved gambling initiatives. Colorado voters approved a state sweepstake. In Georgia, they approved a constitutional amendment legalizing nonprofit bingo games, and in Vermont they agreed to ask the state legislature to approve a state-run lottery. New Jersey voters approved casino gambling in the state's best-known resort, Atlantic City.

Already there was talk of Atlantic City as the Las Vegas of the East. Atlantic City, that dilapidated municipality with 17 percent unemployment, an average family income of $7,000, high crime rate, slums and no future, had hit the jackpot.

Land values were up, the old hotels became prize properties to be renovated. And Resorts International (the investigated firm with casinos in the Bahamas) had substantial holdings in Atlantic City. Playboy Enterprises and some of Las Vegas's operators—Del Webb, Caesar's World, MGM—were rumored to be interested in prospects for big-time casino gambling on the East Coast.

17

NUMBERS

Most authorities on gambling and crime agree that the gambling lottery called Numbers is bet on more then any other and amounts to the richest gambling setup in the nation. More people play it and more money is put into it than into horse racing, cards, dice, or roulette. Numbers is illegal almost everywhere in the nation, yet it is estimated that twenty million people a day play it.

In its simplest form, a player puts down anything from a dime to five dollars on any three numbers he chooses. To make the game foolproof and insure that it is not rigged, the winning number is usually taken from the last three digits in the U.S. Treasury daily report or from the last three digits of the final sum of the Stock Exchange daily trading. One group pushing numbers also used the number of people reported attending a New York Yankees baseball game that day. Whatever the source of the winning numbers, it seems fair to the bettor and above suspicion.

Numbers is not a new game. It goes back to the London lotteries of the 1700s, when pennies were bet on some numbers to support certain charities.

The American form of this personal faith in numbers came over in the late 1880s as a "policy shop," using what was called a policy wheel to pick winners. It was a racket, as most of the money went to the policy-wheel owners. One Al Adams had nearly a thousand policy shops in New York City. Adams rigged the winning numbers. All of his shops were active and ran free with the approving wink of Tammany Hall, the corrupt political machine that ran the city under Boss Tweed and his gang. When Tweed fell from power, a reform group got

Adams sentenced to Sing Sing for a year and a half. He committed suicide afterward. The Treasury figures came in then, as foolproof assurance that the winning number could not be tampered with.

The lure of numbers was the fact that it could be played for as little as a nickel, and so the poor took to it. From the turn of the century until the Depression, Harlem was the home grounds of the numbers game. In Chicago's white and black slums in New Orleans and Washington, D.C., numbers continues to be popular to this day.

The numbers big men were called "bankers," and the games, or *"banks,"* were often a family affair, handed down like red hair or a silver tea service.

In Harlem, Madam St. Clair ran numbers as her personal policy wheel, claiming magical potency for customers. She did so well that she had her own bodyguards once it became known she had cleared a million dollars. She had inherited her game and then perfected the system of banker, operators, distributors, agents and runners. It was a pecking order that left the top operator and banker safe from the law and exposed the agents and runners to the dangers of the streets.

As numbers grew in popularity, it became big business, necessitating the bribery of the police and often of the courts. Murder and terror in the 1920s and 1930s came when the numbers game became the racket of the white Mafia and their black operators. Today, black mobsters have pushed the Mafia out of much of the Harlem and Brownsville numbers games. The move is only ethnic, and numbers continues to be a crime-controlled form of gambling.

Numbers moved deeply into the black ghettos when World War II sent country blacks into urban war industries. Whites began to hear of numbers and soon played it. Agents and runners for policy wheels infiltrated the war plants, the shipyards, and even the Army camps. Agents became union officials in the Detroit auto plants, and some claimed membership in the Teamsters Union. The workers and their families took to numbers with such enthusiasm that it began to have a bad effect on the war effort in the factories. The Ford Motor Company, although it had its own goon squads and head-busters, called in the police and took action, causing the arrest of over two dozen numbers agents in its employ. Records show that in one area nearly 100,000 workers in Ford plants were playing numbers, and in one factory employees had laid out $1,500,000 on the numbers.

By the 1950s the mobs were deep into the numbers banks, and shootouts resulted in riddled corpses in the streets and the nearest body of deep water. Some operators lost their lives when they refused to pay off. This had no effect on the popularity of the game.

How much does the "honest" banker pay out of his huge collections? Only about 25 cents of every dollar collected goes back to winners. The remainder goes into the hands of the policy boss, less what he pays out to agents and runners, and, as the Knapp Commission Report proved, to the police and political figures.

Numbers supports a small army. Thousands of people in New York City are full-time numbers runners. They write out numbers and take money from anyone—child or adult, white or black—from the five boroughs. The runner is expendable. He rarely knows the men he's working for; he knows only the man above him, never the policy boss in his section. Payoffs, too, are made by people who don't know the real top boss in their sector. It is almost a foolproof system of staying clear of the law. The Knapp Report on the police clearly showed that on almost all levels there were payoffs to keep most gambling heads free of arrest and conviction.

Arresting runners is futile. Eager replacements wait by the hundred in every ghetto and rundown district to be picked for the honor of being runners. To the player it seems little worse than playing checkers or doing a crossword puzzle. Most players begin with a daily bet of a small coin, and dream big. But soon it's a compulsive action and the player can go to a dollar or more a day on a number.

To get the money to play numbers, youth of both sexes turn to crime or prostitution. Prostitutes aged twelve and upward play numbers. Numbers and drugs are two of the chief causes of crime in the nation. Yet most citizens brush off numbers as a harmless sport, like matching pennies.

The money bet on numbers adds up. Some put it as $10 billion a year. Is it really gambling? The take is so huge for the syndicates, and the payoffs so scant, that it's really just a racket to skin the players. It also gives the Mafia and the syndicates they control billions of dollars to buy hotels, trucking companies, laundries, construction firms, and other businesses while financing the smuggling of heroin and other drugs. It shows the worst side of the American interest in gambling.

Social workers involved in welfare and health have estimated that 60 to 65 percent of the people in Harlem and Brownsville bet on a daily number. The runner gets 25 percent commission on every sale. The agent to whom he passes his scores and cash gets 10 percent. What is paid in "grease" (police protection) hasn't been figured out. The odds against a player winning on a number is 1,000 to 1. Sometimes no payoff occurs. The ordinary banker who works for the mob can make $200,000 to $300,000 a year. The mob, of course, makes millions.

What of the player who makes all this possible? As a runner told me, "It's like the horse that wins the Kentucky Derby. If he's lucky, he gets a bag of oats." Billy C. told me it pays for his education. "Sure, I'm a runner for the policy bosses. I mean, I need books and a typewriter and scuff [food], and there isn't much bread to be made by a black boy who doesn't take a kick in the ass from whitey. I've been a runner in New York and Chi and up in Frisco. And now I'm working out in Watts, all along Central Avenue. I take numbers from charlies [whites], too. But mostly I'm with the brothers and sisters. They play numbers like it was a new form of God. It's their fun, you know; it's their dreamboat side—kind of the mystery of life; you catch? They vision up a number, or spook up six narcs and two needles and five rats eating garbage, and they have 625. Or they have an old gypsy dreambook and horoscope readings, and they spend maybe half a day figuring out one lousy number. Numbers is their theater, their way of being plugged in with the cosmos. So I take their money and put down their numbers. Maybe it's welfare or unemployment or pension dough. So? Where the money comes from doesn't matter. Social Security widows of black dudes who got the deep six in Vietnam get their check from Washington. Sure, it's a safety valve. Houseworkers, too, play numbers. And of course just plain stealing goes on. Muggings pay for numbers, too. The police? Don't make me laugh. The police know every runner in every city I worked. They know the agents, maybe they even know the banker, but I doubt that. And the law, the feds don't faze bankers. The syndicates have the best lawyers, real dignified gents that wear vests with $400 suits. How to stop a thing like the numbers? Why, you breed up a new kind of lawyer, a new kind of policeman.

"I have this old biddy that fences stolen radios and television sets and she is always betting on 963. She's got a system, like most gamblers. 'Now Billy, the world comes in threes, *not* twos or ones—like triangles, the Holy Trinity. Last night I had this vision, see. God came to me and said nine; and then Martin Luther King, Jr., he appeared and held up six fingers; and Lester, my dead husband, hovered over me with his front teeth showing—three of them were missing. So I'm still betting 963 today.'

"I mean that's the kind of jazz I've heard all week on why they bet a number. You should hear some of the reasons I hear for gambling on a number that turns them on. If I told you, you'd think I was putting *you* on. But, know what I think? Gambling gives a lot of people their jollies, jolts them out of a sad rut, a bad vibe."

18

NICK THE GREEK

His name was Nicholas Andrea Dandolos, but the several times I met him everyone called him Nick the Greek (not to be confused with Jimmy the Greek, the Las Vegas odds-maker). From the 1920s on, until his death at eighty-four in 1966, he was pointed out as the most fabulous gambler of all time, having won or lost, it was estimated, $50 million. I found him to be a very polite gentleman. In the 1950s, with his great days behind him, he felt his life was full. My friend the late Cy Rice, who wrote the authorized biography, *Nick the Greek,* quoted Nick's famous self-scrutinizing remark: "The greatest pleasure in my life is gambling and winning. The next greatest pleasure is gambling and losing."

One reason for his introspection may be that when he could lose a million at poker or dice and shrug it off with dignity, he hardly ever gambled with his own money. Usually he was backed by a syndicate. Rich Greeks who believed in Nick's skill and luck would support him. Even after a huge loss, they never failed to back him.

I found Nick to have that steady gaze and the kind of graciousness one finds in long-time professional gamblers. He differed from the hotshot, fast-talking, exhibitionist gamblers. He was more like the sporting colonial Virginians, the well-tailored chance-takers of New Orleans of the post-Civil War, and the turn-of-the-century gamblers who worked the ocean liners. Nick proudly carried the tag "the Last of the Gentlemen Gamblers."

Nicholas Andrea Dandolos was born on the island of Crete in the sun-baked village of Rethimnon near what some think was the birthplace of El Greco, another wandering Greek. Nick left for the United States, and in 1902, at eighteen, he became an American citizen. He made a modest living as a fig salesman to the Greek colony in Chicago. His dreams, he later said, vacillated between extremes. By frugal living he managed to save up $250, and, attracted by poker games in a downtown saloon, he lost it all in one night. He was, however, delighted with the game and found it a better way of life than carrying around fifty-pound boxes of figs. For him the decisive moment was just ahead.

The prosperous Greeks in the Middle West and elsewhere heard of Nick's style, his interest in good food, fine clothes and beautiful women. He became a kind of folk hero. He gambled first as a student of and finally as an expert at cards and dice. Unlike most gamblers, he was never one to rely on superstition. Like most card players, he also bet on horses and tried to get inside information on fixed rides, which in those days meant that a horse had been drugged with a powder called "foo-foo-fum." Nick smoked $1.50 cigars and was a bookmaker for a while. He even ran horses in Canada, where he was barred from the tracks. As he told me, "Anybody who thinks horse racing is all honest would bet you water isn't wet."

As a gambler, Nick avoided slot machines, roulette and blackjack. "You have to play a game you are easy with, and I never was with them. I like to sit in on a fine gentlemanly poker game and begin by buying $10,000 to $50,000 worth of chips. I secure self-esteem that way."

He was known to lay down $50,000 in a dice game on the man shooting to make his point. In the 1920s, when he was nearly fifty, he was often at Hot Springs, a place good for stewing out losses and looking for a game. The remote little gambling spot just southwest of Little Rock in the Ouachita Mountains was the stomping ground of moonshine makers and gamblers. Nick, lolling in a steam box, liked the therapeutic sensation of being steamed alive like a lobster in a pot.

But the bigtime didn't last. The shadow and substance of a gambler shifts quickly. By 1949 Nick was on the decline and seeming to lose his touch. He was the victim of what he claimed was a crooked poker game in Las Vegas, and he sued for his loss of over half a million. Gamblers don't go to court very often, and he lost the case.

"Why do people gamble, Nick?"

"Why do you paint and draw and write? Why not sell shoes, be a pork butcher, or go dishonest and enter politics?"

"Seriously, what makes a compulsive gambler? I've been talking to doctors and mental-health specialists, and I don't get one definitive answer.

"But they're not gamblers. They're shrinks, head-feelers, the Freudian couch specialists asking questions. Look, I've met them, these shrinks, gabbed with them. They have cooked minds, with one-way vision for selling their specialties. People gamble. Why? Because they find ordinary life a swindle, a sellout, a ripoff. It's just eating, working, dying. The nose to the ground and the boss chewing out your ass. Attached to one woman, she growing wrinkled and mean before your eyes. Okay, okay; most people accept it. Most people accept anything and do not balk. But the few who don't accept, that's your lifelong gambler. They're out after the adventure, the chance, seeing the new town, opening the fresh deck, having new women. The gambler senses, has the feel he's his own destiny. Being Greek, I know the fates and furies have us charted, have it all planned with tragedy in the end. The deep six, the death scene, with the good-bye Charlie prayer for your soul from somebody who never met you saying you're gone."

"The shrinks, as you call them, have deeper reasons."

"Soft mothers? Tough fathers? Drunken parents? Childhood traumas? Gamble or you'll switch to buggery? A fear of authority, or a failure in bed? A wanting to be punished by Big Daddy up in the sky?"

"Some claim all that makes gamblers are losers."

"Some losers are the dropouts of the world. But they don't all gamble. Some punish themselves by booze, or heisting a bank, becoming flashers, drag queens. But I'm talking of real gamblers who want to grab life by the throat, rape it, toss it over their shoulders. They want the excitement of never knowing if there is bread or caviar tomorrow. They are the kind of gamblers who in times past became Columbus, Jesus, or Jesse James."

"But isn't it a sickness, Nick?"

"Isn't life a sickness? And don't we know the cure? Forest Lawn or Potter's Field. Once you know *that*—what the

Elizabethans called 'the skull beneath the skin'—what have you got to lose? Knowing there's no big final jackpot, no royal flush possible? You can only push your luck, play out the hand dealt you, knowing there is no tomorrow. The gambler, he's the only philosopher who has figured it out right. Take it all in while you can. And if the next day you're scuffing for coffee and cakes, still you've had something. Something shoe clerks and the people with savings accounts never have or can get—a thumbing of your nose at the whole frigging universe."

"Let's get back to the wreck of human lives that gambling often causes. The embezzlers, the suicides, the broken homes, the disgrace."

"Only if you admit it's often the same end result in big business, beating the stockholders by going bankrupt. Or ordering a frontal attack in a war, being screwed, ruined by a lawyer or a woman. Truth is, more people kill themselves because they hate life than over gambling losses."

Nick figured he had won $15 million in his great days, and lost $15 million (he never gave the same figures twice). "I was even: I felt good. I stood just even—about where I was when I started gambling."

He remained voluble and proud, but he never again climbed up to the top of the gambling world. In his seventies he had a series of heart attacks. He borrowed money to return to the gambling tables. He still had some credit, and one unlucky night at the Horse Shoe Club he lost $200,000, not in cash but in markers—notes promising to pay. Changing his scene, he then lost $60,000 at the Golden Nugget. Yet he still sneered at Greeks like Onassis and Niarchos: "No card sense in any of those bookkeepers."

He kept a last thousand dollars in his hatband, and he lost the hat, too. The gambling grapevine reported, "Nick the Greek is tapped out." He was down at times to betting two dollars on a horse at Hollywood Park. Nick was now making touches, borrowing, practically panhandling. It was fadeout for the King of Gamblers. People of dubious loyalty began to avoid him. He descended to selling "Nick the Greek's Winning Gambling System." Yet he admitted in private, "There are no winning systems. But what am I to do? To quote the poet Yeats, 'There is no country for old men.' "

He died on Christmas Day 1966. Money had to be collected to pay for his funeral. Someone suggested an epitaph for his tombstone: "The Aristotle of the Don't Pass Crap Table Line." The FBI sent observers to the funeral, which was well attended by gamblers and Mafia representatives: the shrewd, the intemperate and eccentric of the gambling world. A governor, two senators, a sheriff and a county commissioner were also present.

There is no need to moralize on the life of Nicholas Andrea Dandolos. However, once as he left, a loser, after an all-night session, he quoted a phrase from the Psalms that could sum up his life: ". . . because I was flesh, and a breath that passeth away, and cometh not again."

Appendix

THE GAMBLER ON THE COUCH

A scientific paper that appeared in the *American Journal of Psychiatry* in 1953 describes the work of Dr. Nathan Kline et al. that had opened the door to a new "technique of control of human behavior." Could the habitual gambler, the uncontrollable plunger, be lifted from his compulsive ruin of himself and his family? Dr. Kline had been interested in *Rauwolfia serpentina,* a plant used in India for insomnia, mental breakdowns, fevers, and other maladies. It was also called *pagla ka dacra*—"the insanity herb"—from its use with those whose actions were often beyond reason, certainly the state of the habitual gambler-loser.

Dr. Kline, using reserpine, an alkaloid derived from *Rauwolfia,* experimented with the drug as a medication for problem patients. It had an amazing effect as therapeutic treatment for unstable people.

On the subject of reserpine, David Hendin in his book *Life Givers* (Morrow, 1976) quotes from a paper given at the New York Academy of Science in 1954: "There is thus indication that, although obsessions and compulsions do not entirely disappear, the discomforting motivating drive is reduced to livable proportions."

Certainly this was a ray of hope for the grievous condition of the compulsive gambler, without doing harm to his other functions. It does not seem to act as a numbing tranquillizer.

In preparing this study of American gambling games and gamblers, I have questioned doctors and psychiatrists on the use of this drug in the control of compulsive gamblers.

Few doctors would admit they had tried it or were willing to give any data on their progress with it. One Mexican doctor did say that he had used it several times on gamblers and that his results were successful in 80 percent of his cases. Two of his patients were women. Even those who were not fully helped (he did not like the word "cured") tapered off their wild gambling habits, and played cards or backed horses with a little better control.

However, he did not want to publish anything on his case histories, or even to allow the use of his name, as he was fearful of criticism from the Mexican medical societies. I had heard of two doctors who used the drug on gamblers in the United States, but they refused to comment on the results.

As for the psychiatrists I had contacted about reserpine, the majority turned down the idea of a better psychiatric discipline than theirs. They were couch-bound as Freudians; or, if they practiced more than taking notes, they stuck to their faith in such treatments as the injection of insulin.

In hunting down what I hoped would be scientific knowledge as to why men and women become compulsive gamblers, I have come across many theories, and in interviewing doctors, psychiatrists and followers of Freud, Jung and Adler, I have gained some knowledge, though nothing conclusive. Some have good reputations as experts in the field of gamblers' problems. A New York psychiatrist says, "Gambling is a form of self-flagellation and masochism. Many compulsive gamblers come from broken homes. Most had domineering mothers who showed them little affection when they were young. The compulsive gambler is buying love or a substitute form of love. Obsessive gamblers are self-destructive—they have a subconscious wish to lose."

Is it a problem for the national government—like drugs, firearms, spying, air and water pollution? No full official investigation of the nation's gambling habits existed until the late 1970s, when the Department of Justice set up "a federal survey on gambling," conducted by a team from Harvard and M.I.T. Major police departments throughout the nation are taking part in the study, which is seeking to determine the extent of gambling in the United States and to assess the "social costs" involved and the pros and cons of state control.

The inquiry is still in its early stages, so of course none of its expected findings can be predicted.

In his book, *The Healing Mind,* Dr. Irving Oyle (Celestial Arts, 1975) notes the following type of person: "There are people who can leave the day's worries at the office; they know how to relax . . . allow themselves lapses of daydreaming and are able to periodically shut off empirical reality. Most of them would subscribe to the old idea of the power of positive thinking. There are many groups who use this philosophy in teaching their followers that if they constantly see their situations in the most positive light, everything will be fine. 'If you want to have lots of money,' they say, 'act as if you already have it. See yourself spending it! Assume that you have it and it will come to you.' "

I know a dozen compulsive gamblers who think the money will come to them—by gambling.

One psychologist who had treated gamblers believed their way of life was "a retreat from a world that is broken down. It is a retreat to a dream where the edge of reality is beginning to blur. A retreat from a failed civilization to magic and incantation, a retrogression to a child's safety, with normal adult rules and demands pushed aside."

Are gamblers refugees from our society? Some do show symptoms that afflict real refugees. In May 1976, Dr. Jean Carlin, associate dean of psychiatry at the University of California (Irvine), spoke at the 129th annual meeting of the American Psychiatric Association on the adjustment of children and their families. "Six to eight months after their arrival in America, many Vietnamese started becoming quite depressed. They began having horrendous nightmares, mainly violent dreams in which their relatives or friends were being killed. Some are so haunted and depressed that they need professional help." The patterns of dreams of refugees and some gamblers are amazingly alike.

Dr. Carl Jung, Freud's one-time disciple, wrote abstractly of forces that move people compulsively. In *Psychology and Alchemy* he says, "There is within the psyche a process that seeks its own goal independently of external factors. . . . Choose a dream or some other fantasy image and concentrate on it by simply looking at it. . . . Try to find out what image expresses this mood (or symptom). Fix this image in your mind by concentrating on it. In this way conscious and unconscious are united."

For the gambler at the crap table, at cards, roulette, betting on horses or sports, these are certainly united. As Jung explains it further, "Take the unconscious in one of its handiest forms, say a spontaneous fantasy . . . concentrate on it and observe its alterations. This fantasy is a real psychic process which is happening to you personally. . . . If you recognize your own involvement, you enter into the process with your own personal reactions, just as if you were one of the fantasy figures, or rather, as if the drama being enacted before your eyes were real. Healing comes only from what leads the patient beyond himself and beyond his entanglement with the ego."

In "Controlling the Mind" in *The Osteopathic Physician,* June 1974, Jack Leahy states that ". . . as much as 80% of human problems involve psychosomatic disease, either totally or as a contributing factor . . . that a certain section of the brain . . . learned a bad habit . . . and is functioning in an undesirable manner. Research is showing that these bad habits can be voluntarily eliminated by retraining, using biofeedback to tell us what is happening in the physiological domain so that we can become aware of, and use, specific existential changes that are co-related with specific physiological changes. . . . If we can get physiologically sick from responding psychologically to stress in some inappropriate way, we can perhaps get well by learning to control the physiologic response."

Can simple hypnotic technique help? Carl Simonton, M.D., in *The Dimensions of Healing,* Los Altos, California: *The Academy of Parapsychology and Medicine,* 1972, writes of the work of the Silva Mind Control School. It teaches an average individual effective mind control in a short period of time by concentrating an "increased intelligence, an improved memory, heightening of extrasensory perceptive abilities, more incisive and intuitive problem-solving powers, and better control of human emotions and bodily functions . . . to correct physical conditions ranging from migraine headaches . . . drug and alcohol addiction, overeating and cigarette smoking . . . just a few of the undesirable behavioral manifestations which mind control also can correct . . ." Clearly, I was told by psychiatrists, gambling belongs with these addictions.

Dr. Edward Stainbrook, for fifteen years head of the Department of Psychiatry at the University of Southern California, at present head of the Department of Human Behavior there, in a press interview in the midsummer of 1976, has attempted to explain why many people deviate greatly from the so-called norm of their daily lives. Part of their behavior he blamed on life on the West Coast. "It's become a world of constant change, where nothing lasts forever. In that kind of a world, it becomes increasingly difficult for people to sort things out. They get lost in the tempo of change, and they begin to question whether there is any meaning to their lives."

It is on the question of meaning in their lives that most gamblers I interviewed explained their addiction to gambling. They felt it gave them a different viewpoint, that they were, in the doctor's words, involved in "a world of constant change." I did not find that the Western gambler was any more reckless than the Eastern or Middle Western gambler, perhaps only a bit more flamboyant in dress.

Dr. Stainbrook, however, believes there is a coastal difference, that in the pull of environment ". . . our cultural restraints aren't as strong. It's easier for people here to be innovative, easier to be unconventional. People who don't like constraints are attracted by the prospect of new life styles, or deviant behavior . . . plunging into a new life style involves abandoning an old one. It may be more exciting, at least at the beginning, but it also places more stress on the individual. . . ."

I read this to an habitual gambler I've known for years, and he said, "That's me; that's fifty guys I know who live only for gambling, win or lose. We've all got the stress and maybe ulcers to prove it."

Here, with identification disguised, are some actual cases of deeply addicted gamblers:

The Case History of Joseph B.

He is forty-two years old, born of a well-to-do middle-class family. Has been a compulsive gambler since the age of nineteen. He attended one year of high school, ran away from home, and held various jobs until the age of twenty-four, when he began to write popular music with a friend, but he has never been able to support himself by his music. He has lived by gambling and playing the stock market. He is an extremely skilled poker player, and has a mind that understands the odds-on-favor in betting at the dice table and the intricate dealings of the stock market. He avoids roulette and the slot machines. A few times he has had large winnings gambling, but mostly he manages to leave Las Vegas with $200 to $1,000 or so in winnings. In the stock market he gambles in wheat futures, hog bellies, flax, and soybeans.

He first sought psychiatric help six years ago, when, after winning $22,000, he ran his car into the back of a trailer. He also managed to get his hand caught in a closing door, breaking two fingers, after his mother died. He had just borrowed gambling money from her. In a series of long sessions over a period of eighteen months, the psychiatrist felt there was a pattern of several accidents, each coming soon after a gambling win.

The history of Joseph B. shows that he is a highly sensitive person with a quick temper, a sense of failure as a composer, and a dependence on his mother to bail him out when his gambling losses were heavy. When he won, he paid back some of his borrowings, but seems to have had a strained relationship with his mother, the result of his refusing to take an interest in the family business when his father died. It failed in time—and he feels his mother blamed him.

He has been married four times. All the marriages were failures, with hints of feeble sexual potency. Since his last divorce, he has had casual affairs—one-night stands, as he calls them—with some Las Vegas showgirls, but mostly for the sake of their company; he suffers from insomnia and hates to be alone late at night.

He continues to be a successful gambler, but it seems that he resents having to support himself in this manner. The psychiatrist felt it likely that the so-called accidents were triggered after a bout of gambling by his unconscious need to punish himself. At first, Joseph B. refused to accept this theory, but eventually he has agreed that perhaps his subconscious did direct self-punishment. He is well above average in intelligence, drinks very little, overeats, and has, at times, certain shaking spells. He has been withdrawing from most of his friends (he never had many) in the popular-music and show-business world. He feels that he has missed his chances to be taken seriously as a composer and has given up serious musical work. He has continued to gamble, and while his winnings have not been as large as before, he has been winning more than losing. His gambling impulse is as strong as ever. He no longer drives a car.

The Case History of Judy V.

A one-time honor student (Phi Beta Kappa) at a Northwestern university, then a highly paid advertising copywriter for women's fashions and cosmetic products in the East, she spent some time in a private sanitarium after a suicide attempt at the age of twenty-eight. An attractive, slim young woman, at twenty-two she married a lawyer, and later lost a child at birth. She divorced her husband when she discovered he was having an affair with a client. She had an affair with the art director of the advertising agency she worked for, where she was considered one of the star copywriters. It was while she was intimate with the art director that she began to gamble in a private club in New Jersey. It released in her a further breaking away from a rather dismal childhood.

She was attracted to blackjack and roulette and spent weekends gambling, at first with some luck. Then after a series of losses, she sold her car, sublet her apartment to cover gambling losses, swore off gambling and moved to Chicago, where she took an editorial job. She married a booking agent for summer-stock companies, who she soon discovered was a horse player and in debt to bookies. Before long she too was betting on horses and usually losing. When her husband's life was threatened by the mob trying to collect for lost bets, she embezzled funds from the publishing company by false invoices for fashion photos and articles. The couple went out to Reno and had a run of luck, winning $28,000 in several clubs during a four-day spree. They paid off their Chicago losses and moved to New Orleans, planning to start a local weekly about Southern cuisine and fine living. The Chicago publisher began criminal proceedings against Judy, but they were eventually withdrawn.

The new publication never got past the stages of a paste-up. Judy's husband, who had been drinking heavily, was drowned one weekend at Lake Pontchartrain.

Judy got a job dealing blackjack at a gambling house across

from New Orleans in St. Charles Parish. She was dismissed when she refused to participate in cheating some rich card players from Austin. It was then that she sought advice from a psychologist. She could not break away from gambling and had begun to take up with any man who would back her at roulette. When sober, she was revolted by what she had done.

Judy had had a strict upbringing. Her father was untouchable; her mother was a DAR who had refused sexual contact with her husband after Judy's birth. Judy had broken all connections with them, but they had offered to bring her home if she promised not to gamble. Judy refused. She had loved her father, disliked her mother, feeling her father was too kind and soft in his relationship with his snobbish, stern wife. Judy had been sexually shy in school and college, did not permit liberties on dates, and was a virgin when she had first married. She found sex exciting, but somehow always felt the disapproval of her mother at "this disgusting animal grunting and thrashing about." Judy said she was completely frigid in her later sexual adventures to get backing for her gambling. When it was suggested that her gambling was a protest against her mother's cold, puritanical standards, she left off treatment and six weeks later committed suicide in the flat of a numbers banker.

The Case History of Willard S.

He is sixty-six years old and was born in Tulsa, Oklahoma. His father had been a fairly successful wildcatter who had made a great deal of money but lost it drilling dry oil wells. Will had had a rich boy's upbringing but little schooling. He was driving expensive cars by the time he was fourteen. At sixteen he ran off to marry a part-Indian girl; his family had the marriage annulled.

He was nineteen when his father and stepmother were both killed when his father's Cessna crashed. There was nothing left but a bankrupt estate consisting of a few tons of pipe, a dozen trucks, and the remains of rigs and rotary drills. To finance a well, Will went partners with his former wife's brother, and they began setting up a drilling company on shares sold to small ranchers, local lawyers and doctors. They found no oil, but they continued small-time operations, moving around to get backing for other wildcat ventures. Will became a fairly good poker player during this time, playing in games in Oklahoma, Texas and Louisiana. After the partners' rig was seized by a bank for unpaid loans, Will ventured into poker playing. Lean, tall, with corn-colored hair under a Stetson, he acted out the accepted version of a Western card player.

His skill at poker improved. While Will never became one of the top gambling heroes like Amarillo Slim, Texas Dolly, or Cadillac Jack Grimm, he had to be a really good player to end up, in a lucky year, $15,000 to $20,000 ahead. He had no home, lived in a beat-up trailer with various women: a girl rodeo rider, a country-music singer, or small-town girls who thought he looked like Gary Cooper. Will was a kindly man, "sexy as a mink," he admitted, and a heavy drinker when not engaged in some week-long poker contest. He treated the girls well, "bought them pretties" when he was in the money, never turned them off without a fifty-dollar bill. Then, a sergeant in the Korean war, he fought and gambled and made a stake of over $10,000, playing poker with all comers. He was decorated and discharged, and he went back to wildcatting, hoping to give up gambling, settle down and buy a ranch.

He had a partner he didn't trust, and when he caught the man cheating him by "cooking" the books, Will shot him. The partner didn't die, but Will got two years behind bars. In prison, he organized the gambling—with a guard's acquiescence in return for a share—and was paroled with $4,500 in winnings.

Will was soon playing poker on the circuit with the best of them, and doing better with the inferior players. Seeking help when he developed ulcers, he was advised the cure might be treatment by a psychologist. Will submitted to a series of interviews. He said he was aware that his ulcers were the result of his poker playing, together with the knowledge that he'd never be up there with the top ten players. But he had to go on gambling, even if he died of it. He said it was as good a way as any to be handing in his chips. As a decorated war hero, the government would give him a free casket and a grave. . . . He was later reported recovering from a serious operation for a perforated ulcer, and playing poker in the ward of a Veterans Hospital in the Southwest.

There are case histories of former compulsive gamblers that

end on a happy note. In two cases satisfactory results were achieved without the help of psychologists, psychoanalysts or any other special counseling.

Waldo M.

He is short, blond, stocky and very soft-spoken. Born of upper-middle-class parents in a Southern city on the East Coast, he is thirty-one, but looks twenty.

"My great-grandfather bred race horses; my grandfather gambled in railroad stocks and lost a lot of the family holdings, so we didn't keep the old family house. My father played bridge, but not for money. I played good poker when I was twelve, in military school; I was sent down from college in my second year because of some card-playing scandal in the fraternity house. I worked on a trade paper, and I was county inspector of roads. But my real interest was gambling. Mostly horses, with a little high-stake bridge. I had no interest in marriage or in women. Nor men, either. Sex just doesn't hold anything for me. By the time I was twenty-eight I had gambled away the stocks my folks had left me, and I had taken out loans on my life insurance to pay off gambling debts. I had done a bit of paper-hanging [issuing bad checks]. In fact, I was on the run in Canada because of bad paper I gave bookies for about $7,000 on bad bets on the Preakness and the Derby.

"I was wandering around; there was this big noisy meeting with holy band music and an evangelist holding open house for anyone in need of help and guidance. I went in. This preacher was talking—he was a tall, thin man with a Southern accent. He was from Alabama, I found out later. He was talking about those of us who had fallen by the wayside, and how Jesus was always about us, forgiving those who saw their errors, and how one could regain the true life of faith. He was a Baptist, this preacher. I had been raised as one; I even went to Sunday school. The preacher read from the Bible. I'll never forget it: 'Behold, I make all things new. . . . I will give unto him that is athirst of the water of the fountain, of the water of life freely. He that overcometh shall inherit all things, and I will be his God.'

"Maybe I was ready for it; maybe all the time I was needing it. Faith. I do know I came forward to the platform with a few others and knelt. I confessed out loud I had been careless of my belief in Jesus. I came back to the preacher the next night and the next—until he left town—and talked. I remember his quoting: 'And he showed me a pure river of water of life, clear as crystal proceeding out of the throne of God and the Lamb.'

"I promised never to lose my faith in Jesus again. I haven't placed a bet since. People are amused when I say I was saved by God's miracle there in Canada. Well, let them smile. Maybe someday they too will find faith in Jesus, my true Saviour."

Mitchell G.

I met him at a meeting of Gamblers Anonymous in a West Coast city. A graying, straight-backed, gray-eyed man in his sixties, he walked with a limp, aided by a cane, the result of a war wound. He had been an officer in World War II, a soldier all his adult life.

"I've done everything in my time but kiss boys. I was Regular Army from the start. I enlisted at seventeen, working my way up. I went to Leavenworth Officers' Training School. I screwed everything with tits, drank a lot, and gambled in every army post, every officers' club that knew me. If there was a track nearby, I was on the rail. I've been married three times. *Two* people can't both give orders in *one* household. I gambled away two wives' estates. I have a son and two daughters someplace. They don't know where I am, I don't know where they are. . . . Almost got kicked out of the service twice for owing money to people for gambling debts. But with my war record and my medals, three battle wounds and all that, they let me off. I was never a lucky gambler. I never really cared for money—I wanted the excitement.

"When I was going to be arrested for draining off my second wife's estate to pay [gambling] markers, the judge sent me to this head-feeler. I had been fooling those docs in army tests for years. But this psychologist—and me facing the stockade—took me through a rough course. He showed me I liked war excitement, liked battles, liked being a good hard-balls ramrod officer. And so when there was peace, and dull living in some army post, I used gambling to get a little of the old battle-smoke excitement back. I needed action, danger. He sent me to Gamblers Anonymous to get my reactions. I've been coming to meetings for a year now. I don't gamble anymore; I get my jollies talking about old times to other compulsive gamblers who drop in to G.A. And I paint. That's right. I'm a kind of Grandpa Moses; the local bank hangs my pictures in the lobby. If I were gambling on women, I might even get married again."

Della-Mae R.

Forty-five years of age, she is now married and the mother of two children. She is black. At twenty-eight she was a book-keeper for a plastics factory near Philadelphia and was convicted for embezzling $20,000 of the firm's money. She had been secretly gambling for three years, placing bets on horses. While on vacation in Las Vegas, she dropped $11,000 at blackjack and roulette.

"I hated being a Negress when I was young, and I didn't see myself married to any of the shiftless black studs I grew up with. I had this kooky dream of meeting some different man, out of some movie, not real at all. But I didn't meet him, of course. And after some church bingo and winning a TV set in a lodge-club lottery, I began to put money on some tips on horses, and that's how I got into cooking the firm's books. I was mean inside and sour on the world. I grew careless and bet recklessly. They got me up before a judge, and I pleaded guilty, but promised to show how I finagled the books. I did a year and six months, and this social worker talked to me. But I wasn't taking any help. I was still real dog-mean. But I figured it out all by myself. I was a high-assed snob, ashamed of what I was. I was black, and that was that. I was also normal in my needs, and I wanted love and wanted sex. The prison showed me that. The gambling was my way of punishing the world for my cockeyed view of it—and my misery. Anyway, when I got out, I met this good man; he knew I had done time. I had learned hair-styling up there, so we opened this beauty parlor. We got married. And we're getting by. I handle the money, the bank account, the checks. Sometimes, sure, I get this big urge to place a bet on a horse, when I've had a hard day. But I haven't gone back to the bookies. Not so far. I hope never."

Herbert K.

"I have a fine life. I love being a landscape artist, working with plants and flowers in special ways. I get good fees. I'm happily married, have three great kids, own my own ranch-style home. I have good health, and I was voted the most popular landscape creator last year by the Landscape Association. So why did I gamble big for ten years? Nobody has been able to figure it out. I had a happy childhood and fine, understanding parents, good marks in high school, three wonderful years in college. So figure it out, my gambling. No one could. Not my minister, the marriage counselor, a doctor who had all this Freudian knowledge. Then one day—no reason—I stopped reading the *Racing Form*, took down the colored pictures of me and Grace [his wife] we had taken in Vegas and in Monte Carlo the year we actually went there. I stopped gambling just like *that*. I don't know why. Just like I don't know why I began. I don't let it puzzle me, and everything is fine. But this psychologist still keeps bugging me; he claims there isn't a case like mine on record."

Several big-time professional gamblers have expressed the opinion that they gambled because life was a dull routine and gambling was the needed change of pace they looked for in creating excitement.

Dr. Thomas Szasz, Professor of Psychiatry at the State University of New York Upstate Medical Center, appears to agree with them in his book, *Heresies*. When discussing a person's conduct, he writes, "Life is potentially a big empty hole, and there are few more satisfying ways of filling it than by striving for and achieving excellence."

Professional gambling certainly calls for achieving excellence. The great American playwright Eugene O'Neill, in an interview he gave to the *New York Tribune* in February 1921, made what seems the proper statement about the gambler's unattainable dream: "The people who succeed and do not push on to a greater failure are the spiritual middle-classers. Their stopping at success is the proof of their compromising insignificance. . . . The man who pursues the mere attainable should be sentenced to get it. . . . only through the unattainable does man achieve a hope worth living and dying for. . . ."

At this writing, some forty-four states have some kind of legalized gambling, from bingo to poker parlors, horse and dog racing and lotteries and casinos. Thirty-seven states have bills in the works to add to the type of gambling permitted. Nevada,

Delaware and Montana permit betting on football and basket-ball. At present, thirteen states have legal lotteries.

While gambling addiction seems to be a one-way road (68 percent of all men and 55 percent of women are involved in some form of gambling), there is a small trickle away from gambling. Gamblers Anonymous—founded in 1957 with two members—today claims 5,000 members in 450 chapters across the country. Of those confirmed gamblers who come to G.A. for a look, only 10 percent join up. Of members who stay with the organization's weekly meetings, only half can give up the lure of gambling in time. There are two offshoots of G.A.: Gam-Anon is for the wives and husbands of gamblers, and at Gam-a-Teen, children can talk over their parents' gambling problems.

One who doesn't look at the bright side is Professor Edward G. Devereux, Jr., of Cornell:

"Our society is moving more and more toward secularization, to rationalization, to the collapse of real commitment to public morality. Gambling fits into our whole Machiavellian rationale that anything goes *if* it works."

Wanna bet?

GAMBLING TERMS

Nothing gives a special activity color and reality like the graphic language used. For many years, when compiling research for my histories of popular music, *The Real Jazz, Old and New* (1956) and *Sportin' House* (1965), I kept a record of jazz and brothel talk, the jargon and street argot of the people and their admirers. In hunting these fields for expressive talk, I came across much that had to do with gambling, for the jazzman and the cathouse person is usually an ardent horse player, dice shooter and card handler. Starting with these sources, I have been compiling gambling language and terms that have come into common everyday use, often by people who are unaware of the gambling connotation.

I have been helped in this search over the years by talks with Nick the Greek, Cy Rice and Damon Runyon, and by Mencken's *American Language*. J. L. Dillard has produced a fine book, *American Talk*, that has reinforced many of my notes. The most helpful person was the late Wilson Mizner, a card shark, con man and professional gambler, who had wit and a keen sense for the sound of words.

Penny-ante is a small game, or a meager bettor; *to sweeten the pot* is to raise the bets; a *pigeon* is a sucker to be plucked; to be *topped out* is to be beaten by a suspected better hand; it goes against the *poker face* of the *deadpan* player; *to call a bluff* is to call a hand or shut up. The word *brag* (used in a card game) comes from a braggart boasting of his skill.

Acey-deucy is used in a noncard sense now as all-okay. *Stud* from stud poker is a *macho* term that could come from the synonym for "stallion." *Passing the buck* is handing on a buckhorn knife to indicate no desire to deal, but it also relates to

253

buck fever, the inability to shoot to kill. *Hitting the jackpot* did not begin as winning at the slot machine, but as the use of *jack* (money) in the *pot* (the money wagered) in high-play, hard-won card games. A business proposition is a *deal* only because it began as a term for getting down to serious card playing by passing or dealing out the cards. A *square deal* is an *unrigged game.* A *rig* is a cheating device, also called a *brace.* Sometimes there is a call for a *new deal,* hinting at a *big deal, dirty deal,* or even a *wheeler-dealer.* All come from the simple distribution of card hands. *Bottom dealer* becomes *dealing from the bottom of the deck;* Sam Goldwyn's press agent started *deal me out,* a reversal of *deal me in.*

The term *bluff* is obscure, and was unknown until about the middle of the nineteenth century. It appears to have originated as the ability to fool or baffle the other players and get them to pay to *see your hand,* to *call your bluff,* expose your cards, or *call your hand. Feeding the kitty,* or *pussy is hungry,* may have begun from a call to set something aside for the gambling house cat. *Aces, you're aces, aces all around* are used for good guys, or to set up top reliance on someone, like *holding an ace,* or placing two *aces back to back;* terms that have entered show biz and television, as two hoped-for good things placed one after the other. *Tochis abn tish* is Yiddish, meaning "Put up or shut up." The unseen card is the *ace in the hole,* the hidden valuable asset. An *ace up the sleeve* in a card game is cheating, but in popular usage it means clever hidden assets that are not at all dishonest.

To have something *stacked against* you relates to a *stacked deck* or *stacked cards; readers* means marked cards. But a person saying *the cards are stacked against me* does not have to be referring to a game, but to destiny, kismet, bad luck, or the stars. A *fast shuffle* is a quick card action to baffle or confuse, and it too no longer has only a card-game meaning. Games once played with stacks of silver or gold coins were in time replaced by discs that came to be called *chips. In the chips* means well-heeled. The *chips are down* means playing for real. On Wall Street solid stocks are called *blue chips*; chips in blue often have a $100 value in play. To die came to be called *handing in* or *cashing in one's chips,* whether leaving the game or this world. *Chipper* means feeling like a winner.

It was most likely Bret Harte who originated *not a Chinaman's chance,* assuming the Oriental didn't have the skill or wit to beat a white man. Some think it also comes from the Chinese in the West working discarded mining claims where there was little hope of gain.

A player who slaps the table or pats it with the edge of a card to show he's staying in, *stays pat* or *stands pat,* and a good hand of cards thus becomes *a pat hand. Something up one's sleeve* is used every day for some clever move; a *pat hander* in cards can be a cheater with hidden cards or a player who's bluffing.

A fast, tough dealer was most likely the first to be told by a player waiting for a card: *hit me.* From jazzmen comes the card expression *lay it on me,* asking for a card or cards. I've heard the queen called *a lady* or *the ladies,* and the king, *top dog* and *Mr. Big;* in Canada jacks are called *pimps.* Playing cards have been called *the pasteboards;* marked cards are *markers.* IOUs are also called *markers.* A check is *paper;* a *paper-hanger* is a bad-check passer. A *welsher* is one who avoids paying. H. L. Mencken said it originated from a Welshman who was wary of settling a debt. A *tinhorn* is a man who brags that he is a good card player, but isn't. A *fourflusher* is a phony who can't play out to a fifth drawn card. *Playing close to the vest* is protecting one's hand from being seen by holding it against one's chest. The term now describes any crafty, careful fellow. *Lay a few bob* (British) means show money.

In the sporting world, gambling terminology carries over to all sports. A ticket to a sporting event can be called a *ducket* (once an ancient coin—ducat), and a free ticket an *Annie Oakley* (free tickets are often punched with holes so as not to be counted; Annie Oakley shot holes in things). A *deadhead* is also a free-ticket holder. *Ice* is the extra money a *scalper* pays to get hold of tickets to some event he wants to *scalp* (from the Indian game of tearing something off).

A *shill* or *tout* in any gambling game or sports event is some-one who cons the sucker to play. Besides being a *pigeon,* the lured victim is also a *mark,* a *patsy, pushover, gilpin fish, rube, setup,* and often the *meal ticket.* A *sting* is a crooked setup.

Money used in gambling used to be called *spondulics, jack, china, green goods, lettuce;* all are rather obsolete now. Even to-day's popular word *bread* is fading out of fashion, but a *finif* (from Yiddish) is still five dollars. Change is constant for some words used in the gambling world. Others have survived over a hundred years.

BIBLIOGRAPHY

The sources and authorities for much of what went into this book of American gamblers, beyond unpublished journals, personal tapes and interviews, letters and court records, and the files of yellowing newspapers, are contained in many rare books and in volumes mostly out of print. Those that were most helpful in checking data and separating myth from fact are listed here:

Abbot, Wilbur C., *New York in the Revolution*, Scribners, New York, 1925

Amory, Cleveland, *The Last Resorts*, Harpers, New York, 1935

Annals of San Francisco, New York, 1855

Asbury, Herbert, *The Gangs of New York*, Knopf, New York, 1927

————, *Suckers' Progress*, Dodd, Mead, New York, 1938

Asinof, Eliot, *Eight Men Out: The Black Sox Scandal*, Holt, New York, 1963

Ballinger, Kenneth, *Miami Millions*, Hastings House, New York, 1936

Beebe, Lucius, *The Big Spenders*, Doubleday, New York, 1966

Benham, W. Gurney, *Playing Cards*, London, 1931

Blanche, Ernest E., "You Can't Win," *Public Affairs*, n.d.

"Booz," *The Laws of Bridge*, De la Rue Co., London, 1885

Bradley, Hugh, *Such Was Saratoga*, Doubleday, New York, 1940

Brolaski, Harry, *Easy Money*, Cleveland, 1911

Brown, Warren, *Chicago White Sox*, Putnam, New York, 1952

Canfield, Kid, *Gambling & Cards, Sharpers' Tricks*, New York, n.d.

Carralho, S.S., *Complete Auction Bridge*, Current, 1922

Carrington, Hereward, *Gamblers' Crooked Tricks*, Girard, Kansas, 1928

Cavendish, Henry Jones, *The Laws and Principles of Whist*, London, 1864

Chafetz, Henry, *Play the Devil*, Clarkson N. Potter, New York, 1960

Chapman, John, *Incredible Los Angeles*, Harper & Row, New York, 1960

Charles, Robert Henry, *Gambling and Betting*, Edinburgh, 1924

Clarke, Donald Henderson, *In the Reign of Rothstein*, Vanguard, New York, 1929

Cohen, John, *Chance, Skill and Luck*, Penguin, New York, 1960

Collier, Wm. Ross, and Westrate, Edwin Victor, *The Reign of Soapy Smith*, Doran, New York, 1935

Dillard, J.L., *American Talk*, Random House, New York, 1976

Dodge, Harry P., *The Autobiography of an Old Sport*, New York, 1885

Dovol, George H., *Forty Years a Gambler on the Mississippi*, New York, 1892

Drury, Wells, *An Editor on the Comstock Lode*, Farrar & Rinehart, New York, 1936

Edward, Eugene, *Jack Pots*, Chicago, 1900

Erdnase, S.W., *Expert at the Card Table*, n.d.

Esquire's Book of Gambling, Harper & Row, New York, 1972

Ezell, John Samuel, *Fortune's Merry Wheel*, Harvard, n.d.

Fisher, George Henry, *How to Win at Stud Poker*, Los Angeles, 1934

Fitzgerald, J.C. (ed.), *George Washington Diaries*, n.d.

Foster, R.F., *Dice and Dominoes*, New York, 1897

Frarken, Glenn L., *Inside Nevada Gambling*, Exposition, New York, 1965

Frey, R.L., *The New Complete Hoyle*, Doubleday, New York, 1947

Gaming Institute of Nevada, *Gambling in Nevada*, n.d.

Garcia, Frank, *Marked Cards, Loaded Dice*, Lippincott, Philadelphia, 1969

Gardner, Alexander, *Canfield, The True Story of the Greatest Gambler*, Doubleday, New York, 1930

Ging, Eng Ying, and Grant, Bruce, *Tong War*, Little, Brown, Boston, 1924

Glasscock, C.B., *Lucky Baldwin*, Indiana, 1933

Glick, Carl and Hong, Sheng-Hwa, *Chinese Secret Societies*, Whittlesey House, New York, 1947

Green, J.H., *The Secret Band of Brothers*, Philadelphia, 1847

Hargrave, Catherine Perry, *A History of Playing Cards*, Houghton Mifflin, Boston, 1930

Havemann, Ernest, "Gambling in the U.S.," *Life*, June 19, 1950

Hendin, David, *Life Givers*, Morrow, New York, 1976

Houdin, Robert, *The Card Sharper Exposed*, Chapman & Hall, London, 1863

Hoyle, Edmond, *Hoyle's Games*, New York, 1914

Irwin, Will, *Confessions of a Con Man*, B.W. Huebsch, New York, 1909

Jacoby, Oswald, *On Poker*, Hart, n.d.

———, *On Gambling*, Hart, n.d.

Josephson, Matthew, *The Robber Barons*, Harcourt, Brace, New York, 1934

Jung, Karl, *Psychology and Alchemy,* n.d.

Katcher, Leo, *The Big Bankroll—Arnold Rothstein,* Harper, New York, 1959

Kefauver, Estes, *Crime in America,* Doubleday, New York, 1951

Kendall, John Smith, *History of New Orleans,* Chicago, 1922

Kimball, Nell, *Her Life as an American Madam, by Herself,* Macmillan, New York, 1970

Kofoed, Jack, *Moon over Miami,* Random House, 1955

Lillard, John F.B. (ed.), *Poker Stories,* New York, 1896

Longstreet, Stephen, *Chicago, 1860–1919,* McKay, New York, 1973

MacDougall, Mickey, *Gamblers Don't Gamble,* Classic Reprints, Nevada, n.d.

Mackay, Margaret, *Los Angeles Proper and Improper,* Goodwin, 1938

McCable, James D., Jr., *Lights and Shadows of New York Life,* Philadelphia, 1872

McIlwaine, Shields, *Memphis Down in Dixie,* Dutton, New York, 1948

McQuaid, Clement, (ed.), *Gamblers' Digest,* Follett, Chicago, 1961

Marlo, Ed, *Riffle Shuffle System*
———, *Patented False Shuffle*
———, *Control System*
     (privately printed, n.d.)

Martin, E.W., *The Secrets of a Great City,* New York, 1868

Messick, Hank, *Syndicate in the Sun,* Macmillan, New York, 1968

Messick, Hank, & Goldblatt, Burt, *The Only Game in Town,* T.Y. Crowell, New York, 1976

Meyers, Gustavus, *Great American Fortunes,* Modern Library, New York, 1936

Mizner, Addison, *The Many Mizners,* Sears, New York, 1932

Morrell, Parker, *Diamond Jim,* Simon & Schuster, New York, 1934

Morris, John, *An Exposure of the Arts & Miseries of Gambling,* Cincinnati, 1843

Muir, Helen, *Miami, U.S.A.,* Holt, 1953

Nolan, Walter I., *The Facts on Baccarat*
———, *The Facts on Craps*
———, *The Facts on Keno*
———, *The Facts on Slots*
     (all by Gamblers' Book Club, n.d.)

Official Rules of Card Games: U.S. Playing Card Co., n.d.

Orth, Samuel P., *The Boss and the Machine,* Yale, 1920

Oyle, Dr. Irving, *The Healing Mind,* Celestial Arts, 1975

Parmer, Charles B., *For Gold and Glory,* Thoroughbred Racing, Garrick & Evans, 1939

Phillip, Dare, *Stacked Cards,* London, 1934

Pines, Philip A., *Complete Book of Harness Racing,* Grossett & Dunlap, New York, 1970

"Professor" Hoffman, *Baccarat, Fair and Foul,* Rutledge, London, 1891

Quinn, John Philip, *Fools of Fortune,* Chicago, 1892

———, *Gambling and Gambling Devices,* Canton, Ohio, 1912

Redford, Polly, *Billion Dollar Sandbar,* Dutton, New York, 1970

Reid, Ed, *The Shame of New York,* Random House, New York, 1953

———, and Damaris, Ovid, *The Green Felt Jungle,* Trident, New York, 1963

Revere, Lawrence, *Playing Blackjack as a Business,* Mann, Las Vegas, n.d.

Rice, Cy, *Nick the Greek,* Funk & Wagnalls, New York

Richardson, Albert D., *Beyond the Mississippi,* 1867

Rickard, Mrs. Tex, with Oboler, Arch, *Everything Happened to Him,* Stokes, New York, 1936

Riddle, Major A., *Weekend Gamblers Handbook,* Signet, New York, 1965

Royal, H.W., *Gambling and Confidence Games,* New York, 1896

Scarne, John, *Scarne's Complete Guide to Gambling,* Simon & Schuster, New York, 1974

Sergeant, Philip, *Gamblers All,* London, 1931

Shampaign, Charles E., *The Handbook of Percentages,* Treybol, St. Louis, 1930

Smith, Harold S., *I Want to Quit Winners,* Prentice-Hall, Englewood Cliffs, New Jersey, 1961

Smith, Matthew Hale, *Sunshine and Shadow in New York,* 1868

Sonnett, Robert, *Guide to Las Vegas,* Ritchie, 1927

Stead, W.T., *Satan's Invisible World Displayed,* New York, 1968

Sullivan, Edward Dean, *The Fabulous Wilson Mizner,* Henkle, New York, 1935

Szasz, Dr. Thomas, *Heresies,* New York, 1976

Taylor, Rev. Ed S., *The History of Playing Cards,* London, 1865

Thorp, Edward O., *Beat the Dealer: A system to beat the blackjack dealers,* n.d.

Tully, Andrew, *Era of Elegance,* Funk & Wagnalls, New York, 1947

Ullman, Joe, *What's the Odds?,* New York, 1903

Van Every, Edward, *Sins of New York,* Stokes, New York, 1930

———, *Sins of America,* 1931

Van Rensselaer, Mrs. J.K., *The Devil's Picture Book,* Dodd, Mead, New York, 1893

Veblen, Thorstein, *The Theory of the Leisure Class,* Viking, New York, 1948

Walker, Stanley, *The Night Club Era,* Stokes, New York, 1933

Waller, George, *Saga of an Imposing Era,* Prentice-Hall, Englewood Cliffs, New Jersey, 1966

Warren, John H., Jr., *Thirty Years' Battle with Crime,* New York, 1874

Warshow, Irving, *Bet-a-Million Gates,* New York, 1932

Wendt, Lloyd, and Kogan, Herman, *Bet a Million,* Bobbs-Merrill, Indianapolis, 1948

Werner, M.R., *Tammany Hall,* Doubleday, Doran, New York, 1928

Wilson, Neill C., *Silver Stampede,* Macmillan, 1937

I have hunted pertinent matter in the following:

Miami Beach Sun
Miami Herald
Las Vegas Sun
The National Observer
The New York Evening World
The New York Times
The New York Journal
The New York American
The Chicago Tribune
Los Angeles News
Los Angeles Times
San Francisco Examiner
San Francisco Chronicle
San Francisco Call Bulletin PM
Daily Telegram (New York)
New Orleans Item
Harper's Weekly
Leslie's Weekly

The Police Gazette
Sporting Times
Theatre News
The Literary Digest
Review of Reviews
Life
Time
Newsweek
The Wall Street Journal
The Saturday Evening Post
Collier's
Horizon
American Heritage
Chicago Herald & Examiner
Philadelphia North American
The Sporting News
The Baseball Magazine
Chicago American

INDEX